J.P. MORELAND

THE
GOD
QUESTION

D1056095

HARVEST HOUSE PUBLISHERS

EUGENE, OREGON

J.P. Moreland is part of a faith-based online community called ConversantLife.com. At this website, people engage their faith in entertainment, creative arts, science and technology, global concerns, and other culturally relevant topics. While you're reading this book, or after you have finished reading, go to www.conversantlife .com/jpmoreland and use these icons to read and download additional material from J.P. that is related to this book.

  Resources: Download study guide materials for personal devotions or a small-group Bible study.

 Videos: Click on this icon for interviews with J.P. and video clips on various topics.

 Blogs: Read through J.P's blogs and articles and comment on them.

Podcasts: Stream ConversantLife.com podcasts and audio clips from J.P.

conversant **life** .com

engage your faith

To Beth and Klaus Issler

*Two fellow sojourners who have
accepted the invitation gladly*

Contents

Preface

Once upon a time there was a man who thought he was dead. His wife tried everything she could to convince him he was very much alive. But try as she may, he would not change his mind. After several weeks of this, she finally took him to the doctor, who assured the man he was alive. Sadly, it was to no avail. Suddenly, the doctor got an idea. He convinced the man that dead men do not bleed, subsequently stuck him with a needle, and smiled as blood ran out of the man's finger.

The man was downtrodden for several days. He had been certain he was dead, but he could not dispute the fact that he could bleed. Finally, he figured out what to do. Returning to the doctor, the man blurted out, "Good Lord, dead men do bleed after all!"

Our friend had a view of things that he clung to regardless of the evidence that came his way. His "worldview" was immune to revision. As a result, he continued to embrace and assert his view without integrity. If you are like me, you want to live a life of integrity. But there's a problem. I find myself to be a broken person in so many ways, and these areas of fracture and fragility easily distract me from living a full, rich life with the sort of wisdom I deeply desire. Therein lies a big story that I will unpack in the pages to follow.

But my purpose is not merely to inform you of our brokenness, such as it is, and of our need for wisdom. I need more than that, and I suspect you do too. No, I want to give you the hope of a way out and a way forward. And I very much wish to share with you some deep insights that have helped in my own journey. As much as anything, the pages to follow are an invitation to a full life, to an adventure, filled with meaning and drama. And along with that invitation, I offer as much wise counsel and practical advice as my 60-something years have afforded me.

Unfortunately, it is precisely here that the story of the man who thought he was dead challenges us. Receiving counsel is sometimes difficult if it requires us to adjust our view of things and adopt the resulting sort of life that follows. This is especially true when we think we have heard that counsel before and find it angering, threatening, boring, silly, or worse. Familiarity does indeed often breed contempt. This book offers fresh new insights that I trust will be intellectually stimulating and personally enriching. But we humans have been at this thing called life for a considerable time. And you, the reader, should rightly be suspicious of anyone who completely reinvents the wheel without taking any advice from the accumulated wisdom of the ages.

I have eagerly appropriated that wisdom and woven it into a tapestry that combines fresh new ideas with (quite often) forgotten ancient ones. The result is, I hope, something that will be as exhilarating and life changing for you as it has been for my entire family and me. I ask of you only that in the pages to follow, when you encounter something familiar, give it a fair hearing. Let me, perhaps, shed new light on the topic. You have nothing to lose by doing this and much to gain. You may discover that it makes a lot more sense to believe that dead men don't bleed than to hold on to cultural myths that have deadened Western culture to an ancient path that is more relevant today than ever and that leads to a rich and full life.

Part 1

WHY CAN'T
WE BE HAPPY?

Why Can't I Be Happy?

In the mid 1980s, hard evidence revealed that something was seriously wrong with the American way of life. Rumors about the problem were prominent since the 1960s, but when the evidence was published, the rumors became public knowledge, though few today know what is going on. And more evidence has piled up in the past 20 years.

Some of the causes and symptoms of the problem shape the way we approach our lives and make it difficult to face this evidence. Not long ago, I was watching reruns of television commercials of the 1950s. In one quite typical ad, a medical doctor encouraged viewers to smoke cigarettes for their health. Smoking, he assured the viewers, calmed nerves, aided one's appetite, and helped people sleep better. This widely accepted belief hindered Americans from realizing that cigarettes actually harm one's health. Similarly, the conditions of contemporary life make the evidence mentioned above hard to accept.

And even if someone accepts this evidence, it is very, very difficult to know what to do about the situation. And I say to you with all my heart that you have been hurt by what the evidence shows. No, it's worse than that. You and your loved ones have been *harmed,* not merely hurt. In the following pages I have some good and bad news. Let's start with the bad news. What are the problems and the evidence to which I have been referring? What are the causes and symptoms that have hindered us from facing the evidence and overcoming our dilemma? Let's look at these in order.

Americans Don't Know How to Be Happy

The cover story of the December 2006 issue of *The Economist* was about happiness. *The Economist* is about as far from a pop psychology magazine as you can imagine, so the topic must have been something of great concern to the editors. Based on research data from 1972 to 2006, the article concluded that people in affluent countries have not become happier as they have grown richer, had more leisure time, and enjoyed more pleasurable activities and a higher standard of living.[1]

In 2005, the results of extensive study on American happiness were released with similar findings: Americans are on average twice as rich, far healthier, more youthful, and safer than they were 50 years ago, but they are not as happy.[2] Since the 1960s the percentage of Americans who say they are "very unhappy" has risen by 20 percent, and depression rates are ten times higher than they were during and before the 1950s. Each year, 15 percent of Americans (approximately 40 million people) suffer from an anxiety disorder.

For decades, University of Pennsylvania psychologist Martin Seligman has been the nation's leading researcher on happiness. His study released in 1988 sent shock waves around the country. Seligman studied the happiness quotient and depression rate among Americans at that time compared to those of their parents, grandparents, and great-grandparents. Are you ready for this? He discovered that the loss of happiness and the rise of depression were tenfold in the span of one generation—the baby boomers. Something has gone terribly wrong with American culture, said Seligman, and the tenfold, short-term explosive loss of happiness and growth of depression—a factor that has continued to increase since the 1980s—is clearly epidemic. What is going on?

Digging Deeper

Without being harsh, I must say that we would be naive if we didn't believe this epidemic has affected all of us. There is a way out of this mess, and the chapters that follow are my best offerings for embarking on a journey to a rich, deep, flourishing life. In fact, I would like you to read this book as my invitation to you for such a life—one that is brimming with drama and adventure, flowering with meaning and purpose. However, I am not interested in merely offering you an invitation. I also want to give you wise counsel that has been repeatedly tested and found trustworthy and helpful for the journey.

A journey has to start somewhere, and the best place to start this one is by digging more deeply into the causes and symptoms of our cultural crisis. We are looking for broad cultural factors that have generated a shift in the way we do life, a shift that has caused the epidemic. These factors are not likely to be things we regularly think about. If they were, most people would have made a priority of avoiding them, and that is not the case. I am not suggesting that people will reject the alleged factors once they are made explicit. Quite the opposite. I believe that once they are laid bare, most folks will experience an ah-ha moment and readily identify with them. No, in order to do their destructive work, these factors have to fly under the radar. They must be so pervasive that they are hardly noticed.

In their excellent book on anxiety and depression, psychologist Edmund Bourne and coauthor Lorna Garano identify three causes for the epidemic: (1) the pace of modern life, (2) the loss of a sense of community and deep connectedness with others beyond the superficial, and (3) the emergence of moral relativism.[3] The increased pace of life does not merely refer to more work and less free time, though those are certainly factors. Well into the late Middle Ages, Europeans had 115 holidays a year![4] Besides free time, the sheer pace and speed at which we live—our language is filled with terms like "rush hour," "hurry up," and "fast food"—and the technology we use (including iPods, e-mail, television, and cell phones) make it difficult to be quiet and hear from ourselves. As a result, we feed off of adrenaline, our brain chemistry is not normal, and we are not capable of handling the stress of ordinary contemporary life. Maybe we were never intended to, but I get ahead of myself.

On the surface, the loss of community reflects two things: Western individualism (which is a good thing in moderation) gone mad, and the supposed lack of time required to cultivate deep friendships, especially among contemporary men, who have often been described as "the friendless American males." On a deeper level, it reflects misplaced priorities due to a shift on our view of the good life. I will say more about this in the next chapter, but for now I simply note that we define success in terms of the accumulation of consumer goods and the social status that they and a culturally respected line of work provide. We seldom measure a successful life by the quality of family and friendship relationships we cultivate.

Regarding the factor of moral relativism, Bourne and Garano make this note:

> Norms in modern life are highly pluralistic. There is no shared, consistent, socially-agreed-upon set of values and standards for people to live by...In the vacuum left, most of us attempt to fend for ourselves, and the resultant uncertainty about how to conduct our lives leaves ample room for anxiety. Faced with a barrage of inconsistent worldviews and standards presented by the media, we are left with the responsibility of having to create our own meaning and moral order. When we are unable to find that meaning, many of us are prone to fill the gap that's left with various forms of escapism and addiction. We tend [to] live out of tune with ourselves and thus find ourselves anxious.[5]

I cannot resist making an observation about their insightful point concerning moral relativism. The damage it does is one reason why the contemporary idea of tolerance is really an immoral, cold, heartless form of indifference to the suffering of others. The classic principle of tolerance is both true and important: We take another group's views to be wrong and harmful, but we will treat the (alleged) errant people with respect, will defend their right to promote their views, and will engage in respective, civil debate in attempting to persuade them and others to reject their viewpoint. The contemporary idea is grotesque: We are not to say others' views or behavior is wrong. This is immoral because it allows for genuine evil, such as racism and child molestation. We must judge the behavior to be evil before we can stop it! Bourne and Garano show us that it is also cold and heartless: If you think another is engaged in a lifestyle that is deeply immoral and flawed, the most loving thing to do is to help that person face and get out of that lifestyle. Even if you are wrong in your assessment, at least you cared enough to try to help. By contrast, contemporary tolerance creates indifferent people who don't have the moral vision or courage to intervene in the lives of others and try to help.

We might summarize Bourne and Garano's insights this way: First, our resistance to depression and anxiety is weakened by the pace of our lives. Second, we don't have the relational connection we need for support and strength in finding a way out of unhappiness. And third, we lack the intellectual framework required to admit that there is a right and wrong way to approach life and to fuel the energy we need to seek, find, and live in light of the right approach. In fact, believing that there actually is a right approach seems intolerant to many.

I have spent hours thinking about these three points and how they inform my own journey. If I may say so, it wouldn't hurt if you set the book down, took out a sheet of paper, jotted down these three factors, and brainstormed about how they have had a negative impact on you or your loved ones. Nevertheless, I do not believe that Bourne and Garano have identified the heart of the matter. We must probe more deeply.

Digging Deeper Still

Psychologist Carl Jung once observed that "neurosis is always a substitute for legitimate suffering."[6] Jung is referring to our tendency to avoid feeling genuine emotional pain and facing real personal suffering and dysfunction by creating, usually subconsciously, a neurotic pattern of thinking or behaving that allows us to be distracted from our real issues.

When I was attending seminary, my roommate was in constant fear that he had committed the unpardonable sin, an act for which there is no forgiveness. Try as I might, I could not reassure him that he had done no such thing. One day while probing him more deeply, I realized that his real issue was fear of abandonment, loneliness, and feelings of inadequacy due to harsh treatment in his early years by his father. However, it was too painful for him to feel and face these— something he needed to do to get well. Such self-awareness would have been legitimate suffering in Jung's terms. Instead, he projected his anxiety on something more manageable, on something that distracted his anxiety from the real issues—the unpardonable sin—and neurotically worried about this repeatedly throughout his daily life.

I am convinced that this inability to face our deepest anxieties is at the heart of why we have trouble being happy. In chapter 2, I will expose why this inability is a distinctively contemporary problem for Western culture since the 1960s. For now, I want to mention two forms of "neurosis" characteristic of many of us. Just as my roommate obsessed about the unpardonable sin, we use these two items to manage our anxiety and cope with life while avoiding the deeper issues we have trouble facing.

The two items to which I am referring are *hurry* and *worry*. When I speak of hurry, I am not simply referring to the (sick) pace at which we live our lives. That's a problem in its own right. No, I am referring to the role that busyness and being in a hurry plays in coping with our fears in an unhealthy way. People are afraid to slow down and be quiet. As one thinker put it, the hardest thing to get Americans to do today is nothing. We fear solitude, silence, and having nothing to do because we fear what will happen if we aren't busy. What do we fear? We fear that our anxiety will bubble up. We dread feeling insignificant. We fear hearing from ourselves because we might experience pain if we do. We all have responsibilities in which we invest time and effort. But if you compare our lifestyles with folks in earlier generations, it becomes apparent that our busyness and hurried lives are avoidance strategies.

We all have worries and things that could hurt us. But the degree to which we worry is, again, symptomatic of something much deeper. When I refer to worry as a coping strategy, I am not referring to worry about a threatening situation—losing one's job, being sick, not getting married, and so on. I am talking about worry as an approach to life. In this sense, worrying is actually a learned behavior. As dear as she was, my mother was a very anxious person who worried about everything. I lived around her and absorbed her approach to life, so by the time I was a young adult, I had learned how to worry from an expert. And now I was the expert!

What roles do hurry and worry play in your life? I encourage you to spend some time pondering this question. As a help to you, I suggest you find some safe friends or family members and ask them to give you honest feedback about this. This issue is so deep and so much a part of the warp and woof of American life that it is hard to get in touch with the way we neurotically use hurry and worry to avoid problems.

One of our main fears is boredom and loneliness, and hurry and worry keep us from facing these fears. In fact, some patterns of ideas and beliefs that permeate the arts, media, and educational institutions of our culture make it all but impossible to face boredom and loneliness. More on that in chapter 2. Here I want you to ponder an additional fact: It takes a lot of emotional energy to "stuff" our real problems and manage appropriate anxiety by the hurry and worry strategy. And given the three pervasive cultural patterns we mentioned earlier—our pace of life, the loss of community, and the emergence of moral relativism—we have a very dangerous situation in our culture.

To live the way many of us do takes a lot of energy, so we are vulnerable to addiction. Various addictions provide some form of relief from a neurotic life and offer some reward on a regular basis in the form of the satisfaction of desire, usually bodily desire. However, all such addictions obey the law of diminishing returns. The more one turns to addictive behavior, the less it pays off and the more one must turn to the addiction. It may be social recognition, sexual stimulation, drugs or alcohol abuse, eating, acquiring consumer goods, and so on. Over time, we shrivel as authentic persons, and we become less and less in touch with our real selves. Instead, we must project a false self to others—a self we wish others to believe about us, a self that is a collage of parental messages, strategies for remaining safe and hidden, and behaviors that avoid shame and guilt. The range of our free will diminishes, and we become enslaved to safety, social rules, and bodily pleasures and their satisfaction.

It's time to summarize. For at least 40 years, Americans have become increasingly unable to find happiness and, instead, are ten times more likely to be depressed and anxiety filled than Americans of other generations. Clearly, something about our culture is deeply flawed. As a first step toward identifying the flaws, I noted the adrenalized pace of life, the loss of a sense of community, and the emergence of moral relativism in American culture. Digging more deeply, I noted that for these and other reasons, we find it hard to face our real, authentic emotional pain and, instead, opt for lifestyles of hurry and worry that allow us to cope with our boredom, emptiness, and loneliness without having to face our true situation. Such an approach takes a lot of emotional energy and, partly to comfort ourselves, we turn to addictive behaviors that increasingly turn us into false selves who no longer know who we are.

An Invitation and a Word of Concern

I have received much help from others in my own journey, and I believe I have some genuinely good news for you in the pages to follow. I invite you to read on with an open mind and heart. However, I'm concerned about something. I am troubled that you may not be willing to think afresh with me about what follows and won't benefit from whatever wisdom is offered. Why am I so concerned? It's because of my topic and the two primary types of people with whom I want to travel.

Beginning with chapter 2, I am going to mention the *G* word— "God"—more specifically, the Christian God and Jesus of Nazareth. As we will see, whenever we focus on living a rich life and face our inability to be happy, broad questions about the meaning of life inevitably surface. This is as it should be. And lurking in the neighborhood will be questions about God. It has been said that the single most important thing about a person is what comes to mind when he or she hears the word "God." This is a trustworthy saying.

So why am I concerned? Because it is so very hard to invite someone in this culture to give this topic a fresh hearing, especially from my two audiences. The first person to whom I am writing is not a follower of Jesus. You may be an aggressive atheist, mildly agnostic, or inclined to think that religion should be a private matter and that "Live and let live" should be one's motto. If you fit this category, you may have picked up this book at a bookstore or found it online, or a friend or relative may have given it to you. If the latter is the case, you may feel defensive about reading the book. You may feel that your friend or relative wants to fix you or to "win" in your longstanding dialogues about Christianity. If you read this book with an open mind and fresh start, and if you come to agree with some of my offerings, you could lose face, as it were. Others could say you were wrong all along and this proves it.

I completely understand such defensiveness, having practiced it myself in various contexts. But to be honest, if you are concerned about such matters, you are actually not being true to yourself. Instead, you are letting others control you. You are giving them free rent in your mind. It's as though they are looking over your shoulder as you read, just waiting to jump on you if you come to see things as they do. My advice is that you not let others have such power over you. Be yourself. Think for yourself. Give me a hearing, and when you have read the entire book, step back and decide for yourself what you think about these matters.

Besides friends or relatives, if you fit into this first group, I actually have a deeper concern—really, two concerns—about you being defensive in reading what follows. Having talked to atheists and agnostics for 40 years, I've seen that many of them don't want God to exist. In a rare moment of frankness, atheist philosopher Thomas Nagel makes this admission:

> I want atheism to be true and am made uneasy by the fact that some of the most intelligent and well-informed people I know are religious believers. It isn't just that I don't believe in God and, naturally, I hope that I'm right in my belief. It's that I hope there is no God! I don't want there to be a God; I don't want the universe to be like that.[7]

Such an approach to life is hard to sustain. Influential young atheist Douglas Coupland frankly acknowledges how difficult it is:

> Now—here is my secret: I tell it to you with an openness of heart that I doubt I shall ever achieve again, so I pray that you are in a quiet room as you hear these words. My secret is that I need God—that I am sick and can no longer make it alone. I need God to help me give, because I no longer seem capable of giving; to help me be kind, as I no longer seem capable of kindness; to help me love, as I seem beyond being able to love.[8]

Fathers and Freedom

If you are an atheist or something close to it, I believe there may be two reasons why you think this way. I am sharing these with you to be helpful, not to throw this in your face. No one is here but you and me, so please see if these describe you. The first reason you may approach the question of God with anger or rejection is unresolved conflict with your own father figure. I have spoken on more than 200 college campuses and in more than 40 states in the last 40 years, and it has become apparent to me that atheists regularly have deep-seated, unresolved emotional conflicts with their father figures. To think that this plays no role in their atheism would be foolish. Paul Vitz, a leading psychologist in this area claims that, in fact, such conflict is at the very heart of what motivates a person to reject God or be indifferent to religion.[9]

Let's be honest. You owe it to yourself to see if this is causing you to be defensive about the topic of God. If it is, I urge you in the safety of our conversation to follow, to try to set this aside.

The second reason you may not want the Christian God to be real has been identified by Dinesh D'Souza: People want to be liberated from traditional morality so they can engage in any sexual behavior that satisfies them without guilt, shame, or condemnation.[10] The famous atheist Aldous Huxley made this admission:

> I had motives for not wanting the world to have a meaning;
> consequently I assumed that it had none, and was able without
> any difficulty to find satisfying reasons for this assumption…
> For myself, as no doubt for most of my contemporaries, the
> philosophy of meaninglessness was essentially an instrument
> of liberation. The liberation we desired was…liberation from
> a certain system of morality. We objected to the morality
> because it interfered with our sexual freedom.[11]

If you have a vested interest in wanting to look at pornography or to engage in sexual activity outside of a traditional marriage, your hostility to God may well be a way of enabling yourself to sustain your lifestyle while flying in a no-guilt zone. I take no pleasure in saying this, and I am not trying to be harsh or judgmental toward you. The opposite is the case. I have help for you and will offer it in the chapters to follow. All I ask of you is that you give me a hearing and not allow these factors to fuel your defensiveness in such a way that you are not teachable and open to exploring these issues together.

Caricatures of Christians

My first concern about defensiveness, then, is due to the role that unresolved father issues and sexual practices may play in preventing you from facing this topic honestly and with a good and open heart. My second concern is the associations that come to mind when people in our culture think of conservative Christians, most of whom would be called Evangelicals. You may see red at the very thought of Christians. They are hypocrites, intolerant bigots, nosy members of the Religious Right who try to tell others what to do and how to think. Christians are irrational, unscientific, nonthinking sorts who will gullibly believe anything. Comparing Christians (and other religious zealots) and secularists, University of California at Berkeley professor and former Secretary of Labor Robert Reich gave this warning:

> The great conflict of the 21st century will not be between the West and terrorism. Terrorism is a tactic, not a belief. The true battle will be between those who believe in the primacy of the individual and those who believe that human beings owe their allegiance and identity to a higher authority; between those who give priority to life in this world and those who believe that human life is mere preparation for an existence beyond life; between those who believe in science, reason and logic and those who believe that truth is revealed through Scripture and religious dogma. Terrorism will disrupt and destroy lives. But terrorism itself is not the greatest danger we face.[12]

With friends like that, who needs enemies! Reich needs to lighten up a bit. Still, you may share his opinion of what it means to be a Christian. May I suggest two counterarguments that may help you get something out of this book. First, Reich's statement and the description of Christians in the preceding paragraph are gross caricatures that are far from the truth. It's a cultural lie that the more educated you become the more you reject Christianity. A few years ago, University of North Carolina sociologist Christian Smith published what may be the most extensive study to date of the impact of contemporary culture on American Evangelicalism. Smith's extensive research led him to this conclusion:

> Self-identified evangelicals have more years of education than fundamentalists, liberals, Roman Catholics, and those who are nonreligious...Of all groups, evangelicals are the least likely to have only a high-school education or less; the nonreligious are the most likely. Furthermore, higher proportions of evangelicals have studied at the graduate-school level than have fundamentalists, liberals, or the nonreligious.[13]

Sure, there are a few bad (ignorant and bigoted) eggs in our basket, but the whole basket should not be judged on this account.

Even if this demeaning picture of Christians contains more than a small grain of truth, becoming a follower of Jesus doesn't have to make you like this. And there's still the issue of you and your own life and welfare. You have a life to live, and if you are anything like me, you need all the help you can get to live it well. The real issue is whether the Christian God is real and can be known, whether Jesus of Nazareth was really the very Son of God, and whether the movement He started is what you need and have been looking for (consciously or not). At the end of the day, the issue is not whether Christians are hypocrites, Republicans, or whatever. The issue is Jesus of Nazareth and your life.

Familiarity

The second person to whom I am writing is a Christian who has become too familiar with the form of Christianity often present in our

culture. If this is you, you may have become inoculated from the real
thing. You are bored with church, you don't like religious games, and
you believe you have given the Christian thing a try and it isn't what
it was cracked up to be.[14] In a way, you've lost hope. The fire in your
belly has dimmed, and you despair of finding more as a Christian. You
think you have already heard and heeded the invitation I am about to
unpack, and you are not interested in hearing the same old stuff again.
Been there, done that, bought the T-shirt.

Dallas Willard puts his finger on this problem:

> The major problem with the invitation now is precisely over-
> familiarity. Familiarity breeds unfamiliarity—unsuspected
> unfamiliarity, and then contempt. People think they have
> heard the invitation. They think they have accepted it—or
> rejected it. But they have not. The difficulty today is to hear
> it at all.[15]

I'm asking you to listen again to the invitation as though for the
first time. In some cases, that won't actually be true. You will likely
read things in subsequent chapters that you have heard before. If so, I
promise to try to give these things new life, to cast them in a new light.
In other cases, that may actually be true. Some brand-new insights may
follow. If you are a Christian who fits my description, all I can do is to
ask you to read on with an open heart.

So let's move on. You and I have lives to live. How can we get better
at it? In chapter 2, we jump out of the pan and into the fire. We move
to what I believe is at or near the bottom of why you and many of our
fellow Americans can't find much happiness in life. The central issue
revolves around broad cultural ideas about life, reality, and confidence.
The fundamental issue involves the mind and how we think about and
see things. But before I can tell you that story, I'll need to let you in
on something about your brain.

Hope for a Culture of Bored and Empty Selves

You Are What You Think

According to a famous song, it's never supposed to rain in Southern California, but my wife and I drove toward the campus of UCLA in a downpour. I was scheduled to participate in a debate with two other scholars on whether humans have a soul and free will. One professor could not come, so I was to square off with one of the nation's leading neuroscientists—UCLA professor Jeffrey Schwartz. I was in for a big and pleasant surprise.

As it turned out, Schwartz and I were in almost complete agreement that the soul or self is a spiritual substance different from the brain and that people therefore have free will. So the debate turned into a rich evening in which a philosopher and brain scientist shared evidence for the same conclusion from different academic disciplines. During his presentation, Professor Schwartz shared something of deep importance to you and your journey toward a rich and full life.

Several years earlier, Schwartz had taken brain scans of obsessive-compulsive people who engaged in repetitive hand-washing rituals.

They all had a very distinctive, abnormal brain configuration. Schwartz then told the patients to do something for a few weeks and come back: Every time they felt the compulsion to wash their hands, they were to exercise free will, choose to think different thoughts (for example, *I don't need to wash my hands; a little dirt isn't going to kill me*), and repeatedly practice this. When new scans were performed, all the patients had different and normal brain configurations. Lesson: By exerting free will, the mind can change the physical structure of the brain.[1]

Subsequently, Schwartz has done experiments in which people's brains are monitored as they watch videos of carnage from automobile accidents. The anxiety center of the brain goes wild. Then he tells them to pretend they are paramedics who must make snap decisions about whom to treat first and what to do. When showed the same scenes the anxiety center remained calm. We can alter our brain and its role in facilitating anxiety, anger, and so forth by changing the way we think and adjusting our perspective. Here was Schwartz's punch line: People who see the glass half full regarding their lives are healthier, happier, and more functional than those who don't. And, he said, Christian theists who have a background belief that God is real, good, and caring will have a substantial leg up on those without such a belief.

The bottom line: You are what you think. Even better, you are what you believe because studies show that to change your brain chemistry, defeat anxiety and depression, and have a pervasive sense of well-being, you must spot false ways of thinking about life and replace them with thoughts you take to be true. As it turns out, your beliefs are the rails upon which your life runs. You almost always live up to—or down to—your actual beliefs. Your worldview—the set of things you actually believe about God, reality, meaning, value, what counts as success, what constitutes a good person and whether or not you are one, what we can and cannot know, and other significant topics—is the most important factor about your life. It's more important than having a flat stomach, being healthy, or fulfilling the American dream.

This is the conclusion of the studies reported by Seligman and

Campos to which I referred in chapter 1. Campos explicitly states that we are healthier, live longer, are twice as wealthy, have more leisure time, and are better off than our parents and grandparents. But we are less happy. Why? According to Campos, our lives are built on a mistaken premise: If we achieve the American dream and the items just listed, we will be happy. But that doesn't work. What should we do about this? Campos says that we should seek meaning and purpose in life instead of pleasure and so forth.

Seligman comes to a similar conclusion. According to his study, the baby boomer generation is ten times more depressed and less happy than earlier generations. Why? Because boomers stopped trying daily to live for something bigger than they are—such as God, country, or extended family—and instead lived for themselves and their own happiness 24/7.

I wonder if you can identify with all this. Without being judgmental, think for a minute about your neighbors, relatives, coworkers, and other acquaintances. What exactly are they living for? What picture of success makes the most sense of the way they spend their time, money, and efforts? Now, think about yourself and ask the same question. Be ruthlessly honest about this. Take a personal inventory, and if you have trouble being self-aware, ask a loved one or close friend to give you feedback.

One thing was missing in Seligman's and Campos's reports. Neither could explain why Americans in the 1960s made this sudden and harmful shift. There's an answer to this question, and I'm going to tell you what I think it is in the remainder of this chapter. Before I do, two further preliminaries must be put in place.

First, let's take stock of what we've learned so far. Since the 1960s, most of us struggle with unhappiness, boredom, and emptiness, according to all the data. Fewer and fewer of us experience a deep, full sense of well-being day-to-day. The surface reasons for this include our pace of life, the loss of community, moral relativism, hurry and worry. But there is a deeper root cause. Something about the way we think, something about our pervasive belief patterns, something about our culture's plausibility structure (the things we take to be plausible or implausible as an unconscious default position inherited from our culture) has shifted. It has contributed to the formation of people who see the glass half empty, who do not have a set of life-enhancing, brain-restoring beliefs, who no longer exert the effort to live for something bigger than their own lives and instead focus all their energies on personal pleasure and affluence.

From what we have learned, this much is clear. But before I can give you my take on what underlies all this, there is another preliminary to ponder. We must probe the current situation from a slightly different perspective.

Rumors of Emptiness

In 1979, Christopher Lasch's bestseller *The Culture of Narcissism* appeared on the scene. It remains one of the most insightful analyses of American culture I have ever read. Lasch analyzed cultural patterns during the previous 21 years, and the book's subtitle was grim: *American Life in an Age of Diminished Expectations.* According to Lasch, beginning around 1958, therapists began to face an escalation of patients who did not suffer from any specific problem. Instead, they suffered from vague, ill-defined anxiety and depression that seemed "to signify an underlying change in the organization of personality, from what has been called inner-direction to narcissism."[2]

Something had gone wrong with the American psyche itself, which had become numb with pervasive feelings of emptiness and a deep fracture in self-esteem. More and more Americans were preoccupied with their own self-absorbed, infantile needs, along with the instant gratification of desire. As a result, they found it impossible to form intimate relationships with others and to live for something bigger than they were, to identify with some historical stream (for example, the outworking of the kingdom of God or the progression of American ideals and values) that gave meaning to their lives and with respect to which they could play a role.

The epidemic explosion of pervasive American narcissism since the 1960s is a manifestation of an underlying shift in the meaning of the word "happiness" away from a steady understanding of the word from the time of Moses and ancient Greece up to the 1700s in Great Britain and the 1960s in America.[3] The current understanding of happiness identifies it with a pleasurable feeling, a sensation we experience when our team wins, we get a raise, or something exciting happens to us. In fact, the lead definition of "happiness" in the fourth edition of *Webster's New World College Dictionary* is "a feeling of great pleasure." Thus, today we have "happy hour." The classic definition of happiness—a life well lived, a life of wisdom and virtue—has dropped out of the dictionary. Now, pleasant feelings are surely better than unpleasant ones, but the problem today is that people are obsessively concerned with feeling happy. People are enslaved and addicted to such feelings.

There are two problems with this. For one thing, while pleasurable satisfaction is a good thing, it is not important enough to be the goal of life. As we will see in a moment, we have bigger fish to fry. Second, the best way to find pleasurable satisfaction is not to seek it, but rather to seek something else—objective meaning in life and the classic sense of happiness—for which pleasurable satisfaction is a by-product. In general, feelings are wonderful servants but terrible masters. When people make happiness their goal, they do not find it, and as a result, they start living their lives vicariously through identification with celebrities. People literally need to get a life. They have to find something bigger and more important to live for than pleasurable satisfaction, and they have to find a new strategy for daily life besides self-absorption.

Here we must confront the classic understanding of happiness embraced by Moses, Solomon, Jesus, Aristotle, Plato, the church fathers, medieval theologians, the writers of the Declaration of Independence, and many more, the understanding now replaced by "pleasurable satisfaction." According to the ancients, happiness is a life well lived, a life of virtue and character, a life that manifests wisdom, kindness, and goodness. For them, the life of happiness, the life about which to dream and fantasize, for which to hunger and seek, and which should be imitated and practiced, is a life of virtue and character. At its center, such a life includes a very deep sense of well-being, but this sense should not be confused with pleasurable satisfaction. This chart may help clarify the difference:

Contemporary Happiness	Classical Happiness
1. pleasurable satisfaction	1. virtue and well-being
2. an intense feeling	2. a settled tone
3. dependent on external circumstances	3. springs from within
4. transitory and fleeting	4. more permanent and stable
5. addictive and enslaving	5. empowering and liberating
6. split off from rest of self, doesn't color rest of life, creates false and empty self	6. integrated with entire personality, colors everything else, creates true self
7. achieved by self-absorbed narcissism; success produces a celebrity	7. achieved by a life of self-denial for an objective, larger good; success produces a hero

The abandonment of the classic notion for its trivial, superficial contemporary counterpart has given rise to what psychologists call the empty self. The empty self, now an epidemic in America (and much of Western culture), is that to which Lasch, Seligman, and Campos refer. Philip Cushman agrees:

> The empty self is filled up with consumer goods, calories, experiences, politicians, romantic partners, and empathetic therapists...[The empty self] experiences a significant absence of community, tradition, and shared meaning...a

lack of personal conviction and worth, and it embodies the absences as a chronic, undifferentiated emotional hunger.[4]

Pop teenage culture provides a clear example of a social system that produces and contains an abundance of empty selves. Sadly, the traits of the empty self do not leave at the age of 20; studies show that these traits continue until around 40 years of age, and increasingly, they last longer than that.

Whether we like it or not, you, I, our neighbors, and our coworkers have been damaged by this shift in culture. The empty self is a culturally pervasive phenomenon. Its emergence is due to a widespread, generalized sense of existential angst—a deep dread or fear that something is wrong with the world, that something very deep is absent. The empty self cannot face this deeper issue, and narcissism is the result. Neurosis is always a substitute for genuine suffering. Note very carefully that this cultural situation is a distinctively contemporary phenomenon of Western culture. So, what happened? Why the shift in the meaning of happiness?

The Fundamental Cause of the Empty Self

I neglected to tell you Lasch's concluding description of the narcissistic personality ubiquitous in our culture: "The ideology of [narcissistic] personal growth, superficial optimism, radiates a profound despair and resignation. It is the faith of those without faith."[5] In referring to "those without faith," Lasch is talking about the rise of secularism, along with religious skepticism, cynicism, and indifference that goes with it. And secularism is responsible for the "profound despair and resignation" that lies in the subconscious bosom of many of us.

We are fed secular ways of thinking at our mother's knee. We are socialized into a naturalistic, atheistic (or agnostic) way of seeing the world. It is the very air that we breathe. Recently, the *New York Times* published an article claiming that the difference between Europe and America is that Europe embraces secularism and America embraces religion.[6] The article recommends that America follow in Europe's steps. Secularizing factors such as this pelt us daily, and they are so widespread and frequent that they are hardly noticed.

Indeed, their stealth nature explains how secularization gets past our defenses and forms the deepest part of the American psyche, even for religious believers. My graduate students from Africa, South America, and Asia tell me that they regularly see miracles of healing (including blind or lame people made well through prayer) in their services. They are befuddled by the weak faith characteristic of the American church. Dallas Willard makes this note about the negative impact of secularism:

> The crushing weight of the secular outlook…permeates or pressures every thought we have today. Sometimes it even forces those who self-identify as Christian teachers to set aside Jesus' plain statements about the reality and total relevance of the kingdom of God and replace them with philosophical speculations whose only recommendation is their consistency with a "modern" mind-set. The powerful though vague and unsubstantiated presumption is that *something has been found out* that renders a spiritual understanding of reality in the manner of Jesus simply foolish to those who are "in the know."[7]

The subconscious fear that God is dead is responsible for the loss of real, classic happiness among the American people. With real insight, Lasch correctly saw a connection between a secular perspective and a profound sense of despair and fatalism about life. To see why this connection is correct, suppose I invited you over to my house to play a game of Monopoly. When you arrive I announce that the game is going to be a bit different. Before us is the Monopoly board, a set of jacks, a coin, the television remote, and a refrigerator in the corner of the room. I grant you the first turn, and puzzlingly, inform you that you may do anything you want: fill the board with hotels, throw the coin in the air, toss a few jacks, fix a sandwich, or turn on the television. You respond by putting hotels all over the board and smugly sit back as I take my turn. I respond by dumping the board upside down and tossing the coin in the air. Somewhat annoyed, you right the board and replenish it with hotels. I turn on the television and dump the board over again.

Now it wouldn't take too many cycles of this nonsense to recognize that it didn't really matter what you did with your turn, and here's why. There is no goal, no purpose to the game we are playing. Our successive turns form a series of one meaningless event after another. Why? Because if the game as a whole has no purpose, the individual moves within the game are pointless. Conversely, only a game's actual purpose according to its inventor can give the individual moves significance. For example, if the purpose of Monopoly were to see who could lose their money first, all of a sudden the utilities would be treasures, and Boardwalk and Park Place would become lethal properties!

Two things follow from our little thought experiment: (1) If we are playing Monopoly, yet the game has no purpose, then what we do with our turns doesn't matter. In fact, the very act of taking a turn becomes pointless and empty. (2) If the game was actually invented by someone who established its goal or purpose, players must know what that purpose is. Misinformation about the purpose could easily harm players if their efforts are directed at an end inconsistent with the game's actual goal. Sincerity is not enough.

It's the Epistemology, Stupid!

This is where we stand today. Pervasive, subtle, almost subconscious patterns of ideas in our culture imply that life has no meaning. All that is left is addiction to contemporary happiness, the instant satisfaction of desire, and deep anxiety. Let me explain.

Epistemology is the study of knowledge itself: What is it, what are its limits, how do we acquire it? The fundamental characteristic of contemporary secularism lies in an epistemological principle. Given the two worldviews (which I'll describe in a moment) that permeate the marketplace of ideas, the central defining feature of our secular culture is this epistemological principle: Knowledge is limited to what can be tested by the five senses and the hard sciences are our *only* sources of knowledge of reality. There is no non-empirical knowledge (knowledge outside the five senses), especially no theological or ethical knowledge. Science *alone* carries authority in culture because knowledge gives people authority and science alone has knowledge.

Unfortunately, science cannot even formulate (much less answer) the central questions of importance to life: Is there a God, is there meaning to life, is there such a thing as right and wrong, what is a good person and how do I become one, and so on and so on.

It can hardly be overemphasized that the primary characteristic of modern secularism is its view of the nature and limits of knowledge. It is critical to understand this because if knowledge gives one power—we give surgeons and not carpenters the right to cut us open precisely because surgeons have the relevant knowledge not possessed by carpenters—then those with the cultural say-so about who does and doesn't have knowledge will be in a position to marginalize and silence groups judged to have mere belief and private opinion.

There simply is no established, widely recognized body of ethical or religious knowledge now operative in the institutions of knowledge in our culture, such as the universities and schools. Indeed, ethical and religious claims are frequently placed into a privatized realm of nonfactual beliefs whose sole value is that they are "meaningful" to the believer. Such claims are judged to have little or no intellectual authority, especially compared to the authority given science to define the limits of knowledge and reality in those same institutions.

The pervasive denial of truth, knowledge, and rationality outside the hard sciences has left people without hope that true, knowable forms of moral and theological wisdom can be discovered as guides to a flourishing life. As a result, people have turned to emotion and the satisfaction of desire as the decisive factors in adopting a worldview. In turn, this affective approach to life, now embodied in art and culture generally, has created the conditions for the emergence of the empty self I have described. And I repeat an important point: Never before in the history of Western culture has this personality type been seen so pervasively and profoundly; indeed, it is a post-'60s phenomenon. And this destructive phenomenon results from a shift in worldview from a Judeo-Christian one to two alternatives to be mentioned shortly. The result is a shift in our culture's default position about knowledge: It is limited to the hard sciences and is not available as guidance in the most important areas of life.

Just yesterday, I spoke to a woman who is a doctor at the University of California at Irvine. She is a Christian, and her colleagues regularly express shock and disgust to her that she believes such superstitious things.

The two worldviews that have created this situation and have replaced a Judeo-Christian worldview are scientific naturalism and postmodernism. I want to provide a brief sketch of these secularizing ideologies and explain how they have impacted your life.

Naturalism

Just what is scientific naturalism (hereafter, naturalism)? Succinctly put, it is the view that the spatio-temporal universe of physical objects, properties, events, and processes that are well established by scientific forms of investigation comprise all there is, was, or ever will be.

Naturalism has three major components. First, it begins with an epistemology, a view about the nature and limits of knowledge, known as scientism. Scientism comes in two forms: strong and weak. Strong scientism is the view that the only things we can know are things that can be tested scientifically. Scientific knowledge exhausts what can be known, and if some belief is not part of a well-established scientific theory, it is not an item of knowledge. Weak scientism allows some minimum, low-grade degree of rational justification for claim in fields outside of science like ethics. But scientific knowledge is taken to be vastly superior to other forms of reasonable belief—so much so that if a good scientific theory implies something that contradicts a belief in some other discipline, then the other field will simply have to adjust itself to be in line with science.

Second, naturalism contains a creation story—a theory, a causal story, about how everything has come to be. The central components of this story are the atomic theory of matter and evolution. The details of this story are not of concern here, but two broad features are of critical importance. First is the explanation of macro-changes in things (a macro-change is a change in some feature of a normal sized object that can be detected by simple observation, such as the change in a leaf's color) in terms of micro-changes (changes in small, unobservable entities at the atomic or subatomic level). Chemical change is explained in terms of rearrangements of atoms; phenotype changes are due to changes in genotypes. Causation is from bottom-up, micro to macro. We explain why heating water causes it to boil in terms of the excitation of water molecules. The second feature of the creation story is that all events that happen are due to the occurrence of earlier events plus the laws of nature, regardless of whether the laws of nature are taken to be deterministic or probabilistic.

The third component of naturalism is that it has a view about what is real: Physical entities are all that exist. The mind is really the brain, free actions are merely happenings caused in the right way by inputs to the organism along with its internal "hardware" states, and there is no teleology or purpose in the world. History is just one event following another. The world is simply one big cluster of physical mechanisms affecting other physical mechanisms.

Postmodernism

Postmodernism is a loose coalition of diverse thinkers from several different academic disciplines, so it is difficult to characterize postmodernism in a way that would be fair to this diversity. Still, it is possible to provide a fairly accurate characterization of postmodernism in general because its friends and foes understand it well enough to debate its strengths and weaknesses.[8]

Postmodernism is both a historical, chronological notion and a philosophical ideology. Historically, "postmodernism" refers to a period of thought that follows, and is a reaction to, the period called "modernity." Modernity is the period of European thought that developed out of the Renaissance (the fourteenth to seventeenth centuries) and flourished in the Enlightenment (the seventeenth to nineteenth centuries) in the ideas of people like Descartes, Locke, Berkeley, Hume, Leibniz, and Kant. In the chronological sense, postmodernism is sometimes called "post modernism." So understood, it is fair to say that postmodernism is often guilty of a simplistic characterization of modernity, because the thinkers in that time period were far from monolithic. Indeed, Descartes, Hume, and Kant have elements in their thought that are more at home in postmodernism than they are in the so-called modern era. Nevertheless, setting historical accuracy aside, the chronological notion of postmodernism depicts it as an era that began after and, in some sense, replaces modernity.

As a philosophical standpoint, postmodernism is primarily a reinterpretation of what knowledge is and what counts as knowledge. More broadly, it represents a form of cultural relativism about such things as reality, truth, reason, value, linguistic meaning, the self, and other notions. On a postmodernist view, there is no such thing as objective reality, truth, knowledge, value, reason, and so forth. All these are social constructions, creations of linguistic practices, and as such, they are relative not to individuals, but to social groups that share a narrative. Roughly, a narrative is a perspective such as Marxism, atheism, or Christianity that is embedded in the group's social and linguistic practices. Important postmodern thinkers are Friedrich Nietzsche, Ludwig Wittgenstein, Jacques Derrida, Thomas Kuhn, Michel Foucault, and Jean-Francois Lyotard. Some postmodernists are thorough-going relativists, though most allow that the hard sciences provide reliable knowledge of reality.

Worldviews and You

Naturalism and postmodernism come to us daily in a dozen different ways, some subtle and some not so subtle. They create an impression about the way the world is. They provide a context within which we decide what we will believe and what we will reflect. They form the context within which we define success, set goals for living, and carry out our sojourn between birth and death. And naturalism and postmodernism imply that there is no objective meaning or purpose to life. Homo sapiens are a short-lived swarm of organisms hurling through space on an infinitesimally small piece of dust called earth with no overarching reason why they are here. Atheist Bertrand Russell (1872–1970) gives a nice description of the implications of scientific naturalism:

> That man is the product of causes which had no prevision of the end they were achieving; that his origin, his growth, his hopes and fears, his loves and his beliefs are but the outcome of accidental collocations of atoms; that no fire, no heroism, no intensity of thought and feeling, can preserve an individual life beyond the grave; that all the labors of the ages, all the devotion, all the inspiration, all the noonday brightness of human genius, are destined to extinction in the vast death of the solar system, and that the whole temple of man's achievement must inevitably be buried beneath the debris of a universe in ruins—all these things, if not quite beyond dispute, are yet so nearly certain that no philosophy which rejects them can hope to stand. Only within the scaffolding of these truths, only on the firm foundation of unyielding despair, can the soul's habitation henceforth be safely built.[9]

You must understand that Russell's statement is not some ivory tower pontification that does not impact your life. His statement is now the view of life certified by the academic community, the arts, and the media. If naturalism is true, then you are a physical object, namely, your brain and body. And because you are a chunk of matter—nothing more and nothing less—all your behavior is fixed by your environment and your genetic and brain structure. All your "actions" (they are actually just body movements on this view) are determined by the laws of physics and chemistry. This is grasped by the cultural movers and shapers. For example, Cornell professor William Provine flatly asserts that "free will as traditionally conceived...simply does not exist. There is no way the evolutionary process as currently conceived can produce a being that is truly free to make choices."[10]

And there is no such thing as real, objective right and wrong. Thus evolutionary naturalist Michael Ruse makes this note:

> Morality is a biological adaptation no less than are hands and feet and teeth. Considered as a rationally justifiable set of claims about an objective something, ethics is illusory. I appreciate that when somebody says "Love thy neighbor as thyself," they think they are referring above and beyond themselves. Nevertheless, such reference is truly without foundation. Morality is just an aid to survival and reproduction...and any deeper meaning is illusory.[11]

This means that there is no difference between Mother Teresa and Adolph Hitler, and no real significance to anything your physically and chemically determined body does or does not do. Finally nothing—and I mean *nothing*—happens for a purpose. The ascendancy of naturalism in the West squeezed out the so-called teleological outlook. To help you understand this, I must digress a bit and make a philosophical distinction between an efficient and a final cause.

An efficient cause is that by means of which an effect is produced. When ball A moves ball B, A is the efficient cause of B's motion. A final cause is that for the sake of which an effect is produced. Ball A was made to hit B in order to put B in the side pocket. We can cite efficient causes for what makes water boil, and we can refer to final causes when we give the reason why it is boiling (such as to make tea). Teleology refers to something taking place for an end, a purpose, a goal, a final cause.

Darwin rejected final causes and replaced them with efficient causes regarding living organisms, their behaviors, and their parts. Instead of explaining the eye's existence and nature as being there in order for the organism to see, Darwin told a story about the eye coming to be what it is solely in terms of efficient causes—mutation, variation, natural selection. Drawing to a climax the long war against teleology in human action started by Freud, B.F. Skinner and others of the early and mid twentieth century claimed that no one really acts for the sake of an end. Instead, actions are efficiently caused by various subconscious motives, drives, and so forth.

If there are no purposes, no goals, no ends in the cosmos, then the same must be said for human life and action. One of my philosophy professors at the University of Southern California finished class by saying that the lack of ultimate purpose and meaning was liberating to him because it meant that he could do anything he wanted to without worrying about any ultimate consequences of his actions. This attitude is undoubtedly true of no small number of naturalists.

Note carefully that the question put to Gould—"Why are we here?"—is an irreducibly teleological one. The questioner is asking, "Is there some purpose or end for the sake of which we are here?" But Gould, understanding clearly the implications of Darwinian naturalism, did not answer this question. Instead, he changed the subject and told an efficient causal story of how we got here (the three uses of "because" all cite efficient causes). That's the best a naturalist can do. Ironically, upon Gould's death, his naturalistic friends employed teleology to eulogize his life: He lived in order to combat ignorance, promote genuine science education, defeat creationism. Here is the unavoidable hunger for purpose, a hunger that can neither be explained nor satisfied in a naturalist view of things.

At the end of the day, the naturalist answer to the question of whether there is meaning to life doesn't get much better than a slogan I recently saw in a Valvoline commercial: You're born, you die; in between, you work on cars.

What is true of naturalism is true of extreme secular postmodernism. Because everything is relative to one's culture or personal choices, the difference between right and wrong, virtue and vice, good and bad, true and false, real and unreal, meaningful and pointless is utterly arbitrary. As a result, nothing—such as the prohibition against child abuse, the desire to be a good inner-city teacher, living a life of frugality so your grandchildren can go to college—is really praiseworthy or subject to moral outrage. In fact, all these dichotomies reduce to the level of pure custom and taste, just like decisions about whether we drive on the right or left side of the street, prefer Fords or Chevrolets, or have a one- or two-point conversion in football.

Two other features of postmodernism prevent people from thriving and having deeply meaningful lives. The first is the fact that, according to postmodernism, the self is a social construction, a creation of language and therefore a culturally relative, historically conditioned construct. As Philip Cushman asserts, "There is no universal, trans-historical self, only local selves; no universal theory about the self, only local theories."[12]

Two things follow from this. For one thing, there is no unity to the self and no enduring ego.[13] You do not actually have a real self or "I." Rather the self is a bundle of social roles and relations that are expressions of the arbitrary flux of the group. At different times you are a sports-fan self, a wife self, a salesperson self, a political self, and so on. This has disastrous implications for helping people separate and individuate from others in any objective sense, draw appropriate boundaries, and accept responsibility for their actions. If postmodernism is true, then when people try to deal with their issues and grow as persons through therapy or forms of self-help, all they can do is disown one arbitrary socially constructed self (such as an angry-husband self) and accept another one (such as an innocent-salesman self). Is such a trip even worth the effort?

For another thing, this view gives people no reason to own their pathologies because they can simply distance themselves from an arbitrary, fleeting, constructed self in which their pathologies are embedded.

Second, as postmodern critic Terry Eagleton points out, if the self is a passive social construction, "there are no subjects sufficiently coherent to undertake...actions."[14] Active agency and free action disappear under the postmodern cloud of constructivism. The result is the culture of victimization in which we now live.

A Proven, Reliable Way out of This Mess

I am talking about your life and mine. I am describing the world in which your children are growing up. If you adopt a passive approach to your life, you will drift along in the stream of cultural inertia toward boredom, emptiness, anxiety, unhappiness and addiction, hurry and worry. If you are identifying with these insights and a light is going on in your understanding, you have to be proactive, take responsibility for your welfare, and find a way out of this mess. And fortunately, you don't have to reinvent the wheel. There is an alternative view of the world that alone provides a context that runs in the opposite direction from naturalist, or postmodern pathways. So what exactly would I recommend that you do?

First, you need to formulate a *rational life plan* for yourself, a well-thought-out, reasonable approach to the way you will live your life so as to be a rational person. Such a plan will include what you should value, how you should spend your time, what sort of person you should want to become, and so forth. Second, such a plan needs two features if it is to help you in the remainder of your journey on this earth and beyond: (1) It should be reasonable; it should make sense; there should be some solid grounds for thinking that it is true and correct. (2) It should provide you with a safe place to stand graciously yet firmly in the midst of and against the cultural patterns discussed above, and it should include an account of and reasons for believing in a bigger meaning to life, a larger purpose for which you can live and from which you can derive significance and well-being.

I do not believe that such a life plan is possible unless God really exists, He is a certain sort of being, and we can know that He's real, what He's like, and how He thinks about things of relevance to our lives. Otherwise, we have no way of escape. In a fascinating televised interview with cannibalizing serial killer Jeffrey Dahmer just before he was murdered in prison, Dahmer articulately explained the process that led him to a life of serial murder. Dahmer pointed out that we all have desires—for food, recreation, recognition, and so on—and that we will seek their satisfaction unless we have overriding reasons not to. As a teenager, the world became devoid of purpose for Dahmer. He became an atheist who believed human beings evolved out of slime and that there was no God, no reason why any of us is here, no afterlife, no judgment for what we have done in this life. Dahmer quite correctly could not find room for objective values in such a pointless world, and as he explained, he came to see moral rules as mere social conventions on the level of principles of etiquette for proper eating or dressing for different occasions. Social conventions were not weighty enough to constitute overriding reasons to refrain from seeking the satisfaction of his desires, and the rest is history.

If you think carefully about this, it becomes apparent that Dahmer is correct: If there is no God and so forth, then his conclusions follow. But was Dahmer correct about the nonexistence of God? No, he was not, and in the next chapter we will see why.

Part 2

IS THERE A REAL SOLUTION TO OUR DILEMMA?

The Question of God, Part 1

We've Got a Problem

I want to have a serious conversation with you about God. But I fear it won't go well, and in fact, I feel at a bit of a disadvantage. I'm troubled with two concerns. First, without being mean-spirited, I have to say that the cultural understanding of this topic is so illiterate, so completely wrong, and so politically correct that it seems almost impossible to get a fresh hearing about God. You may think that getting serious about God requires you to accept some blind, illogical viewpoint for which there is no evidence. This attitude is the way we naively take things to be. We assume it without explicitly formulating it ourselves; it lies so deep within our culture that it is part of the very structure of the Western psyche's subconscious.

To see this, consider the following very typical example. Marilyn vos Savant writes a weekly column in *Parade Magazine* called "Ask Marilyn." People send her brainteasers, tough questions, and the like in order to stump her. The column features her answers to these queries. In one such column, a man writes Marilyn asking for guidance. He loves the religion of his parents, but his friends have invited him to explore other religions, and he wants to know what Marilyn thinks of adults who unquestioningly accept their parents' religion without considering alternatives. Here is Marilyn's response:

> Let me tell you what I think of *you* instead. You're smarter than those friends. Religions cannot be proved true intellectually. They come from the heart—and your parents—not the mind. In my opinion, you have behaved wisely.[1]

On the other hand, you may fear that to give careful consideration to the existence of God will eventually require you to adopt a posture of some spokesperson for the Religious Right. You may associate religious commitment with the behavior of some televangelist or with trying to become religious (whatever that means). You can fill in your own blanks here.

As if our cultural understanding were not bad enough, a second and perhaps deeper concern is lurking in the neighborhood. I am speaking of our tendency to project onto God our own distortions, hurts, and disappointments. Sigmund Freud was partially correct when he said that we tend to project onto God our own unhealthy attachments to dysfunctional father figures, whether they be authoritarian or weak and passive. But Freud was not the first to discover this problem. Centuries ago, the Bible itself warned about this difficulty. In Psalm 50:21 (NCV), God warns, "You thought I was just like you," thereby noting the ubiquitous human tendency to create God in our own image. To make matters worse, narcissism has affected all of us and, as Christopher Lasch observed, the narcissist "sees the world as a mirror of himself and has no interest in external events except as they throw back a reflection of his own image."[2]

May I suggest that you have nothing to lose by giving me a fair hearing in the next few chapters. I want to explain how the world looks to me—what I think about God and why I think that way. My views are not idiocyncratic. In their general contours, my views have been held by many of the greatest thinkers and heroic people through the centuries and today. These include outstanding philosophers, theologians, historians, and scientists. My views are consistent with the single, greatest book ever written—the Bible.

I believe two things: (1) that God really exists, has a certain nature, and has a set of ideas about various things that He has disclosed to us; and (2) that the things claimed in the first premise can be known to be true and need not be accepted by a blind, arbitrary act of privatized faith exercised by weak people who need such a crutch. It should go without saying that within the span of a single volume, much less within the limits of three chapters, adequately defending these claims would be impossible. So I won't try. However, what I will do is talk my way through considerations that have been central and persuasive in my own journey in the hope that you will find something of value for your own pilgrimage. And I will provide footnotes that can guide you into fuller, more sophisticated treatments of these themes in case you wish to pursue these matters further.

Getting Started

So how should you approach this topic? How does one search for God, anyway? First, let me tell you how not to do it. You don't want to look for something that works for you or helps you irrespective of whether it's true. To see why, consider the case of a fictitious figure I'll call Wonmug.

Wonmug was a hopelessly dull physics student attending a large Western university. He failed all of his first semester classes, his math skills were around a fifth-grade level, and he had no aptitude for science. However, one day all the physics students and professors at his college decided to spoof Wonmug by making him erroneously think he was the best physics student at the university. When he asked a question in class, students and professors alike would marvel out loud at the profundity of the question. Graders gave him perfect scores on all his assignments even though he deserved Fs.

Eventually, Wonmug graduated and began to work on his Ph.D.

The professors at his university sent a letter to all the physicists in the world and included them in the spoof. Wonmug received his degree, took a prestigious chair of physics, regularly went to Europe to deliver papers at major science conferences, and was often featured in *Time* and *Newsweek*. Wonmug's life was pregnant with feelings of respect, accomplishment, expertise, and happiness. Unfortunately, he still knew absolutely no physics. Everyone laughed at Wonmug behind his back. In short, he was a dunce.

Do you envy Wonmug? Would you wish such a life for your children? Of course not. Why? Because his sense of well-being was built on a false, misinformed worldview. If you approach the question of God in this manner—with no regard for truth, guided only by what you will get out of it—you will trivialize your life and should be pitied just like Wonmug. And you would be naive to think that if you are an atheist, agnostic, or mildly irreligious person, you have somehow escaped Wonmug's problem. I would like you to consider the fact that if you satisfy one of these descriptors, you may very well have chosen your view of God—perhaps unconsciously—precisely because your view works for you; it allows you to live the lifestyle you currently exhibit without threat of being wrong.

Now, if truth is going to be our concern, a problem immediately confronts us. Some of the surface principles and moral rules of various religions may be similar, but when it comes to their deeper aspects— what is real; what God, the self, and the afterlife are like; what the purpose of life is—deep contradictions arise among them. Atheists and conservative Buddhists deny there is a God, but popular Hinduism says there are millions of gods. Islam says the greatest source of infidelity is to believe Jesus is God, yet that is precisely what Christians claim. These diverse viewpoints contradict each other and cannot all be correct.

To see this, consider an illustration I used while speaking at a fraternity house at the University of Massachusetts. Though I had never met them before, I asked three young men to describe my mother. Here's what resulted: She's five feet two, has blond hair, and weighs 105 pounds; she's five feet four, has brown hair, and weighs 125 pounds; she's five feet seven, has black hair, and weighs 140 pounds. I pointed out two things to the young men in attendance. First, they couldn't all be right. My mother could not simultaneously satisfy all three descriptions. Second, sincerity is not enough. For example, the first young man could sincerely believe he was correct and even persuade a million people he was correct, but if my mother did not satisfy his description, then he and all his followers were wrong.

A good way to think about the diversity of religions is in terms of a maze. The most famous maze in the world is located in the gardens of Hampton Court near London. The maze, consisting of eight-foot-tall hedges, was planted in 1702. It covers a third of an acre, and its winding paths are more than half a mile long. When entering the maze, you immediately face a dilemma—*Which path should I take?* The goal is to reach the center of the maze, but which path will take you there? Some routes quickly lead to a dead end; others take you deep into the maze only to eventually fail. Some paths run parallel to each other for long periods of time only to have one hit a wall while the other continues. The challenge is to find the one path that leads you to the final destination—the center.

This analogy is a good one for several reasons. First, the maze analogy places a value on exploration and self-discovery. The only way to assess the effectiveness of a route is to consider where it takes you. Does the route lead you to a dead end or take you to the center? If you are to be a serious seeker of God, you need to carefully assess the different routes that competing religions offer. What deficiencies found in a route will cause you to abandon this route and look for another?

Second, viewing religions as a maze with multiple routes heading in different directions acknowledges the religions' wildly contradictory views. In a maze, participants are confronted with choices that will send them in completely different directions. Heading into the maze, the participant accepts the challenge of finding the one path that will lead him or her to the center.

Third, as in any maze, some routes will at times head in the same direction or run parallel to each other. The Muslim, Jewish, and Christian routes run parallel to each other in their belief that God is one (they are monotheistic). Hinduism and Buddhism run parallel to each other in their belief in the law of karma and reincarnation. The maze analogy lets travelers acknowledge similarities as paths head in the same direction even though only one will ultimately arrive at the center.

I don't want to press the point further except to say one thing. Given such diversity of religious worldviews (including atheism or agnosticism), you are going to have to find a way to increase your chances of arriving at the truth of the matter. In the past 40 years, I have watched literally thousands of people navigate this issue in the wrong way. And before I give you my take on the correct way to seek God, I owe it to you to warn you about this popular but mistaken pathway.

The approach I'm referring to is a smorgasbord approach. Here one considers various religions, picks and chooses a little from each, and formulates his or her own picture of God as a collage. The reason why this approach virtually guarantees failure should be obvious. When people seek God in this way, they always end up with a picture of God that looks strangely like the person who went looking for Him! If one is a liberal Democrat, a conservative Republican, or lives in Kansas City, then God will turn out to be a big Ted Kennedy in the sky, a Rush Limbaugh figure, or a Chiefs fan, respectively! No, this approach is really nothing but a projection of one's own likes and dislikes onto reality in order to feel safe without having to change.

Let me remind you that you don't want to make a mistake in the view of God you eventually embrace. Here's why. The other day our yardman mistakenly pulled a flower he mistook for a weed. It was no big deal. We bought a new flower, planted it as a replacement, and informed the yardman about the situation. Contrast this incident with someone who desperately needs brain surgery and, upon meeting a brain surgeon to schedule the operation, hears the surgeon say, "Of course I will do the operation for you. By the way, isn't the brain located right near the navel?" If this ever happens to you, please find another doctor! Here's the lesson: The more important the issue, the greater the damage done by holding to a false belief. One's view of God is more like brain surgery than flowers and weeds. I labored in chapters 1 and 2 to convince you that the question of God is momentous.

So where does that leave us? I suggest that the only approach to seeking God worthy of the decisive nature of the quest and adequate to be done with integrity is one in which you are guided by your mind. You must think hard, carefully, and as non-defensively as you can. You must look for and at the evidence, weigh it along with alternative explanations, and make the most reasonable decision you can. In short, this issue should lie at the foundation of your rational life plan.

Facts, Explanations, and Proof

Can anyone prove God exists? In my view, this is the wrong question because the notion of a proof sets such a high standard. It invites one to imagine a situation in which one's intellectual opponents have to admit that they are completely wrong with no possibility that your position could be mistaken. This sort of proof is so rare that it is almost impossible to think of an example that satisfies it. About all I can come up with is proof in logic and math. For example, one might say he can prove that $y = 8$, given that $x = 5$ and $y = 3 x -7$. But even here, there will be dissenters. A professor in my doctoral program at the University of Southern California did not believe the simple statements of arithmetic (such as $1 + 1 = 2$) were true. According to him, they were useful fictions. I disagree with him, but my point is that a proof in the sense described above is hard to come by.

Besides, we all have more than adequate grounds for believing many things that fail to live up to the proof standard. We may have doubts and unresolved questions about them and be willing to admit that we could possibly be mistaken, but we can be confident they are true. I know I had coffee this morning, that $1 + 1 = 2$, that kindness is a virtue, that my wife is a person, that I am feeling pain in my ankle, that the banana on the table is yellow, and a host of other things. Yet each of these claims has its critics. I can't prove any of them, but I know them nonetheless.

A better way to approach the question of the existence of God is similar to a technique that is successfully practiced in science, history, law, philosophy, and other areas. I'll call it "a cumulative case inference to the best explanation." This intellectual strategy has two characteristics. First, as the name suggests, it involves an inference to the best explanation. This occurs when we identify a range of data to be explained, formulate a pool of possible explanations, and judge that one is the best among that pool. When this happens, the data provide evidence that the explanation is true. For example, if we observe lightning, static electricity, and so forth, and if we postulate that there are such things as electrons with certain characteristics (a certain charge and mass), we are entitled to believe in electrons if they provide the best explanation of the data. Similarly, if a range of data surfaces in a jury trial, and the best explanation is that the defendant committed the crime in a certain way, then we are entitled to believe that this is so. In what follows, I will identify a range of factual data that find their best explanation by far in the existence of a single, personal God.

Second, this intellectual strategy involves a cumulative case. This occurs when several independent strands of evidence support the same conclusion. In this case, it could easily happen that no single piece of evidence warrants accepting the conclusion, but nevertheless, one still ought to believe the conclusion in light of the combined weight of all the evidence taken together. This regularly happens in trials, in historical explanations, and in science. In what follows, I will offer a range of factual data that, taken together, provide sufficient grounds for believing in God. I actually believe some of these data are sufficient by themselves to warrant belief in God. But all I am asking of you is that you take the cumulative evidence into account as you reflect on the issues to follow.

The Existence of the Universe

The rest of this chapter and a few places in the next may be intellectually difficult for you. Then again, they may be too simplistic. The problem, of course, is that I don't know you. So I am going to write at a level I trust will be challenging and helpful, and I will fill in the gaps with endnotes of sources that vary in level of difficulty. That said, let's plow ahead.

In quiet moments, I suspect you have taken a walk at night, gazed up into the starry heavens, and felt a strong inclination to believe that all of this had to have a cause. My parents were blue-collar workers who never finished high school, but this line of thinking seemed so evident to them that it passed as common sense. And I think they were correct. I am impressed with two features of our universe: (1) It had a beginning, and (2) it didn't have to exist. Let me explain these in order.

The first argument is sometimes known as the *kalam* argument. (*Kalam* is an Arabic word that refers to speech.) It goes like this: The universe came into existence. It hasn't been here forever. There was a beginning. Now, things don't pop into existence from sheer nothingness with no cause at all. Something completely different from and outside the universe had to bring it into being. And the best candidate for that cause is God. Consider the following.[3]

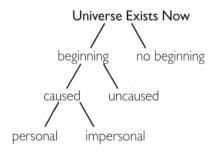

The defender of the argument tries to establish one horn of each dilemma and thus to argue for these three premises:

(1) The universe had a beginning.

(2) The beginning of the universe was caused.

(3) The cause of the beginning of the universe
     was personal.

The Beginning

Let us look briefly at each premise starting with (1). The fact that the universe had a beginning has received overwhelming philosophical and scientific support in recent years. One important philosophical argument for premise (1) involves the impossibility of crossing an actual infinite number of events. For example, if a person started counting one, two, three…he or she could count forever and never count an actual infinite amount of numbers. This is due to the nature of infinity—it is infinitely larger than any finite number. The series of numbers counted could increase forever without limit, but it would always be finite. Trying to count to infinity is like attempting to jump out of a pit with infinitely tall walls—walls that literally go forever without top edges to them. No matter how far one counted, no meaningful progress would be made because there would always be an infinite number of items left to count!

Now, suppose we represent the events in the history of the universe as follows:

The present moment is marked zero and each moment in the past (such as yesterday or 1500 BC) are points on the line. If the universe never had a beginning, the left side of the line has no end. Rather, it extends infinitely into the past. If the universe had no beginning, the number of events crossed to reach the present moment would be actually infinite. It would be like counting to zero from negative infinity.

But one cannot cross an actual infinite (regardless of whether you count to positive infinity from zero or to zero from negative infinity), so the present moment could never have arrived if the universe were beginningless. This means that since the present is real, it was preceded by a finite past that includes a beginning or first event!

One important objection has been raised against this argument.[4] According to some critics, the argument assumes what it is trying to prove, namely, a beginning. They claim that the argument pictures a beginningless universe as a universe with a beginning time, infinitely far away, from which the present moment must be reached. But, they claim, a beginningless universe has *no* beginning, not even one infinitely far away. These critics go on to assert that if one begins with the present and runs through the past one event at a time (yesterday, the day before yesterday, and so on), one will never come to an event from which the present is unreachable.

Unfortunately, this criticism represents a gross misunderstanding of the argument. It does not assume a beginning time infinitely far from the present. It is precisely the lack of such a beginning that causes most of the problems. If there were no beginning, then coming to the present moment would require crossing an actual infinite number of events—analogous to counting to zero from negative infinity—and such a cross is impossible, as was pointed out above.

Further, coming to the present moment by crossing an infinite past would be a journey that could not even get started. Counting to positive infinity from zero can at least begin, even if it cannot be completed. Counting to zero from negative infinity cannot be completed or even started. The whole idea of getting a foothold in the series in order to make progress is unintelligible. Take any specifiable event in the past. In order to reach that event, one would already have to traverse an actual infinite, and the problem is perfectly iterative—it applies to each point in the past.

Critics of the argument go wrong in picturing a beginningless universe as an indefinite, unspecified past, not an infinite one. They invite us to start at the present, work through the past mentally by forming a growing series of events as one works backward, and try to specify a point you could reach that is unreachable from the present! But that is not the correct picture. If we count backward a day at a time, the problem will not be in trying to reach the present from the day we have counted (say we count back 50 million years, stop momentarily, and ask if the present is reachable from that moment). The problem will reside in the fact that for each point we count (such as the moment that was realized 50 million years ago), that point is no better off than the present moment—it could not have happened either if the universe was beginningless, because it would require crossing an actual infinite to reach it, just as the present moment requires.

We have, then, a good philosophical argument for the fact that the universe had a beginning. But premise (1) can also be given scientific support from at least two sources: the Big Bang theory and the second law of thermodynamics. The Big Bang theory is currently the most reasonable and widely respected theory regarding the origin of the universe, and it confirms the fact that the space-time physical universe had a beginning. Scientists have discovered evidence that the galaxies are accelerating away from each other. You can picture this by imagining a balloon with dots drawn on it. Each dot represents a single galaxy. Now, as the balloon is blown up, its surface expands and stretches and the dots travel away from each other. This is exactly what is going on in our universe. Now, if you reverse time and extrapolate backward, you reach a point at which time, space, and matter spring into existence at an initial creation event.

A few years ago, my wife and I visited a science museum in Denver. We entered a room with a display about the cosmos. One exhibit stated firmly and without qualification that the Big Bang theory implies an absolute beginning to our universe. This implication should not be controversial.

Regarding the second law of thermodynamics and its applicability to the question of a beginning of the universe, an argument can be developed along the following lines: The second law states that the universe is irreversibly running out of its useful energy. (This is called "entropy" and has to do with the amount of disorder in the universe or, alternatively, the energy available to do work in the universe.) The universe hasn't reached an equilibrium state yet, so it must have had a finite past. Why? If the universe had already existed throughout an actually infinite past, it would have reached an equilibrium state an infinite number of days ago, but it obviously has not done so.

Think of it this way. Suppose you woke up in a room so tightly sealed that there was nothing whatsoever, including matter or energy, that could enter or escape the room. Now, suppose you found a warm cup of coffee and a burning candle. You would know that the room was not beginningless, that it had not been built and sealed an infinite number of years ago. In fact, you would know that the room could not have been built and sealed more than, say, an hour ago. Why? Because had it been longer, all the warm, burning objects would have run out of energy and the entire room would be a uniform temperature (it would have reached equilibrium).

A few years ago, *Time* magazine featured a story about how the universe will end.[5] The bottom line is that a day will come when the universe's temperature will be at absolute zero (–273 degrees centigrade), there will be no local pockets of heat or light (such as the sun), and the objects in the universe will disintegrate into infinitesimally small, motionless fragments. This has not happened yet, so the universe could not be infinitely old, or else this state would have already been reached an infinite number of days ago.

The Cause

Regarding premise (2) of the *kalam* cosmological argument (the beginning of the universe was caused), the principle that every event has a cause is quite reasonable. We may not always know the cause for some event, but it seems reasonable to always believe that any event has a cause. Our entire, uniform experience favors this principle. We simply find the world to be such that events don't pop into existence without causes.

Some argue that certain quantum events (such as the exact time a specific atom of uranium decays into lead or the exact location where an electron hits a wall after being shot from an electron gun through a tiny slit) do not have causes. But premise (2) of our argument involves something coming into existence out of absolutely nothing. So premise (2) does not really rest on the principle that every event has a cause, but on the much more stringent principle that every event *in which something comes into existence from nothing* has a cause.

Things don't just pop into existence from nothing with no cause. To think such a thing could happen is metaphysically absurd. Remember, nothing is just that—nothing at all. A quantum vacuum, quantum ghost particles, or any other entity is something that actually exists, has certain characteristics that can be described, and so on. But nothingness is the absence of anything whatsoever. It is hardly a candidate for generating a universe!

Besides, if something could just pop into existence out of nothing without a cause, then there would be no reason why it would be a whole universe, a dog, a bucket of sand, a tomato, or anything else. Here's why. Coming into existence is not a process like walking into a room. When you walk into a room, you begin completely out of the room, and then you are 10 percent in the room, 20 percent, and so on until you are completely in the room. Coming into existence isn't like that. It's not as though something starts out completely nonexistent, then becomes 10 percent real and 90 percent unreal, then 50/50, and so on. Something either does or does not exist. Coming into existence from nothing is an instantaneous occurrence.

This means that coming into existence from nothing cannot be governed by the laws of nature. The laws of nature can govern only changes or transitions in things that already exist. If something pops into existence from nothing, laws of nature could not determine why one thing rather than any other thing whatsoever came into existence as it did. In fact, if you think about it, since we are imagining something popping into existence from absolute nothingness, nothing at all could be responsible for why such and such as opposed to thus and so came to be. This shows how bizarre the idea is.

Some may also object that if we hold that all events in which something comes to exist must have causes, then what caused God? But we can consistently hold that all such events need causes and that God does not need a cause because God is not an event. Furthermore, the question, what or who made God? is a pointless category fallacy (the mistake of ascribing the wrong feature to the wrong thing) like the question, what color is the note C? The question, what made x? can only be asked if x is makeable.

But God, if He exists at all, is a necessary being. That means He could not *not* exist. He must be the self-existent, uncreated creator of all else, who simply exists in and of Himself, period. This definition is what theists mean by "God" even if it turns out that no God exists. Atheists and theists typically agree about the definition of what God would be if He exists. They differ over whether or not anything exists that satisfies that definition. Now, if that is what "God" means, then the question, what made God? turns out to be, what made an entity, God, who is by definition, unmakeable?

It's important to bear in mind that my response does not presuppose that God actually exists, only that we have a certain concept of God that we are discussing. Suppose someone asked, "How big are the scales on a unicorn?" The question is clearly a pointless category fallacy. Why? Because the concept of a unicorn is about one-horned horses that don't exist, and even if they did, they aren't the sort of thing that has scales. Fish do, but unicorns don't. In the same way, who made God? is just a confusion.

But there's one more thing to be said here. The concept of God as a necessary being who is the self-existent, uncaused—indeed, an uncauseable—creator of everything else is far from arbitrary. In fact, it is the only logical explanation for the existence of everything else.

Here's why: If God was caused by some other thing, that thing itself would also have to have been caused, and the cycle regresses infinitely with no beginning. And without a beginning, nothing could exist. The regression only stops with something that just exists without being brought into existence by something else. And such a thing cannot be any physical object or indeed the universe itself, which did in fact come into existence. Something supernatural is the only appropriate candidate for the first being.

A Personal Cause

What about premise (3), that the cause of the beginning of the universe was personal? Whatever created the first event existed in an immaterial, timeless, changeless, immutable, spaceless state of affairs (all time, matter, change, and space resulted *from* the first event). How could such an impersonal state of affairs produce the first effect?

The world gives us examples of two basic types of efficient causes (the means that produces an effect). The first kind is the one that governs the behavior of physical or natural causal relationships and is the focus of science. It is called event-event causation. In general, this sort of causation involves one event (the cause) producing another event (the effect) in accordance with the laws of nature. An example is a brick breaking a glass or a ball hitting and moving another one.

It should be clear that the first event could not be produced by such a causal mechanism because the first event must be caused by something that is timeless and changeless and that can spontaneously and immediately produce the first event. Event causal sequences presuppose time, so such a causal relation cannot itself account for the beginning of time and the first event itself. This is why science will never be able to explain the first event. Science cannot start explaining things without objects, space, and time already existing. The laws of nature govern changes in things that exist in space and time. Thus, science cannot explain the existence of the thing that exists before objects, space, and time.

The second type of efficient cause is called agent causation. This type of causation occurs when a conscious person acts, such as when I raise my arm. The cause is a substance or thing (a self), not a temporally prior event or state inside a thing, and the effect (the raising of the arm) is produced immediately, directly, and spontaneously as I (a conscious self) simply exercise and actualize my causal powers to raise my arm. This type of causal relationship does not need an earlier temporal event to cause it, so it is a good model for how a first event could have been generated. It follows, then, that the most reasonable explanation for the beginning of the universe is that it was the result of a free act of will by an immaterial, conscious agent who can exist outside of space and time.

It Didn't Have to Be This Way

At the beginning of this section I mentioned two facts about the universe that impress me: (1) It had a beginning, and (2) it didn't have to exist. I've spent a fair amount of time reflecting on this first fact, and I will close this chapter with a brief discussion of the second. Here's the basic idea: When I contemplate the universe, regardless of how long it has been here, I can easily see that it might not have existed. Why does the universe exist? Something outside the universe had to cause it to exist, and the best candidate for that something is God. Let me elaborate.

An object is "contingent" if it doesn't have to exist. Our world is contingent because it didn't have to be just like it is. The force of gravity, the composition of the atmosphere, and the speed of the earth's rotation all could have been different from the way they actually are.

The following principle is controversial to some, but I really can't see why. It seems commonsensical to me: If something is contingent, then there has to be some reason or cause as to why it exists as opposed to not existing. A particular chair, Pike's Peak, and the Milky Way all satisfy this. Things exist for particular reasons, and in fact, we can actually provide those reasons or causes in many cases. So the universe must have a reason or cause for existing rather than not existing. And whatever that reason or cause is, it must be something outside the natural world itself. In that sense, it must be supernatural.

I claimed above that this principle—that something is contingent, it must have a reason or cause for existing as opposed to not existing— is obviously true to me. But that was not quite the whole truth. There is, in fact, one notable exception to the principle, and to see what it is, consider a person who is deliberating about what to do and is about to make a free choice. Suppose she has two alternatives: to go to the store because she is hungry, or to go to the polling place and vote because she wants to make a difference in local politics.

Now, suppose she goes to the store because she is really quite hungry and doesn't care that much about local politics anyway. I suppose we could look for prior reasons for her choice—perhaps she was raised in poverty with little food and was taught to disdain political involvement. But if actions are really free, then at some point, the regress of further reasons will stop at some final reason on the basis of which one simply acts. It this case, if we ask why she did one thing instead of another, about all we can say is that she just did, and that's all. In other words, she freely chose the way she did, and nothing further can be said about the matter.

So when people exercise free will, there is no reason why their acts exist as opposed to some alternatives. Free acts, therefore, do not conform to our principle. But now we are in an interesting place. If the universe is contingent, it must have some reason or cause for existing rather than not existing, and eventually, we must reach a cause that doesn't have a previous cause of reason for happening as opposed to not happening. And the only type of cause that could qualify is an act of free will. For this reason, the existence of our contingent universe is best explained by an act of free will by a conscious being who is self-existent, that is, who exists and is incapable of not existing.

Remember, the being who causes the universe to exist must be a necessary being (to avoid an infinite regression). But the being's act of causing the universe to exist must be contingent since the effect (the universe's existing) is contingent. If God is a necessary being with free will, then we have an adequate explanation for the universe.

In closing, I must say that these arguments are not merely intellectual exercises for me and they should not be such for you. They are powerful, persuasive reasons for believing in a personal God. Well-known scientist Robert Jastrow mused about these and additional arguments to be mentioned in the next chapter. Jastrow believed that these arguments, especially the scientific aspects to them, have surged in prominence since 1950. But for millennia, said Jastrow, we have known the truth of the statement, "In the beginning, God created the heavens and the earth." Jastrow goes on to comment wryly that the discovery of theistic-friendly evidence in the last 60 years has been a bad dream for the agnostic or atheistic scientist: "He has scaled the mountains of ignorance; he is about to conquer the highest peak; as he pulls himself over the final rock, he is greeted by a band of theologians who have been sitting there for centuries." [6]

4

The Question of God, Part 2

Beginning in the mid-1950s, philosopher Anthony Flew was the most influential, intellectually sophisticated defender of atheism in Western culture. He exercised a magisterial role in debates about God's existence for half a century. But in 2004, Flew shocked the world by announcing that he had changed sides. Since 2004, Flew has become an ardent defender of belief in God.[1] As if this weren't newsworthy enough, his reasons for changing are important and deeply relevant to these chapters. According to Flew, he has no particular interest in God, worship, and that sort of thing, nor does he have concerns about the afterlife. His change had absolutely nothing to do with wanting God to exist. Rather, his change resulted from following the evidence wherever it led, and his conversion was an intellectual one. Flew goes so far as to say that if the recently discovered arguments and evidence for God had been known in 1950, he and other prominent atheists of the twentieth century would have become believers decades ago.

Flew's change of mind is not an isolated incident. For at least 25 years, an explosion of intellectual activity on behalf of theism, particularly Christian theism, has led more and more scholars to convert to or become more outspoken about Christian theism. Chapter 3 featured some of the evidence that was persuasive to Flew and others. In this chapter, I will discuss three additional lines of evidence that have likewise been significant.

Design

The human ear can discriminate among some 400 thousand different sounds within a span of about ten octaves and can make the subtle distinction between music played by a violin or viola. The human heart pumps roughly a million barrels of blood during a normal lifetime, which would fill more than three supertankers. Human eyes are composed of more than two million working parts and can, under the right conditions, discern the light of a candle at a distance of 14 miles. The eye bears a striking analogy to a telescope: The eye was made for vision; the telescope, for assisting it. Both utilize a sophisticated lens. Both reflect and manipulate light. Both are able to bring an object into proper focus. The muscles surrounding the soft lens of the eye move to bring objects into focus, and a telescope uses dials to move the lens.

What are we to make of these facts? These and myriads of additional facts confirm what is obvious—we are the handiwork of a wise Designer. In fact, the evidence for God from design is most likely the most popular argument for God. I find at least four different sorts of evidence to be particularly powerful for justifying belief in God. Before I describe them, however, I should say a word about the basic structure of the design argument which, as it turns out, is pretty commonsensical.

Each day we all try to explain the things that happen around us: Why did the water freeze? Why is it raining today? Why is the car parked on the street and not in the driveway? Why is the water boiling now? In these cases, we use two different forms of explanation: natural law and personal explanations. In natural law explanation, we cite a law of nature and physical conditions. The water froze because water freezes at 32 degrees (the law), and it was 25 degrees last night (physical conditions). When the air reaches a certain saturation point it rains (law), and it is above that point today (conditions). By contrast, we quite often use a personal explanation to explain things. In this case, we cite a person's ability to do something; his motives, intentions, and so forth; and the means he used to carry out his purpose. The car is in the street because Joe is able to drive (by contrast with Sammy, the family's five-year-old), and he wanted to play basketball last night, so he moved the car in order to clear out the driveway.

The design argument goes like this: Certain facts about the world cannot be explained by impersonal causes, conditions, and laws of nature. But a personal explanation works perfectly. We have no reason to think these facts about the world are unexplainable. It is better to use a form of explanation—personal explanation—to explain them. Moreover, some of these facts have characteristics that clearly point to only one source: intelligent agents. So the intelligent action of a Designer is the best explanation for these facts.

Beauty

The first type of evidence that impresses me greatly is the ubiquitous existence of stunning, gratuitous beauty. According to Christianity, the world is not the way it was intended to be. More specifically, death, disease, suffering, and other forms of evil are not part of God's ideal blueprint for the world. But in spite of evil, the world is still overwhelmingly filled with good things. In fact, the widespread presence of gratuitous beauty—beauty that seems to serve no additional function besides just being beautiful—is powerful evidence for a Grand Artist.

Artists skillfully bring parts of a statue or painting together to form symmetry, elegance, and so forth. They effectively use just the right color coordination or the proper harmony of notes and sounds to create beautiful things. But these features and more characterize the world far, far beyond the meager ability of humans to imitate them. In fact, design and beauty should not be discussed in the abstract. The power and force of beauty comes from carefully attending to specific cases of it: a butterfly, the way a baby is formed in the womb, sunset over Maui, the Alps, the fish that fill the oceans. The world is teeming with overwhelming beauty.

Three things about such cases show why they are best explained by a Grand Artist. First, we all know where beauty frequently comes from—skilled artists who generate it day after day. There is no good reason to deny the analogy between human artifacts and the beauty of creation; thus, we should use the same personal explanation for the latter.

Second, beauty is intrinsically good and valuable. If God does not exist, then the best atheistic account of how everything got here would be a strictly scientific account told in terms of chemistry and physics. But science can only tell a story of what is the case. It can say nothing about what ought to be the case; it cannot even use the category of intrinsic goodness or value, much less offer an explanation of how it came to be. But if God exists, the universe begins with a being who is intrinsically valuable, good, beautiful, wise, and so forth. So if God exists, we have a powerful explanation of how subsequent beauty could come to characterize our universe. But if God does not exist, we have no story of how this could be.

Some atheists think they can solve this problem by saying that at some point in the development of matter, beauty just emerged, and that's the end of the matter. But "emergence" is just a name for the problem to be solved; it is not a genuine solution. Further, this sort of emergence is a case of something popping into existence out of nothing. Why? From the Big Bang until some stage at which matter reaches a certain complexity, matter can be fully described by its physical, chemical features. This sort of matter does not contain beauty or even the potential for beauty. Then all of a sudden, matter reaches a certain complexity, and presto, beauty squirts into existence. This borders on sheer magic—indeed, magic without a magician!

Here's the third reason these cases of beauty are best explained by a Grand Artist. To understand this factor, we need to distinguish primary and secondary qualities. Primary qualities are those thought to characterize matter: mass, size, shape, charge, location, being in motion or rest, solidity, and wave characteristics (frequency, amplitude, and length). Secondary qualities are colors, smells, sounds, tastes, and textures. According to science, there (allegedly) are no such things in the world as secondary qualities as commonsense people understand them. Secondary qualities should be reduced to primary qualities: Colors are the same things as wavelengths, sounds are just vibrations, and so forth. But these reductions are all false. Colors may be correlated with wavelengths just as fire may be correlated with smoke. But fire is not the same thing as smoke, and a color is not the same thing as a wavelength. A color is a stationary quality smoothly and continuously spread over an object's surface. By contrast, a wavelength is a colorless, rapidly vibrating, moving quantitative pattern.

Since the time of Newton, Boyle, and others in the seventeenth century, most scientists and philosophers have agreed that if secondary qualities were real, irreducible features of the world, no scientific explanation could account for their origin or their regular, lawlike correlation with primary qualities. The philosopher John Locke gave what is the only plausible explanation for their existence and regular appearance: These were due to God's good pleasure. I think Locke was right. But why God's pleasure instead of His justice or some other attribute of God? Because secondary qualities make the world beautiful and enjoyable. Think of how dull the world would be if it had no sounds, colors, tastes, and so forth, and only had particles and waves moving through space. The sheer existence of secondary qualities and their crucial role in making the world beautiful provide powerful evidence for God's existence, or so it seems to me and many others.

Irreducible Complexity

Scientist Michael Behe has recently called attention to a second and, in my view, very impressive type argument for design called "irreducible complexity." An irreducibly complex system is a "single system which is composed of several well-matched, interacting parts that contribute to the basic function, and where the removal of any one of the parts causes the system to effectively cease functioning." Behe offers a simple illustration of an irreducibly complex system—a common mousetrap.

> The mousetrap that one buys at the hardware store generally has a wooden platform to which all the other parts are attached. It also has a spring with extended ends, one of which presses against the platform, the other against a metal part called the hammer, which actually does the job of squashing the mouse. When one presses the hammer down, it has to be stabilized in that position until the mouse comes along, and that is the job of the holding bar. The end of the holding bar itself has to be stabilized, so it is placed into a metal piece called the catch.[2]

Behe then asks, how effective will the trap be if it's missing the spring? The hammer? The platform? Behe's answer: It won't catch anything! If *one* piece of the trap is missing, it won't perform at all. Yet evolution would seem to claim the mousetrap could evolve slowly, step-by-step. Thus, you would start with a platform, then a hammer, and then a spring, and so on. Here's the problem: According to Darwin, each piece of the mousetrap must be useful by itself in performing its function. But if the purpose of a mousetrap is to catch mice, what good is a block of wood (platform) or an isolated spring?

This same line of thinking can be applied to the eye. What good is a retina by itself? Or ocular muscles without a lens? As an irreducibly complex system, the eye must come as a package deal or it wouldn't be useful. Yet according to Darwin, the eye could not come as a package. If it did, it would violate the very criteria he established for his theory— that living structures had to be capable of evolving in small incremental steps. Darwin said that if a big jump in evolution occurred such that a complex structure came as a package, that would be evidence of a miraculous act of the Deity.

But one does not need to turn to something as complicated as the eye to illustrate irreducible complexity. Indeed, the living world literally teems with it. Consider a much lower, simpler form of life: the bacterial flagellum.[3] A flagellum is a long hairlike filament that acts as a rotary propeller, enabling a bacterium to swim. Look at the following diagram:

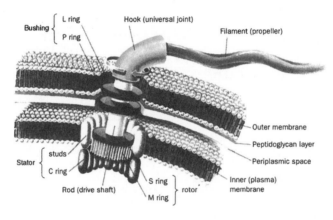

"The Bacterial Falagellar Motor," S.C. Schuster and S. Khan, *Annual Review of Biophysics and Biomolecular Structure*, vol. 23, 1994, p. 524. Used by permission. www.annualreviews.org

The rotary propeller rotates at 100,000 rpms, it can stop on a dime and rotate at that speed in the opposite direction, and it contains at least 50 different parts, which all have to be present and in exactly the right place for the structure to function. It exhibits a structure exactly the same as one that is engineered, and it conforms to the same requirements of functionality. As you can see in the diagram, the bacterial flagellum has three different types of rings, studs, a propeller, a universal joint, and much, much more.

When I ponder this structure—as often happens when I watch a PBS special on some living thing or ecosystem—I find it obvious that the structure is designed by an Intelligence. This is clear even if one does not know the means the Designer used. I struggle to believe that an open-minded person can resist the same conclusion.

Specified Complexity

But other sorts of design are even more powerful, or so it seems to me. One of them—our third argument for design—is "specified complexity." Recently, William Dembski has written a book in which he analyzed cases in which it is legitimate to infer that some phenomenon is the result of a purposive, intelligent act by an agent.[4] Among other things, Dembski analyzes cases in which insurance employees, detectives, and forensic scientists must determine whether a death was an accident (without an intelligent cause) or caused intentionally by an intelligent agent. According to Dembski, whenever three factors are present, investigators are rationally obligated to draw the conclusion that the event was brought about intentionally:

- The event was contingent. That is, even though it took place, it did not have to happen. No law of nature requires that the event happen (unlike the freezing 32 degrees).

- The event had a small probability of happening.

- The event is capable of independent specifiability. That means it can be identified as a special occurrence besides the simple fact that it did, in fact, happen.

To illustrate, consider a game of bridge in which two people each receive a hand of cards. Let one hand be a random set of cards—call it hand *A*—and the other be a perfect bridge hand that the dealer dealt to himself. Now if that happened, we would immediately infer that *A* was not dealt intentionally, but the perfect bridge hand was and, in fact, represents a case of cheating on the part of the dealer. What justifies our suspicion?

First, neither hand had to happen. There are no laws of nature, logic, or mathematics that necessitate that either hand had to happen exactly as it did. In this sense, each hand, and indeed the very card game itself, is a contingent event that did not have to take place. Second, since hand *A* and the perfect bridge hand have the same number of cards, each is equally improbable. So the small probability of an event is not sufficient to raise suspicions that the event came about by the intentional action of an agent.

The third criterion makes this clear. The perfect bridge hand can be specified as special independently of the fact that it happened to be the hand that came about, but this is not so for hand *A*. Hand *A* can be specified as "some random hand or other that someone happens to get." Now, that specification applies to all hands whatsoever and does not mark out as special any particular hand that comes about. So understood, *A* is no more special than any other random deal. But this is not so for the perfect bridge hand. This hand can be characterized as a special sort of combination of cards by the rules of bridge quite independently of the fact that it is the hand that the dealer received. It is the combination of contingency (this hand did not have to be dealt), small probability (this particular arrangement of cards was quite unlikely to have occurred), and independent specifiability (according to the rules, this is a pretty special hand for the dealer to receive) that justifies us in accusing the dealer of cheating.

Similarly, if a woman happens to die at a young age in an unlikely manner even though she is healthy, and if this happens just after her husband took out a large insurance policy on her or a week after proposing to a mistress, then the three factors that justify labeling an event as an intentional act by an intelligent designer are present.

What does all this have to do with the existence of God? In the last several years, scientists have made a discovery so shocking that it played a prominent role in Anthony Flew's conversion to belief in God. In fact, in light of the discovery, Flew says that the universe appears to have known we were coming.[5] Of course, the universe is dead matter and thus cannot know anything, so Flew actually affirms that God was the one who knew we were coming. One of my faculty colleagues—David

Horner—took his doctorate in philosophy from Oxford University. One day while he was walking past a lecture hall, he heard one of the world's leading atheists (I won't mention his name) speaking about this discovery. Horner heard him frankly admit that it provides significant evidence for God's existence, and he really didn't know how to respond to this new evidence as an atheist.

So, what is the discovery? It is this: the universe is precisely fine-tuned so life could appear. More than 30 independent, basic constants in the universe have been discovered that are, scientifically speaking, brute facts and for which there are no further scientific explanations. These include the force of gravity in the universe, the charge of an electron, the rest mass of a proton, and the rate of expansion resulting from the Big Bang. What blows the minds of so many is that if any single one of these—much less all 30!—had been slightly larger or smaller on the order of a billionth of a percentage point, no life could have appeared in the universe. The universe is a razor's edge of precisely balanced, life-permitting conditions.

If gravity's force were infinitesimally stronger, all stars would burn too quickly to sustain life. If ever so slightly weaker, all stars would be too cold to support life-bearing planets. If the ratio of electron-to-proton mass were slightly larger or smaller, the sort of chemical bonding required to produce self-replicating molecules could not happen. The same is true for the electromagnetic force in the universe. If the strong nuclear force were slightly greater, the nuclei essential for life would be too unstable; if it were slightly weaker, no elements but hydrogen would form. If the rate of the universe's expansion had been smaller by one part in a hundred thousand million million, the universe would have recollapsed and could not form or sustain life. Quantum laws are precisely what they need to be to prevent electrons from spiraling into atomic nuclei. If the earth took more than 24 hours to rotate, temperatures on our planet would be too extreme between sunrise and sunset. If the rotation of the earth were slightly shorter, wind would move at a dangerous velocity. If the oxygen level on our planet were slightly lower, we would suffocate; if it were slightly higher, spontaneous fires would erupt.

I could go on and on with additional facts. It should be clear why these discoveries shocked scientists and philosophers. First, these precisely balanced factors are contingent. We can exactly conceive of them being different. Second, they are extremely improbable and balanced to an infinitesimally small degree. And third, they are independently specifiable. Regarding this last point, for the longest time, scientists thought that even if these numbers were significantly different, life still could have appeared. But no longer. They now know that a life-permitting universe has features that are precisely formulated within a range of billionths of a percentage point from what they actually are in the real world. Thus, the actual values fall within razor-thin ranges that are required for life to appear. These values are special (just as are the rules of a card game) quite independently of the fact that the universe's actual values correspond to them.

Think of it this way. Physicist Robin Collins imagines a scenario where human space travelers arrive on Mars and find a fully functioning, life-sustaining biosphere. When the astronauts enter the Martian biosphere, they find a panel that controls the environment.

> At the control panel they find that all the dials for its environment are set just right for life. The oxygen ratio is perfect; the temperature is seventy degrees; the humidity is fifty percent; there's a system for replenishing the air; there are systems for producing food, generating energy, and disposing of wastes. Each dial has a huge range of possible settings, and you can see if you were to adjust one or more of them just a little bit, the environment would go out of whack and life would be impossible.[6]

That's the universe we live in. Each of the 30-plus independent dials (the constants of nature or hard facts about the universe) that we have discovered has a wide range of alternate settings. Yet each dial is exactly set to precisely the correct setting so life can appear. And some scientists estimate that many, many more dials exist that we have not yet discovered. Theoretical physicist Paul Davies draws this conclusion:

> It is hard to resist the impression that the present structure of the universe, apparently so sensitive to minor alternation in the numbers, has been rather carefully thought out...the seemingly miraculous concurrence of [these] numbers must remain the most compelling evidence for cosmic design.[7]

Biological Information

But as impressive as irreducible complexity and specified complexity are, I believe an even more powerful argument for design has to do with *biological information.* To grasp the full force of this sort of design, we must first think for a moment about the SETI research program (the Search for Extra-Terrestrial Intelligence), begun in the early 1960s. Regardless of what you think about SETI or its prospects for success, it is nevertheless a clearly formulated research project that has received millions of dollars of funding during the last half century.

Obviously, before SETI scientists look for intelligent life in outer space, they must first formulate criteria that will tell them when they have found it. And such they have. To grasp these criteria, we must distinguish among randomness, order, and information. As an example of randomness, suppose we had a large pile of alphabet soup noodles composed of numbers and letters and other characters, and I tossed a handful into the air resulting in this sequence scattered on my study desk: x, ½, an upside-down g, %, +, @, 1, q, 7. This sequence is random, and it has two characteristics: (1) Is it simple. To generate a random sequence, you would only have to give a computer two instructions: pick any symbol, and repeat. (2) It is not specific. You tell the computer to pick *any* symbol and repeat with *any* symbol.

Moving from randomness to order, suppose you looked on my desk and saw the letters in a pattern of 500 MEs in a row: ME ME ME...

This sequence is ordered, and it has four characteristics: (1) It is simple. To generate it, you would only have to give a computer three instructions: pick an *M* and then an *E*, and repeat. (2) It is specific (specifically pick an *M* and then an *E*). (3) It is iterative or repeatable—it consists in a unit repeated over and over. (4) The parts (let's call each ME one part) are prior to the whole (which is just a sum of 500 MEs). Here's a test you can perform to tell if the parts are prior to the whole: If you remove a part and it does not do anything to the rest of the whole, then the parts are prior to the whole. For example, if I removed the seventy-fifth ME, there would be a gap there, but the identity of the rest of the MEs would be unchanged. ME number 273 would still be sitting there, quite indifferent to the presence or absence of the ME number 75.

If SETI scientists received a signal from outer space that was random or ordered, they would continue to sip their coffee. Such a signal would indicate nothing at all. But things change dramatically when one is confronted with the third category: information, such as "John loves Mary." Information sequences have four characteristics: (1) They are complex, not simple. To generate our sentence, one would have to tell a computer to produce 15 specific symbols (including spaces) in a row. If we were dealing with the Gettysburg Address, the New Testament book of Romans, or the *Routledge Encyclopedia of Philosophy,* the complexity would be staggering. (2) They are specific (the computer must select very specific symbols). (3) They are not simply composed of an iterative, repetitive unit. (4) The whole (the thought behind the words) is prior to the parts. Here's a test for determining when a whole is prior to its parts: Remove or replace a part. If the entire whole is destroyed, then the whole is prior to its parts. For example, if one replaces *M* in "Mary" with the square root of minus one, you get unintelligible gibberish. If you replace that *M* with a *C* you have an entirely different whole—"John loves Cary."

The movie *Contact,* based on a novel by Carl Sagan, featured Jodie Foster as SETI researcher Ellie Arroway. For a long time, Ellie received only random or simple ordered sequences. But one day she received a signal that told the world an intelligent designer was behind the signal: one that represented the prime numbers from 2 to 101. This signal clearly satisfies the criteria for information. But why did Ellie correctly infer an intelligent designer or communicator as the cause of the signal? The SETI program makes an assumption that seems to me to be almost self-evident: Information only comes from an intelligent agent or mind.

So far so good. But there's a punch line in all this. Perhaps the most important discovery in twentieth century biology was that living things contain a special molecule—DNA—that is composed not of order or randomness, but of information. Indeed, the amount of information in the genetic code of a human being is more than all the information in all the books in the Library of Congress combined! Clearly, if the information in the prime numbers from 1 to 101—measly as it is— legitimately justifies an inference to an intelligent agent as its cause, then by parity of reasoning, an incredibly smart Intelligent Designer must stand behind the information in DNA. Note carefully that one of the intrinsic features of information is that it indicates that it comes from intelligence. So if a critic of SETI claimed that given enough time, chance, and natural law, a signal bearing the prime numbers from 1 to 101 could easily be produced by natural processes, no one would take him seriously. If they did, the entire rationale for SETI would vanish! Even if such an outcome *could* be produced naturally, it would be far more rational to conclude it came from intelligent life. The same sort of reasoning provides a fitting rejoinder to those who would make the same claim about the origin of information in DNA.

These considerations about beauty, irreducible complexity, specified complexity, and information have been defended in a more thorough, sophisticated way than I can do here. But for me, ordinary folk are correct in thinking that the existence of an Intelligent Designer is as plain as the nose on one's face, given the sort of world in which we live. In the remainder of the chapter, I want to share with you two further areas of reflection that I believe provide grounds for the claim that we know there is a God: various features of (1) the moral life and (2) human persons.

Various Features of the Moral Life

You don't have to be a rocket scientist to recognize that our society is in a state of moral chaos. The simple fact that Jerry Springer and his talk show competitors are such popular theaters of moral expression is enough to send shivers down the spine of anyone who has an ounce of moral sensibility. This moral chaos should come as no surprise to anyone who acknowledges the deep connection between the worldview of a culture and its moral beliefs and behaviors. The shift from a Judeo-Christian worldview to an atheistic, naturalistic one is what lies behind much of the moral chaos we now face. In April of 1986, Steven Muller, the president of Johns Hopkins University, got it right when he warned that our crisis in moral values is due largely to the loss of a Judeo-Christian worldview and its replacement with secularism and naturalism.

Conversely, several features of the moral life and the objectivity of purpose in life are, in my view, best explained by the sort of mono-theistic God the Bible describes and who creates human persons in His image:

- the fact that value properties exist and came to be exemplified in the world

- the imperatival force of moral law (they are commands, not mere facts or suggestions) that is best explained by a Moral Commander

- the existence and appropriateness of moral shame and guilt that goes beyond what is owed to other human persons

- the fact that human persons have incredibly high value compared with other entities in the cosmos and that they have equal value as human persons

- the fact that our faculties are such that we have knowledge of value

- the fact that our desire structure causes us to want to do what is right, even when it is not in our self-interests

- the fact that we are so constructed that we can actually make moral progress

- the fact that it is rational to adopt the moral point of view in the first place

Let's unpack some of these points a bit. We all know that moral absolutes exist. By a moral absolute I mean an objectively true moral prescription that, like the truths of math, science, and logic, we discover and do not invent. These prescriptions are true regardless of whether anyone believes them. "One ought not steal, murder, lie," "one ought not torture little babies for the fun of it," "one should be kind, just, and fair-minded..." these are examples of moral absolutes. Anyone who denies the existence of moral absolutes and claims to subscribe to moral relativism is clearly just posturing and not being honest. All you need to do is find out what he or she deeply values, treat that issue as if it were arbitrary and relative, and you will see an absolutist come out of the closet every time!

For example, years ago I met a young man who claimed to be a relativist. After a bit of probing, I found out that he cared deeply for the environment. I then told him that four of my buddies and I had a monthly routine: We would each contribute 50 dollars to a kitty, buy a 100-gallon vat of sulfuric acid, drive to a local lake, dump in the acid, and see how many dead fish floated to the surface. The person whose guess was closest to the number of dead fish won the kitty. Well, you could see the blood vessels popping on his neck. He was enraged. I noted that from his body language, he seemed to think our monthly practice was, well, *wrong!* This young man was a relativist in areas of his life in which relativism was convenient (like his sexual practices), but he was an absolutist when it came to the environment!

The Nuremberg Trials were a series of trials (1945–1949) held in Nuremberg, Germany, prosecuting leaders involved in the Nazi regime. The most famous trial involved 24 key Nazi leaders charged with crimes against humanity. Individuals following the trial were shocked how effective the Nazis' defense team was in arguing against the charges. How is that possible? What defense could be given for the indefensible?

> The most telling defense offered by the accused was that they had simply followed orders or made decisions within the framework of their own legal system, in complete consistency with it, and that they therefore could not rightly be condemned because they deviated from the alien value system of their conquerors.[8]

The lawyers of the Nazis were simply appealing to a moral relativism to plead their case. After all, if morals are determined by culture, then how can you convict Germans for following the values, laws, and beliefs of German culture? If the Germans had won the war, the trial would never have happened.

The trial came to a halt. How would the prosecution respond? The chief counsel of the United States, Robert Jackson, came up with an answer. The only way to judge any culture, he argued, was to appeal to a "law above the law." A "law above the law" transcends culture and applies to both the winners and losers of the war. The trial continued, and justice was served. But from where does such an objective law come? Surely not from plasma or a cloud of electrons! Objective moral values do not come to us as a list of suggestions or simple statements of moral facts. No, they come as thundering imperatives, as commands: Do not murder! And so forth. But commands only come from things with wills, that is, commanders. Thus, the best explanation for the "law above the law," something we all recognize regardless of what we claim in politically correct company, is that it represents the commands of a good, just, loving Commander.

Further, when we violate this law, we feel a deep sense of shame and guilt that goes far beyond what we would experience in front of other human beings. Somehow, we sense that we have done something wrong against—what? The universe itself and some abstract moral law are unconscious, impersonal things—we cannot be ashamed or have rational guilt feelings before them. No, the type of reasonable shame and guilt people feel the world over is best explained if there is a personal source of the absolute moral law, in front of whom we stand guilty.

Here's something else to think about. Consider the statement "The ball is hard." If this statement is true, it has implications for the way the world is. A specific ball exists, and it possesses or exemplifies a real property, hardness. Now consider the following value statements: "Mercy is a virtue." "Friendship is good." "Human beings have worth." These statements are true and, commonsensically, they ascribe non-natural, intrinsically normative value properties to mercy, friendship, and human beings. By a nonnatural property I mean an attribute that is not a scientific, physical characteristic of physics or chemistry. By intrinsically normative I mean a property that is valuable in and of itself and that is something we ought to desire.

Now, anyone would expect to find these properties in the spatio-temporal universe on a Christian view of things. For Christians, the most fundamental entity in existence is not matter or energy or any other physical thing studied by science. It is God, and His attributes include moral and ontological excellence: wisdom, kindness, goodness, and the like. And God created the world to be a place where these values are exemplified and play a role in the course of things. Even if someone claims that value properties are forms that dwell, as it were, in Plato's heaven, it is wildly implausible to believe that if you start with a Big Bang, and the history of the cosmos amounts the rearrangements of particles or waves according to the laws of chemistry and physics, that somehow these ordinary physical processes could reach up into

Plato's heaven and pull these value-forms down into space and time. After all, science describes what is the case, not what ought to be the case; it can only give us descriptions, not prescriptions. Purely physical, natural states and laws amount to what is the case and permit no reference at all to what ought to be the case. The simple fact is that you can't get an "ought" from a mere "is."

Interestingly, naturalist J.L. Mackie agreed and argued that the emergence of moral properties would constitute a refutation of naturalism and evidence for theism: "Moral properties constitute so odd a cluster of properties and relations that they are most unlikely to have arisen in the ordinary course of events without an all-powerful god to create them."[9]

Regarding our ability to know what has intrinsic value, if God exists and is like the way the Bible depicts Him, then He made us to be able to know and live in light of real, objective, intrinsic values. But on a Darwinian atheistic account, the various brain mechanisms relevant to human behavior in general, and rational and ethical behavior in particular, are what they are because they helped (or at least did not hinder) their possessors to adapt to recurring problems over the long course of evolutionary history in feeding, reproducing, fighting, and fleeing, which in turn, aided their possessors in the struggle for differential reproductive advantage. The blind processes of evolution selected sensory and mental faculties apt for interacting with the sense-perceptible world under the demands of survival. However, the ability to be aware of intrinsic value goes far beyond sense experience (you can't see, hear, touch, taste, or smell a moral value). And in any case, the accurate perception of value would make no difference in a world whose successive states are governed entirely by the laws and states of physics. Thus, evolutionary naturalist Michael Ruse makes this note:

> Morality is a biological adaptation no less than are hands and feet and teeth. Considered as a rationally justifiable set

of claims about an objective something, ethics is illusory. I appreciate that when somebody says "Love thy neighbor as thyself," they think they are referring above and beyond themselves. Nevertheless, such reference is truly without foundation. Morality is just an aid to survival and repro-duction...and any deeper meaning is illusory.[10]

Penultimately, we all know that there is a real difference between dysfunctional and properly functional behavior. Child molestation, racist bigotry, and sociopathic narcissism are examples of the former, and behaving kindly, honestly, and lovingly are illustrations of the latter. Now, can a carburetor dysfunction? Of course it can. But sup-pose the Santa Ana winds blew a scattered pile of six leaves on my back porch. Would it make sense for me to say to my wife, "Honey, see the third leaf in the pile, the green one? That leaf is dysfunctional with respect to the whole pile of leaves." It would not. Wherein lies the difference? When we say that the carburetor is dysfunctional, we mean that it isn't functioning the way it's supposed to function. And that means it isn't functioning the way it was designed to function. By contrast, the green leaf was not designed to function a certain way in the pile of leaves—indeed, the entire pile was formed by chance and natural law.

Thus, there is no distinction between dysfunction and function for the leaf. Only with a designer does the distinction make sense. But we all know and act as if such a distinction actually exists in many other cases, and I believe this rational, accurate behavior makes the most sense if we were designed by God to function a certain way. In this case, there is such a thing as proper functioning and real dysfunction-ing. By the way, this is why I think that far from counting as evidence against God's existence, evil actually provides evidence for God. How? Evil is when things aren't the way they are supposed to be or are the way they aren't supposed to be. You can't have real evil without there being a real way things are and are not supposed to be. But again, this distinction is clear to me only if there is a God. But if God does not exist, there just is no way things are supposed to be. Stuff happens and that's the end of the matter.

Finally, Christian theism provides—and atheism utterly fails to provide—a satisfying answer to these questions: Why should I be moral? If I am trying to decide what my life plan will be—what I will care about, live for, and spend my time seeking—and if I want my life plan to be rationally justified and sensible, then why is it reasonable for morality and the life of virtue to be a key part of my life plan? Why isn't it more reasonable to live a life of pure egoism in which my own self-interests, defined any way I wish, are all that should matter to me, rationally speaking? Why should I not just pretend to care for morality when it is in my self-interests to do so, all the while not really adopting the moral point of view at all?

Christian theism says we should be moral because the moral life of virtue is real, we know some truths about it, and to live in disregard of the moral life is to live out of touch with a real and important part of reality made by God. Moreover, God made us to function best when we live the life of virtue. To live in disregard of morality and virtue is to live like a fish out of water, that is, to live contrary to our proper functioning. By contrast, naturalist atheism is too impoverished to be able to explain why I should be moral. Instead, its meager intellectual resources can only justify pure egoism, a grotesque philosophy of life in light of which even atheists cannot live consistently.

Various Features of Human Persons

According to Judaism and Christianity, human persons are made in the image of God. Something about the way we are made resembles the way God is. Now, if this is true, then a very interesting conclusion follows: Some things ought to be true of human beings that don't fit with alternative worldviews, especially those like atheism that deny the existence of God. In my opinion, since the 1930s, various departments in Western universities—biology, anthropology, philosophy, psychology, and sociology to name a few—have repeatedly tried to give an atheistic, naturalistic account of the nature of human persons. But since the 1980s, it has become increasingly apparent that these attempts have failed and that human persons stubbornly resist being accommodated into a naturalist framework, just as Judaism and Christianity predict.

Here's why. Human persons are *conscious*. Consciousness is what you are aware of when you introspect. We have several different states of consciousness: sensations (such as an awareness of red, emotions, or a pain), thoughts, beliefs, desires. Human persons have *free will*. We *act teleologically*—that is, we put together a chain of acts as means to achieve a final end. We act *rationally*—we deliberate, have thoughts about the world, we get insight into the relationship between premises and conclusions of different thoughts we entertain. We are *simple, unified selves;* we are centers of consciousness.

From Particles to Persons

If God does not exist and scientific atheism is true, the universe begins with dead matter that behaves according to the laws of chemistry and physics. So before the first sentient life, there was no such thing as consciousness, no such thing as free will. The history of the cosmos was constituted by the unfolding of a series of events—efficient causes—in accordance with natural law. There was no teleology. There was no rationality—everything was caused by nonrational particles in motion. And all ordinary-sized objects (brains, rocks, dogs) are aggregates composed of myriads of tiny particles. In fact, the processes of nature involve the formation of new combinations of particles from existing combinations according to natural law.

Do you see the problem? How do you get beings with the five features mentioned above if you begin with matter that is capable of being completely described by the hard sciences? Brute, dead matter is bereft of these features. And how do you take such matter, subject it to processes that simply rearrange it and recombine it according to physical laws, and get simple, unified selves that are conscious, possess free will and rationality, and are capable of acting for the sake of final causes? By contrast, if God exists, the universe begins with a being who has these five features, so their origin in the universe is not a problem as it is for the atheist.

Human Value

Two other features of human persons are of importance in this context. The first involves the idea that human persons have equal rights and values, and that they have greater rights and values than other life forms. This is quite rightly a cherished belief of most people. However, this claim is difficult if not impossible to justify given a naturalist worldview. Two things must be true if people have equal rights and value: (1) They must have something in common equally. (2) Whatever it is they have in common, it must be deeply important and valuable and not shallow or trivial.

For many naturalists, the best and perhaps only way to justify the belief that all humans have equal and unique value is in light of the metaphysical grounding of the Judeo-Christian doctrine of the image of God.[11] Such a view depicts humans as individuals with a human nature made in the image of God. Unfortunately, Darwin's theory of evolution has made belief in human nature, though logically possible, nevertheless, quite implausible, as Ernst Mayr has noted:

> The concepts of unchanging essences and of complete dis-continuities between every eidos (type) and all others make genuine evolutionary thinking impossible. I agree with those who claim that the essentialist philosophies of Aristotle and Plato are incompatible with evolutionary thinking.[12]

This belief has, in turn, led thinkers like David Hull—perhaps the leading philosopher of evolutionary biology in the twentieth century—to make the following observation:

The implications of moving species from the metaphysical category that can appropriately be characterized in terms of "natures" to a category for which such characterizations are inappropriate are extensive and fundamental. If species evolve in anything like the way that Darwin thought they did, then they cannot possibly have the sort of natures that traditional philosophers claimed they did. If species in general lack natures, then so does *Homo sapiens* as a biological species. If *Homo sapiens* lacks a nature, then no reference to biology can be made to support one's claims about "human nature." Perhaps all people are "persons," share the same "personhood," etc., but such claims must be explicated and defended *with no reference to biology*. Because so many moral, ethical, and political theories depend on some notion or other of human nature, Darwin's theory brought into question all these theories. The implications are not entailments. One can always dissociate "*Homo sapiens*" from "human being," but the result is a much less plausible position.[13]

Finally, this observation has led a number of thinkers to claim that the traditional "sanctity of life" view of human beings is guilty of speciesism (a racist, unjustified bias toward one's own biological classification) and to attribute our value to personhood and not simply to being human. Thus, value resides in personhood, not humanness. What is a person? A person is anything that satisfies the right list of criteria, that is, has a self-concept, can form meaningful relations with God or others, can use language, can formulate goals and plans, and so on.

There are two key implications of this view: (1) There can be human nonpersons (such as defective newborns and people in comas) and personal nonhumans (like orangutans), and the latter have more value than the former. (2) The features that constitute personhood can be possessed to a greater or lesser degree, so some individuals can be more of a person and thus have more rights and value than other individuals. In my view, (1) is false. Being a person is to being a human as being a color is to being red. There can be nonhuman persons (angels) but there can be no human nonpersons, just as there can be colored non-red things (blue things) but no red non-colored things.[14] Proposition (2) is one that naturalists have worked hard, and in my view, unsuccessfully, to avoid.[15] In any case, it should be clear that the high intrinsic and equal value of all human beings is easy to justify given Christian theism, but they are hard to square with naturalism.

Human Flourishing

Psychologists have recently discovered another characteristic of humans persons that is of great interest to me. To understand the impact of this discovery, let me digress a bit and talk about a certain form of reasoning.

From scientific theorizing to everyday life, we all quite appropriately engage in if-then reasoning: If the moon were in such and such a place, then the tide would be thus and so. But the tide isn't thus and so, so the moon must not be in that place. If oil prices go up, then... You get the idea.

Just the other day I was browsing in Borders, and I came across a book by Laura Smith and Charles Elliot entitled *Depression for Dummies,* and boy, did I find something interesting toward the end of the book.[16] Before I tell you what it was, let's do a little if-then reasoning first. Suppose that God does not exist and evolutionary theory tells the correct story about how we got here. For our purposes, the important thing about that story is that all living things, all their behaviors, and all their parts exist and are what they are because they were successful (or at least were not a hindrance) in the struggle for survival.

More specifically, they effectively contributed toward the tasks of finding food, getting away from danger, fighting when needed, and reproducing efficiently. If this is the correct story of our origins, then the human behaviors that are most conducive to human flourishing should be those that are closely connected to finding food, getting away from danger, fighting when needed, and reproducing. In fact, this if-then form of reasoning is the basis of evolutionary psychology according to which human behaviors—for example, male preferences for certain female body shapes—are what they are because somewhere in our past, they contributed to these survival-enhancing activities (these body shapes were most effective for producing healthy offspring).

Now let's assume a different creation account. Suppose that the God of the Bible is real, He created us, and irrespective of how He did it, He put us here for a purpose. If this is the correct account of our origins, then according to the Bible, certain things will be central to human flourishing: daily gratitude to God for the things of life, learning to give and receive love, seeking and learning to give forgiveness, and finding ultimate meaning and purpose in life according to why we were put here in the first place.

According to the naturalistic evolutionary account, human flourishing should be achieved through behaviors associated with power, sexual attraction, physical health, social position, and wealth (since wealth should make one less vulnerable to living conditions that shorten life). According to the biblical account, human flourishing should be achieved through spiritual and moral behaviors associated with living a righteous, loving, grateful life of objective meaning and purpose according to the way we were created to function, all the while seeking forgiveness for our wrongs and offering it to those who have wronged us. What we have here are two very different if-then scenarios. If a Vulcan were coming to earth with no clue what he would find here, yet he were armed with these two contrasting theories, he could find empirical (observational) evidence for one and against the other by observing what factors are actually conducive to human flourishing.

Well, don't hold your breath for Vulcans to land on earth. Fortunately, we don't have to wait for them to do the empirical research regarding human behavior and human flourishing. And here's where *Depression for Dummies* comes in. Summarizing the findings of empirical psychology, Smith and Elliot note some interesting facts. Contrary to what you might think, power (for example, money, education, and success), health, sexual attractiveness, and being youthful are not all that important as factors conducive to happiness and human flourishing. This finding runs counter to what we should expect if the naturalistic evolutionary story were true. So these findings provide some disconfirming data for this evolutionary story.

But the findings of empirical psychology don't stop there. Smith and Elliot list in this order the factors that are, in fact, conducive to happiness and human flourishing: At the top of the list is living in a constant spirit of gratitude—a sense of thankfulness in life. Next were unselfishly caring for and helping others, learning to give and receive forgiveness, and finding a deep and real sense of meaning and purpose in life by giving oneself to a larger framework than the individual's own life.

Two things stand out about this list. First, they are exactly what one would expect if the biblical account is true. So these findings provide some confirming data for the biblical account.

Second, several items on the list are absolutely absurd and irrational on the naturalistic evolutionary account, but they make rational sense on the biblical account. For example, one can't be grateful for something (a new car) without being grateful to someone (the person who bought it for you as a gift). And one can express gratitude only toward another intelligent, conscious being. One cannot be grateful to a fencepost, the moon, or a collection of atoms. On an atheistic view, one can be happy that the sun is bright or the ocean is turquoise, but one can't be grateful for these things since there is no one to whom to be grateful. And the psychological data show that gratitude brings happiness. Happiness does not create itself.

The same goes for meaning and purpose. If atheism is true, there *is* no ultimate, objective meaning and purpose. We and the universe in which we live are just here, and that's all. Neither it nor we are here *for* anything. Since objective meaning and purpose are conducive to human happiness and flourishing, that flourishing is frustrated on an evolutionary, naturalist view because the things that generate it (objective meaning and purpose) make no sense within naturalist limitations. But meaning and purpose are central to the biblical view. So these findings about human beings provides evidence against atheistic naturalism and for theism.

Summary and Prelude

In the last two chapters, I have briefly provided some of the reasons why believing God exists makes sense. But the arguments presented do not merely justify belief in God; they also provide information about what sort of being God is. From the arguments of chapter 3 (from the universe's beginning and dependency) we concluded that God is immaterial, He is capable of existing outside space and time, and He possesses free will and therefore consciousness. From the design argument, we may conclude that God appreciates beauty and that He is extremely knowledgeable. From the moral argument we may conclude that God is good and virtuous. And from the nature of human persons we may conclude that God is a person with rationality, consciousness, and free will and that He is capable of acting for the sake of ends.

For three reasons, we should also conclude there is one personal God instead of many finite, polytheistic gods: (1) Finite gods (think of the Greek gods or the multitude of Hindu gods) are capable of change, movement, and acting through a span of time and are therefore temporal. That is, they require the existence of time to exist. But the God who must exist to explain the facts of chapters 3 and 4 must exist outside of time (to be capable of causing time to begin). So a plurality of finite gods is ruled out. (2) If two explanations are equally successful, then all things being equal, one should prefer the simpler explanation. Solely for the sake of argument, let's assume that polytheism and monotheism are equally good explanations for the facts. Under these assumptions, the advantage of simplicity requires us to prefer monotheism. (3) Any number of gods greater than one is explanatorily superfluous and impotent. To see this, take some arbitrary number of finite, polytheistic deities and call that number n. Now, why are there n deities instead of n / 2 or n + 50 or...? Any other number of finite deities will do just as well. If this is so, then no particular finite number over one will do a better job of explaining the facts than another number. Thus, any number greater than one is superfluous.

As it turns out, God leads a very interesting life. In fact, He loves His life a lot. He's creative, kind, just, good, completely separate from any wrongdoing and all evil, extremely intelligent, very, very powerful, fair and just, and filled to overflowing with hilarious joy. He's the sort of person who loves to forgive people. He also loves the things He made. And get this: He loves you a great deal. In fact, He actually likes you. In fact, you are on His mind even as you read this. I'm getting ahead of myself, but I just couldn't resist telling you a little bit about the person I have come to love deeply. I'm ahead of myself because we'll need to talk about some things in the next two chapters for all this to make enough sense to you to warrant giving your entire life to God.

The Luminous Nazarene

God exists. This much we know. And this is no small fact. It is, arguably, the single most important fact anyone could know. And knowledge of this fact should prod us to seek God with everything we have. But how do we go about such a thing? Where do we go from here?

Three Criteria for Choosing My Religion

Three criteria are central for choosing (and not losing!) one's religion. First, does the depiction of the Supreme Being in a given religion harmonize with what we already know about God from creation? For example, does it line up with the considerations about monotheism listed in chapters 3 and 4? If it doesn't, the religion is false. If it does, it may be true. We do not bring a blank slate to the table when we assess various alleged revelation sources, and this criterion justifies religions that are forms of ethical monotheism. Note carefully that the explanatory demands of creation, not the Bible or some other alleged revelation, justifies monotheism.

The second criterion for choosing one's religion is this: Does that religion provide the most profound diagnosis of the human condition and the most adequate solution to that diagnosis? Humans everywhere need a threefold reconciliation (people are at odds with God, other people, and even themselves), relief from shame and guilt, meaning to life, hope for life with God and purposeful existence after death, guidance for living well, relational intimacy with God Himself, and empowerment to live the sort of life we all know we should live.

I cannot argue this point here, but while I would admit that most religions have truths in them, the person, deeds, and teachings of Jesus of Nazareth and His apostles, recorded in the New Testament, simply tower over all other ideologies and religious systems. This is true both in its intrinsic content and in its historical impact throughout generations. Regarding its intrinsic content, all one needs to do is read the rich devotional, theological, and ethical literature in the history of Christianity to see that, when it accurately expounds the New Testament, this literature is without rival. Regarding historical influence, counterexamples, such as the Crusades, do not count as genuine counterexamples because the teachings of the New Testament itself show that the counterexamples are not genuine expressions of New Testament religion. Wherever genuine Christianity has thrived, human flourishing has flowered.

And here is the third criterion for choosing one's religion: Does the best explanation of both the origin and continued history of the religion include God's supernatural activity? Is the signature of the divine on that religion? I am convinced by arguments from fulfilled Old Testament prophecy and by historical evidence that the Bible is indeed a divine revelation and that Jesus of Nazareth is the risen, divine Son of God. The historical evidence for Jesus will occupy us in the remainder of this chapter.

A Word of Caution

When we began to talk about God a few chapters back, I expressed my reservations to you. I was concerned to get a fresh, non-stereotyped hearing from you. I am even more troubled about this as we discuss

Jesus. In his deeply insightful book *The Jesus of Suburbia,* Mike Erre
makes this note:

> I think we have lost sight of Jesus among all the trappings
> of the Christian religion. Amid all the hype about the grow-
> ing political power of evangelicals, the growing number of
> megachurches, and the booming, billion-dollar Christian
> subcultural industry, I wonder if we have left Jesus behind.
> Or, worse, if he has left us behind…My primary contention
> is this: Much of what passes for modern, Western Christian-
> ity isn't of Jesus.[1]

The figure of Jesus and the movement He began is covered over
with layer after layer of things that have little or nothing to do with
either. We need to put some cognitive and emotional distance between
ourselves and the distorted cultural stereotypes if we are to approach
the real Jesus. But this isn't easy. As a result, I feel a bit like Donald
Miller:

> In a recent radio interview I was sternly asked by the host,
> who did not consider himself a Christian, to defend Chris-
> tianity. I told him that I couldn't do it, and moreover, that
> I didn't want to defend the term. He asked me if I was a
> Christian, and I told him yes. "Then why don't you want
> to defend Christianity?" he asked, confused. I told him I
> no longer knew what the term meant. Of the hundreds of
> thousands of people listening to his show that day, some of
> them had terrible experiences with Christianity; they may
> have been yelled at by a teacher in a Christian school, abused
> by a minister, or browbeaten by a Christian parent. To them,
> the term *Christianity* meant something that no Christian
> I know would defend. By fortifying the term, I am only
> making them more and more angry. I won't do it. Stop ten
> people on the street and ask them what they think of when

they hear the word *Christianity,* and they will give you ten different answers. How can I defend a term that means ten different things to ten different people? I told the radio show host that I would rather talk about Jesus and how I came to believe that Jesus exists and that he likes me. The host looked back at me with tears in his eyes. When we were done, he asked me if we could go get lunch together. He told me how much he didn't like Christianity but how he had always wanted to believe Jesus was the Son of God.[2]

In like fashion, I am not interested in discussing Christianity, much less Christendom. But I do want to talk about the luminous Nazarene, as Albert Einstein once called Jesus. He is quite simply the most important, influential figure in human history. He himself predicted that He would stand at the center of world history. And so He has, and so He does. Distinguished Yale historian Jaroslav Pelikan offers this word picture:

> Jesus of Nazareth has been the dominant figure in the history of Western culture for almost twenty centuries. If it were possible, with some sort of super magnet, to pull up out of that history every scrap of metal bearing at least a trace of his name, how much would be left?[3]

In his 2002 book *The Next Christendom: The Coming of Global Christianity,* Philip Jenkins, a distinguished professor of history at Penn State, notes that the most significant changes in the world during the last portion of the twentieth century were not secular trends like fascism, communism, feminism, or environmentalism. According to Jenkins, "It is precisely religious changes that are the most significant, and even the most revolutionary, in the contemporary world...We are currently living through one of the transforming movements in the history of religion worldwide."[4] According to Jenkins, the church is exploding at unprecedented rates in the Third World.

Jenkins is not alone in this assessment, and everyone who knows the facts recognizes that in the past 50 years or so, and especially since 1980, revival has been breaking out all over the world. The best-kept secrets of the era are the explosion of the kingdom of God and a harvest of converts and disciples greater than anything the word has ever seen. In fact, the single most explosive movement of any kind—political, military, or whatever—is the spread of the gospel and the advance of the kingdom in the past 50 years. Consider the following: Some estimate that in 1970, there were around 71 million born-again Christians with a vision to reach out to the entire world for Christ. By the year 2000, there were 707 million, roughly 11 percent of the earth's population! Up until 1960, Western Evangelicals outnumbered non-Western Evangelicals by two to one, but by 2000 non-Westerners (mostly Latinos, blacks, and Asians) led by four to one, and the figure will be seven to one by 2010. Today more missionaries are sent from non-Western than Western nations. At a church-planting congress in 1998, representatives from Latin American countries set a staggering goal of planting 500,000 new churches by 2010 and—get this—progress up to 2005 indicates that the target will be reached! In fact, five nations have already reached their target goals and have set new ones![5]

If things continue this way for the next 20 years, a transformation of epic proportions will characterize the global scene. Keep in mind that these numbers do not just represent nominal converts. Transformations of social, cultural, religious, and even economic conditions often accompany these conversions.[6]

How is it that a carpenter from obscure Nazareth commands the allegiance of hundreds of millions of people who have given and would give their lives to Him? The New Testament documents have an answer: Jesus was the very Son of God, that is, He was (and is) God the Son. Jesus was genuinely God and man, He was the incarnation of God, and He is the final, supreme revelation of God to the human race. He lived a sinless life, performed numerous miracles, and rose bodily from the dead three days after His crucifixion. I am convinced that this picture of Jesus is true, and I am going to present historical evidence to support that conviction. As I do, please keep something in mind. I will make reference from time to time to New Testament texts. However, I will not be assuming that the New Testament—or the Bible generally—is a true revelation from God, though I do believe that to be the case. Instead, I will simply assume that the New Testament documents are first-century historical sources for the life of Jesus and the origins of Christianity. My task is to argue that these sources are solid and historically reliable.

Historical Evidence for Jesus

According to a widely held myth, only simpleminded folk trust the New Testament, and intellectuals, on the other hand, are all convinced it is filled with legend. But this myth is shattered by a simple but significant fact: Thousands of men and women with earned doctorates in history, New Testament studies, or first-century culture from world-class institutions accept the reliability of the New Testament documents precisely because of (and not in spite of) their academic training. In fact, highly regarded intellectuals at elite universities who teach in this area of study are convinced by their investigation of the facts that the New Testament is reliable and that the traditional view of Jesus is true. This does not prove the New Testament documents are historically reliable, but it does show that the case for their reliability must be substantial, or one would not find so many scholars, including many at the top of the field, who hold and have contended for this view. Let's look at some of the evidence.

Evidence for Jesus Outside the New Testament

Roman and Greek historians during or shortly after Jesus' life were geographically distant from Judea and Galilee. Moreover, this location was considered to be a remote and unimportant outpost far, far away from Rome, so there was little interest in what happened there. First-century historians did not pay much attention to the many religious figures, social and political movements, and examples of unrest and instability in Judea and Galilee. But they did take note of Jesus. And much ancient literature has been lost, so they may have referred to Jesus more than we know.

Setting aside the New Testament documents, we have clear references to Jesus in Roman, Jewish, and Greek historians. From these we get the following picture: Jesus was a Jewish teacher who had a group of disciples, He was a wonder-worker of some sort, performing healings and exorcisms, He was rejected by the Jewish leaders and crucified by Pontius Pilate during the reign of Tiberius Caesar, the sky turned dark at the time of the crucifixion (the pagan historian Thallus explains this as an eclipse of the sun!), His followers claimed to have seen Him risen from the dead shortly after His crucifixion, and the Christian movement spread so rapidly that within a few decades it had taken root in Rome itself.[7] In AD 49 the Roman emperor Claudius expelled the Jews from Rome because they were disputing over "Chrestus," most likely because the preaching of Jesus in Roman synagogues created a large disturbance in Rome.

The Time Factor

Let us use the term "high Christology" to refer to a picture of Jesus as God Incarnate, the miracle-working Son of God, who rose bodily from the dead. Let's use "low Christology" to refer to a picture of Jesus as a mere man who was a charismatic leader and gifted teacher. The duration of time from Jesus' crucifixion in AD 33 until there is clearly a high Christology in the early church is too short for myth and legend to influence that portrait. The time factor is so short that it is implausible to disregard the early church's high Christology and its portraits of Jesus in the Gospels. Moreover, during this short time span, plenty of friendly and hostile eyewitnesses were available to keep in check extravagant claims about Jesus. And the high Christological view of Jesus begins around the geographic area in which Jesus lived and ministered, not hundreds of miles away. This too provides grounds for trusting the New Testament picture of Jesus. Let me elaborate on these points.

Secular, classic historian A.N. Sherwin-White—an expert in the times prior to and during Jesus' day—claims that even though Roman and Greek historical sources are heavily biased and removed from the events they discuss by as much as two centuries, historians still use those sources successfully to reconstruct what actually happened. He also says that for the Gospels to be legendary, the rate of legendary development would have to be "unbelievable." Using Herodotus as a test case, Sherwin-White argues that a span of even two generations is too short to allow legendary tendencies to sweep away the hard core of historical facts.[8] Given this fact, let's consider the first three Gospels: Matthew, Mark, and Luke.

The Gospel Record

Two facts are virtually beyond dispute: First, the same person wrote Luke and Acts. We know this because of the similar style, grammar, vocabulary, themes, and so on. Second, Acts was written after Luke, and Luke was written after Matthew and Mark. If we can date the book of Acts, Luke should be dated earlier and Matthew and Mark earlier still. In my opinion, overwhelming evidence shows that Acts should be dated around AD 60–62.[9] Here are three reasons for this dating.

1. Acts ends abruptly with Paul in prison in Rome and with no indication of what happened to him after his release. The ending of Acts has a distinctive feel of having been written at the same time of the events it recalls—Paul's imprisonment from AD 60–62.

2. The author of Luke and Acts focuses on events in and around Jerusalem more than the other Gospels. For example, Jesus' resurrection appearances in Luke occur in Judea, but the ones in Matthew and Mark take place in Galilee. The city of Jerusalem and the church there play a prominent role in Acts. Jerusalem was surrounded by Gentile armies in AD 66 and destroyed in AD 70, yet Acts makes no mention

of this. The silence of Acts is even stranger when we realize that in Luke, Jesus predicts that Gentiles will surround and destroy Jerusalem. For the sake of argument, suppose the author made up this saying and placed it on Jesus' lips. What would be the purpose of such a fabrication if the "fulfillment" happened and was not duly noted? The only sensible explanation to me is that Acts was written before AD 66.

3. Acts is careful to record the martyrdoms of figures in the early church, such as James (the brother of John) and Stephen. The three key figures in Acts are James (the brother of Jesus), Peter, and Paul. All three were martyred in the early to mid 60s, yet there is no mention of any of this in Acts. This is best explained if Acts was completed before the early 60s.

Given a date of AD 60–62, Luke should be dated from the early to late 50s. Luke was earlier than Acts, but no evidence exists that they were written in a continuous fashion. A time gap between the completion of Luke and the beginning of Acts is entirely possible. Matthew and Mark were probably written between the early 40s and the mid 50s.[10] And of course, the material contained in these Gospels was in wide circulation years before it was written down.

Paul's Letters

Besides the Gospels, we have 13 of Paul's epistles that were written over a 16-year period from AD 49 to AD 65. When we examine these letters, two facts become obvious: (1) Paul's view of Jesus is static; that is, it doesn't begin with a low Christology in his earlier letters and evolve to a high Christology in his later letters. Throughout this time period, Paul's view of Jesus remained constant. (2) Paul's Christology was uniformly high. He knows nothing of a mere sage or charismatic leader. From the very beginning, Jesus is the Incarnation of God Himself, a miracle worker, the Savior of the world, who rose bodily from the dead. Sometime before AD 49, Paul's view of Jesus was solidified.

Some critics attempt to marginalize Paul by claiming he was in serious conflict with Peter and that Paul's Christology is not representative of the early church. But this claim is a significant exaggeration without sufficient evidence. Their confrontation about certain issues (such as separating from the Gentiles) hardly justifies this hasty generalization. No evidence at all indicates that Paul and Peter were involved in a major rift in the early church. Moreover, not more than four years after the crucifixion, Paul himself checked out his gospel and Christology with the early leaders of the Jerusalem church (Peter, John, and James) to make sure it was in harmony with the rest of the early church (see Galatians 1–2). And he explicitly states that his Christology was authoritative teaching in the early church that he received from others (Romans 1:1-4; 1 Corinthians 15:1-7). This was entirely in keeping with the communitarian worldview of the Ancient Near East. That culture did not value Western individualism, so the idea that Christianity was started by the rogue Paul, who individualistically stood by himself quite apart from the rest of the early Christian community, is a myth. All this means that the early church had adopted a high Christology sometime before AD 49.

A Message in the Music

But there's more. The letters in the New Testament were written in Greek for Greek speakers in the Gentile world. The early Jewish followers of Jesus in the Jerusalem area during the first decade after AD 33 primarily spoke Aramaic and Hebrew (though many also knew Greek). Scholars have discovered various hymns and creeds—ranging from two to seven or eight verses—embedded in New Testament letters (for example, 1 Corinthians 15:3-8; Philippians 2:5-11). These texts are written in the form of Hebrew poetry, they translate easily from the Greek back into Aramaic, they contain Aramaic, and Jewish phrases, and the vocabulary is sometimes different from the way Paul (or Peter or John) typically speak.

These facts have led most New Testament scholars to the view that these are early hymns used in worship services and instruction among Aramaic-speaking Jewish followers of Jesus in the first decade after the

crucifixion—most likely, within three years—in and around Jerusalem. Paul and the others translate them into Greek and incorporate
them into their letters. And get this: Every one of them is about Jesus
Christ, and they exalt Him to the status of God! These texts show two
things: (1) The early Jewish Christian community had a high Christology at a very early date. Within no longer than three to five years after
the crucifixion, Jesus was being worshipped by monotheistic Jews as
God Almighty, and miracle-working deeds and the bodily resurrection
were ascribed to Jesus. (2) This early, high Christology was present in
the very soil where Jesus was alleged to have performed miracles and
risen from the dead. That is, it was present exactly where numerous
friendly and hostile eyewitnesses lived!

New Testament scholar Larry Hurtado claims that within the first
few months, and perhaps within the first few weeks, these early Jewish
converts not only believed Jesus was God but also engaged in devotional practices and worship that exalted Jesus to the status of being
coequal with the Old Testament God of Israel. And Martin Hengel
says that these hymns to Christ as God "grew out of the early services
of the [primitive Jewish Christian] community after Easter, i.e., [they
are] as old as the community itself."[11] Hymns were sung to Jesus, and
prayers were offered through and to Him. His name was called upon
in healing and exorcism practices even though the Old Testament
explicitly commands that one call only on the name of the God of
Israel. And Jesus was viewed as the Lord who stands in the middle
of and unites the early community just as the God of Israel had done
before Jesus' coming.[12] And all this is present from the earliest days
after Jesus' crucifixion!

Other New Testament Time Factors

But there's even more!

1. It is beyond question that Paul wrote the book of Galatians, and
in it, he states clearly that he received his high view of Jesus and his
understanding of the gospel message around AD 34 or 35. Paul states

that he never deviated from this historical understanding, and it was identical to the views of the other apostles. Thus, a high Christology was present within a year after the crucifixion.[13]

2. Acts records the history of the early church. Acts 1–12 are quite different from chapters 13–28. The former feature Peter and his speeches, mostly to Aramaic, Hebrew-speaking Jews at a time when Christianity was still in its infancy. The latter feature Paul and his speeches to Greek-speaking Gentiles in subsequent years.

Now, here's what I find interesting: Cambridge New Testament scholar G.N. Stanton discovered that the grammar, literary style, theological motifs and emphases, tone, and use of the Old Testament are different in Acts 1–12 from those in chapters 13–28.[14] Moreover, the speeches in Acts 1–12 contain a number of Semitic phrases and other features that indicate it is a Greek translation from an early Aramaic source. What is interesting to me is that this is exactly what one would expect if these narratives, particularly the speeches, were historically accurate. Why? Because Peter is the speaker in Acts 1–12, and he is allegedly addressing Jews in Aramaic, whereas Paul is the speaker in Acts 13–28, and he is addressing Gentiles in Greek. This discovery by Stanton increases our confidence in the historical reliability and early dating of the speeches in Acts 1–12. And they express a high Christology.

3. Royce Gruenler has applied what is called the criterion of dissimilarity to the sayings and actions of Jesus with an interesting result.[15] The criterion of dissimilarity says that if a parallel to a saying of Jesus can be found in the Jewish community in which Jesus lived or in the early church He founded (as evidenced by the New Testament materials besides the Gospels), then Jesus did not say it. But if a saying passes this test, then it is so utterly unique (not bearing an analogy to sayings in the Jewish culture or the early church), that Jesus most likely said it, absent other reasons to suspect the saying. Now, this criterion has always seemed crazy to me if it is taken as a necessary condition for accepting a saying as authentically coming from Jesus. Why? It drives a

ridiculous wedge between Jesus and His culture—He can never agree with ideas in His culture—and between Jesus and His followers—He can't say anything that stuck with them which they reiterate in their writings! The criterion is too harsh, too skeptical. If it were applied to historical figures besides Jesus, it would destroy much of what we hold to be accurate history.

But precisely because it is so skeptical, it seems to me that it is a sufficient condition for historical accuracy. That is, if a saying of Jesus passes this test, then treating the statement as a fabrication is irrational unless there are extremely strong independent reasons for doing so.

Gruenler uses this test to isolate a core of 15 sayings of Jesus, ranging from one to twenty verses, that even the most radical skeptic must accept on pain of losing credibility as an honest historian. These core sayings accurately reflect the mind of the historical Jesus. So, what do these sayings tell us? Jesus took Himself to be greater than Moses, Abraham, David, or anyone who had preceded Him. Even more, He took Himself to stand in the authority—indeed, the very place—of God, embodying in His person the power, presence, and authority of God's own kingdom, welcoming outcasts in God's name, and offering forgiveness of sins, which only God could do. He also received worship and saw Himself as a divine figure who would judge the world—and each and every person in it—at the end of the age. So a high Christology goes back to Jesus of Nazareth Himself.

Oral Tradition in First-Century Jewish Culture

Besides extrabiblical data and the time factor, another important issue in my confidence in the historical reliability of the New Testament documents, particularly the Gospels, resides in the nature and role of oral tradition in Jesus' day. Jesus lived in a predominantly oral culture, one which formulated, preserved, and passed down to subsequent generations its history, key events, central narrative, and core values largely through memorization and oral performance. Detailed studies have been done on such cultures, and we have learned that in contrast with contemporary Western culture, people in these groups can memorize a lot of information quite easily and pass it on carefully and without significant change.

The story of Jesus was preserved and passed on in an orally skilled culture during the ten to twenty years from Jesus' death until the first Gospel was written. The information was preserved carefully by people who were capable of such preservation. I find this to be powerful evidence for the historical reliability of the Gospels. However, four additional facts about this oral preservation cement the Gospels' reliability.

A Collective Story

First, the recollections of the early Christians of Jesus' teachings and deeds…

> were not individual memories but *collective* ones—confirmed by other eyewitnesses and burned into their minds by the constant retelling of the story. Thus, both the repetition of the stories about Jesus and the verification of such by other eyewitnesses served as checks and balances to the apostles' accuracy.[16]

The material about Jesus was recited in oral performances when the early church gathered for worship and instruction, and it was the collective memory of those who knew Jesus. The Gospels were not put together as a hodgepodge of the isolated memories of people scattered throughout the Ancient Near East.

An Eyewitness Account

Second, the material was memorized, preserved, and circulated in the very area where Jesus had lived and ministered and thus among eyewitnesses. These eyewitnesses would have provided a check on the tradition when it went astray. Perhaps the leading expert on oral tradition is James D.G. Dunn. According to Dunn, the fact that a community of Jesus' followers gathered to preserve and spread this material in the first place, indicates that it was the material that formed the community and not vice versa:

> If, as I have argued, it was the impact of what Jesus said and did that first brought the disciple group together as disciples, it would follow that the tradition [about Jesus] that gave them their identity as a group of disciples would be treasured by them, particularly during the period of Jesus' continuing mission, during which...much of the tradition began to take its enduring shape.[17]

In other words, the oral tradition began during Jesus' ministry, it was initially formulated by His disciples, and they would have served as guardians for preserving the accuracy of that tradition. So the early origin of this oral tradition, the role of general eyewitnesses in the area, and the influence of the apostles on the tradition all count heavily in favor of its historical reliability.

An Authoritative Tradition

Reference to the apostles provides a fitting occasion to mention the third point. According to Dunn, in oral cultures generally, certain designated and recognized people were entrusted with the responsibility of reciting and preserving the community's tradition.[18] And in the Jewish culture of Jesus' day, rabbis customarily selected certain pupils from among their students to authoritatively memorize the rabbis' words and works and pass them on unchanged after the rabbis' deaths. These designated pupils were given the responsibility of settling disputes about the exact nature of the rabbis' teachings after their deaths. For several reasons, Jesus seems to have intentionally conformed to this pattern: (1) He was called "rabbi" and had pupils like other rabbis. (2) This broad pattern in rabbi-pupil relationships explains why Jesus selected 12 apostles in the first place. Indeed, their job was to serve as authorities in the community in a manner precisely parallel to the broader cultural pattern. (3) Designated rabbinic students had a specific way of referring to how they handled the tradition about the rabbi. They would "deliver over" to others what they had "received." The phrases "delivered over" and "received" were technical terms used to refer to the careful dissemination of the rabbi's sayings and deeds. And this is precisely how the apostles referred to their dissemination of the Jesus tradition (1 Corinthians 15:3-8; Galatians 2:1-10; Colossians 2:7; 1 Thessalonians 2:13). And Paul Barnett notes other key terms from the broader rabbinic practice that is used in the Gospels: "Jesus was called 'rabbi' and 'followed' by 'disciples' who 'sat at his feet,' 'learned from him,' took his 'yoke' upon them."[19]

A Written Record

Fourth, the apostles probably took notes and used written compilations of these notes alongside the oral tradition. This would serve as an additional check for preserving the accuracy of the message. For one thing, we now know that disciples of rabbis often took notes. These notes were sometimes written on wax tablets. Tax collectors in Jesus' day often knew three languages and even had their own form of shorthand, so it may be no accident that Jesus selected a tax collector (Matthew) to be among the 12. It is also significant that the early Jesus movement and its transmission of the Jesus tradition flow from urban Jerusalem and not rural Galilee. This reinforces the idea that a rabbi-pupil relationship is the correct context for understanding the Jesus tradition, along with the note taking that was a part of rabbinic dissemination. Further, the Jesus tradition was passed on in the first decade or so in the context of Jewish synagogues. In such a context, public reading of Jesus' sayings and deeds would have been important, and as with the synagogue, written texts of Jesus' sayings and deeds would have arisen quickly to be read along with oral recitation.

The cumulative weight of this evidence provides substantial grounds for taking the Gospels to be substantially reliable historical sources. Interestingly, when we examine the Gospels, we find exactly what one would expect if Jewish oral tradition and note taking form the background prior to their writing. Much of Jesus' teaching is in poetic form with parallelism, alliteration, and other techniques that aid memorization. In fact, it has been estimated that 80 percent of Jesus' teaching is in rhythmic, easily memorized, poetic form. In addition, we find 64 examples of easy-to-memorize threefold sayings (such as "ask...seek...knock"). All this provides hard evidence for the historical reliability of the Gospels.

Other Features of the Gospels

I have always been impressed by the fact that the Gospels and Acts were written by people who knew the difference between fact and fiction, who attempted to write accurate history that recorded what actually happened, and who were quite capable of success—and actually did succeed—in this aim. Several places in the New Testament acknowledge the importance of eyewitness testimony (for example, Luke 1:1-4; John 21:24-25; Acts 1:21-26; 1 Corinthians 15:1-5; Galatians 1:11–2:5; 2 Peter 1:16; 1 John 1:1-4). And in these and other places, the New Testament writers tell us that they are being careful to record the exact truth of what happened. Of course, they could have been lying or incompetent, but I believe that considerable evidence shows that they intended to record the truth and did a good job of doing so. At least four lines of evidence support this claim.[20]

Embarrassing Details

Historians agree that if a document contains details that are embarrassing to or harm the author's purpose for writing, then the details are quite likely to be historically reliable because of the strong motivation to exclude them. The Gospels have numerous passages that cast doubt on Jesus' divinity, character, or competence and make the leaders of the early church look like fools.

- John baptized Jesus. But John baptized only sinners, and Jesus was supposed to be sinless.

- Judas betrayed Jesus. Was Jesus incompetent when He picked Judas? And why would Jesus' close associate turn against Him?

- Peter denied Jesus. This makes the leader of the early church look like a coward and calls His moral authority into question.

- Jesus was crucified. That form of execution was reserved for criminals.

Eddy and Boyd add these (all references are to the Gospel of Mark):

- Jesus' own family questioned His sanity (3:21). Some thought Jesus was in collusion with, and even possessed by, the devil (3:22,30).

- Jesus could not perform many miracles in His own town (6:5) and was rejected by people who knew Him (6:3).

- Jesus at times seemed to rely on common medicinal techniques (7:33; 8:23), and His healings were not always instantaneous (8:22-25).

- Jesus' disciples were not always able to exorcise demons (9:18), and Jesus' own exorcisms were not always instantaneously successful (5:8).

- Jesus seemingly suggested He was not supremely good (10:18).

- Jesus associated with people of ill repute (2:14-16).

- Jesus was sometimes rude to people (7:27).

- Jesus seemed to disregard Jewish laws, customs, and cleanliness codes (2:23-24) and sometimes spoke and acted in culturally shameful ways (3:31-35).

- Jesus cursed a fig tree for not having any fruit when He was hungry despite the fact that it was not even the season for bearing fruit (11:13-14).

- The disciples who were to form the foundation of the new community consistently seemed dull, obstinate, and eventually cowardly (8:32-33; 10:35-37; 14:37-40,50).

These cases can all be explained, but that is not the point. That these are even present significantly increases the credibility of the Gospels.

Too Much Information—or Not Enough

If the Gospels were largely legendary creations by the church from AD 50 to AD 85 (I am including the latest dating possible for the first three Gospels), how would the authors or their communities decide what to create and what not to create? Clearly, they would invent material that met the needs of the churches during the time when they were invented. For example, if believers were starting to die (and Jesus had not returned yet), then—on this mythological view—sayings of Jesus were invented and placed on His lips that addressed this situation by giving hope about those who died before the second coming.

But this scenario has two problems, and each points to the historical reliability of the Gospels. First, Jesus is silent about a number of important issues facing the churches from AD 50 to AD 85. What must Gentiles do to be accepted into the new community? What is the nature of spiritual gifts, and how are they to be used in assembly meetings? How are congregations to be organized and run? What is the role of women in the church? What attitude should disciples have toward meat sacrificed to idols? How does the Holy Spirit minister? What is the relationship between the church and the state?

Perhaps the single biggest omission is the presence of "Paulinisms" (statements that reflect the way Paul thought and spoke). Many of the churches from AD 50 to AD 85 were planted by Paul, and the others were heavily influenced by him. This means that their way of thinking and talking about their faith would be influenced by Paul. But the Jesus of the Gospels, while not contradicting the teachings of Paul, does not sound like him. If many of Jesus' sayings were inventions of the early church, the Jesus of the Gospels should think and sound a lot like Paul, but He does not.

Second, not only is there a lack of teaching by Jesus that would have been very relevant to what the church was facing in AD 50 to AD 85, a lot of material is included that was, quite frankly, irrelevant to what they were facing. The only motive for including them in the Gospels could be that they were things Jesus had actually said, and even though they were not particularly helpful to their pressing issues, the church retained them in the Gospels because they were accurate. Consider Jesus' attitude of favor toward Israel and its privileged place in God's plan, Jesus' use of "the son of Man" and parables, and His controversies with the Pharisees about distinctively Jewish issues (such as keeping the Sabbath).

Aramaisms and Personal Names

The Gospels were written in Greek predominantly to those who spoke that language. But Jesus most likely spoke Aramaic (though He also knew and on occasion probably used Greek). Aramaic phrases sometimes occur in the Gospels, and these were most likely retained (even though Greek readers would not know what they meant) because they were historically accurate. There is no other good explanation for their presence. These include *talitha cum* (Mark 5:41), *ephphatha* (Mark 7:34), *Golgotha* (Mark 15:22), *bar* (Matthew 16:17). When Jesus said the Pharisees "strain out a gnat but swallow a camel" (Matthew 23:24), He was making a play on Aramaic words (the Aramaic for "gnat" is *galma* and for "camel" is *gamla*). This occurs in a number of other cases.

Two things are significant about the widespread use of personal names in the Gospels and Acts. For one thing, legends don't usually name eyewitnesses to the events they describe, but the Gospels name them quite frequently. Second, Richard Bauckham recently published an incredible study of the personal names in the Gospels, and he has identified two facts that he claims (correctly in my view) provide strong evidence that the Gospels are factual accounts written by eyewitnesses.[21]

Here's the first fact. Historians have discovered grocery lists, letters, and other documents from Jesus' day, and they have developed a database of hundreds and hundreds of individuals' names, along with the frequency of each name's use in the culture. That frequency differs between the strictly Palestinian Jewish community, the Diaspora (the scattered Jewish) community, and the strictly Gentile community. Incredibly, Bauckham discovered that the relative frequency of the various names used in the Gospels corresponds quite accurately with the three thousand names from the Palestinian Jewish community in the database, but not with the other two communities. If the names were inventions prior to or at the time of the Gospels' writing, then the name frequency should correspond to the latter two communities because those were where the Gospels were written. On the other hand, if the Gospels were eyewitness accounts of Jesus' life as it unfolded in the Palestinian Jewish setting, one would expect the names and the frequency of their usage to correspond to that of the Palestinian Jewish community. And that is what we have discovered.

Here's the second fact. Since there were more people than names, a way had to be developed to distinguish several people with the same name, such as Simon. Several strategies were developed, including adding the father's name—"John son of Zacharias." When compared to the database, the strategies used in the Gospels and the frequency of their usage fits the Palestinian Jewish community and no other. According to Bauckham, all this evidence indicates the implausibility of random invention of the names and underscores the eyewitness nature of the Gospels.

Archaeological Confirmation

Over and over again, archaeologists have made discoveries that confirm completely irrelevant, picky little details in Gospel stories.

People who write legends do not take pains to get small details accurate, especially if those details have nothing to do with the reason for writing the account in the first place. Such confirmation shows that the Gospel writers were trying to get it right, even down to the level of insignificant details. Here are two examples of this selected from a much larger pool of candidates.

John 5:1-15 shows Jesus healing a man at a place called the pool of Bethesda. The passage says that the pool was surrounded by five porticoes (rows of columns supporting a roof). Until the 1890s, critics dismissed the entire narrative on the grounds that no one had ever discovered the pool. But then archaeologists discovered the pool, and it had exactly five porticoes, just as John said.

Here's a second example. The author of Luke and Acts was concerned about the geographical area of Jerusalem and surrounding Judea as opposed to Galilee. Thus, the resurrection appearances in Luke occur in Judea, and the Galilean appearances are omitted. Accordingly, Luke is familiar with and interested in customs and events in Judea. Now, Luke 7:11-17 tells the story of Jesus raising the widow of Nain's son from the dead when He comes upon the funeral procession. Jesus speaks to the mother first and then goes back to the coffin. This corresponds exactly to the custom in Galilee (the province containing Nain). In Galilean funeral processions, people walked in front of the casket. But in Judea, people walked behind the casket. Being familiar with and interested in customs in Judea, if the account were a fabrication, one would expect the funeral to be described according to Judean practices. But it is not. Rather, it is accurately described, and this is what one would expect if the account were historically correct.

I wish I had time to discuss the accuracy of the book of Acts. It contains literally hundreds of geographical details, local customs, titles given to local governors, details about army units, descriptions of major routes, pieces of agricultural data, details about the amount of time needed to travel from one place to another, typical weather conditions of different locations, descriptions of topology, and on and on.[22] Acts is one of the most accurate pieces of historical writing we have from the ancient world.

The Resurrection of Jesus from the Dead

I close this chapter with reflections on what I consider to be not only the very heart of Christianity but also an event so well attested that only personal or philosophical bias could justify its rejection. I am speaking of Jesus' bodily resurrection from the dead three days after His execution. I am particularly impressed with four lines of evidence for this fact.

It All Happened So Fast

First, the length of time from Jesus' death until the widespread belief in His resurrection was no more than five years (and many scholars would say a few months or even weeks) after the crucifixion. This is not enough time for legend to develop. Some of the time factors cited above are relevant here. But I cannot resist adding one more consideration. Atheists and Christians agree that Paul wrote 1 Corinthians. Here is one of Paul's assertions from 1 Corinthians 15:3-8:

> For I delivered to you as of first importance what I also received, that Christ died for our sins according to the Scriptures and that He was buried, and that He was raised on the third day according to the Scriptures, and that He appeared to Cephas, then to the twelve. After that He appeared to more than five hundred brethren at one time, most of whom remain until now, but some have fallen asleep; then He appeared to James, then to all the apostles; and last of all, as to one untimely born, He appeared to me also.

Notice three items about this text: (1) It includes the "deliver to... received" formula that indicates the careful transmission of memorized oral tradition. (2) It is usually dated in the mid 30s because of the oral formula, because it is in the form of a Hebrew poem and translates back into Aramaic nicely (making it an early hymn or creed), because the primitive Jewish "Cephas" and "the twelve" are used instead of "Peter" and "the apostles," which were more typical as time went on, and because the term "sins" is in the plural, yet Paul usually uses "sin" in the singular (indicating that this is a text given to Paul, not one of his own writing). (3) Jesus appears to five hundred people at once, many of whom were still alive and could and should have been interrogated by folks who had doubts.

The Empty Tomb

The second and third facts are the empty tomb of Jesus and the resurrection appearances to the disciples. In his hernia-inducing, 817-page defense of the resurrection, N.T. Wright argues that one cannot explain the origin of Christianity, especially the belief that Jesus had risen, without both facts.[23] Given pagan and Jewish beliefs about life after death in those days, neither by itself can explain the early belief that Jesus was raised. If the empty tomb was a fact but there were no resurrection experiences, Jesus' body would appear to have been stolen, and His crucifixion and empty tomb would have been a puzzle and a tragedy. If the resurrection appearances had occurred without the empty tomb, they would have been construed as visions or hallucinations. Let me say a bit more about each fact.

Several lines of evidence convince me that Jesus' tomb was indeed empty three days after His burial. (1) The Gospel narratives are simple, unadorned, and do not exhibit later reflection. (2) The fact that women are alleged to be the first to witness and bear testimony to the empty tomb and to have undergone resurrection appearances simply must be accurate. A woman's testimony was considered worthless in those days, and indeed, a woman could not testify in a court of law except in certain circumstances (such as when a male from her family would back her testimony). The presence of women as the first witnesses would be highly counterproductive, it would raise doubt and suspicion among those who were being evangelized, and it represented an embarrassment to the early church. The only rational explanation for their presence is that this is what actually happened. (3) The description of Jesus' tomb comports with archaeological finds of tombs around Jerusalem in Jesus' day. Joseph of Arimathea is most likely a real historical figure. (You don't invent a name for someone in the Sanhedrin because everyone knew who the members of this body were.) Being a rich man, Joseph would have had such a tomb, and the tomb would have been like those discovered by archaeologists. (4) The earliest Jewish response to the resurrection proclamation was to say Jesus' body was stolen, a response that grants the empty tomb. (5) In Jesus' day, at least 50 tombs of holy men were sites of yearly veneration by the rabbis' and priests' followers, yet Jesus' tomb was never used this way. This could only be taken as a sign of disrespect for Jesus unless, of course, the early church did not associate Jesus' tomb with the place where Jesus was. Indeed, the early church did have such times of veneration, but they did not venerate Jesus' character or teachings. They celebrated the fact that He had been killed! This is odd unless they did not think He was still dead. The veneration took place, of course, in the regular practice of baptism and the Lord's Supper, both of which celebrate the resurrection.

Resurrection Appearances

Almost all scholars agree that the disciples had resurrection appearances of Jesus after His death. They were obviously sincere in their proclamation of Jesus' resurrection and did not invent what they preached. After all, they suffered lives of hardship and were martyred for their belief. Besides, they subjected themselves to damnation in hell if they fabricated something that Jehovah God had done and falsely and intentionally bore witness to a lie. Remember, they believed in the existence of hell and the God of the Old Testament, and they were not about to lie in this way. People often die for mistaken beliefs, but that is not what we have here. We have people dying for something they saw, heard, and physically touched. That's very different.

These experiences could not have been hallucinations. For one thing, Jesus appeared to several groups of people, including 500 folks at once, and these people were not anticipating Jesus showing up after He was killed. There was no wish fulfillment involved. And if the early followers of Jesus had in fact undergone hallucinations, they would never have interpreted them as experiences of a resurrected person. Here's why. In those days, it was universally believed that there was one and only one resurrection at the end of the age, at which time everyone was raised from the dead all at once. There was no concept of a solo resurrection by an individual prior to that end-time event. So they would never have thought of the category of "resurrection" to interpret their hallucinatory experiences. Not only that, but other categories were available that they would have used to interpret their experiences of Jesus after His death, such as a resuscitation or a translation directly to heaven (as they believed had happened to Enoch). These were considered to be entirely different from a resurrection. In my view, the best explanation for these experiences is that Jesus had actually risen from the dead and appeared to various individuals and groups.[24]

Transformed Lives

The fourth line of evidence for Jesus' resurrection serves, as it were, double duty. It not only provides additional evidence but also helps to answer the question, so what? I am referring to the fact that for two thousand years, millions of pilgrims have actually encountered the risen Jesus and had their lives transformed as a result. And that transformation, it seems to me, is precisely the antidote to the loss of happiness and meaning I described in the first two chapters.

So here's where we are. The last three chapters have been a bit cold and intellectual. This was needed, I believe, in order to insist that trust in God and, more specifically, the biblical God and His Son, Jesus, rests on a solid factual, intellectual basis. Such trust is not a step into the dark; it is an expression of confidence in what we know on the basis of the considerations of the last three chapters and much, much more. We have seen grounds for belief in God and considered evidence for Jesus as the risen Son of God. At this point, one further piece of evidence needs to be put in place: If you have not already done so, you should perform a devotional experiment in which you place your trust in Jesus (see chapter 7 for more on this), cast yourself on Him and His kindness, and seek Him with all your heart. Begin to attempt to do what He taught, and you will begin to see the power of His presence and kingdom manifest itself in, through, and around you. This will be the final confirmation that a life of discipleship to the luminous Nazarene is indeed entrance into the Way, the Truth, and the Life. That is what I found, as I shall share in the next chapter.[25]

My Own Journey as Jesus' Apprentice

Harvard professor William James was a leading figure in American intellectual history. An expert in philosophy and psychology, James is, perhaps, best known for his important work *The Variety of Religious Experiences*. In it, James analyzed several different kinds of people who had had a variety of religious experiences and concluded that the best explanation for their changed lives was the hypothesis of a genuine spiritual Reality that caused these changes. James included this comment:

> When we commune with it [spiritual Reality, or God], work is actually done upon our finite personality, for we are turned into new men, and consequences in the way of conduct follow in the natural world upon our regenerative change. But that which produces effects within another reality must be termed a reality itself, so I feel as if we had no philosophic excuse for calling the unseen or mystical world unreal...God is real since he produces real effects.[1]

But for two thousand years, literally multitudes of followers of Jesus have not reported having merely vague, general experiences with "spiritual Reality." People of virtually every conceivable personality type, educational background, cultural context, historical setting, and social class have experienced the risen Jesus Himself, along with God the Father and the Holy Spirit. They have experienced not only the Triune God Himself, but also powerful, life-enhancing changes they were impotent to bring about themselves. And as if this were not enough, they have experienced countless specific answers to prayer and seen miraculous healings and other events done in Jesus' name.

For example, in the early second century, Quadratus emphasized that some whom Jesus had healed were still around, and their presence strengthened the faith of the church:

> But the works of our Savior were always present, for they were true, those who were cured, those who rose from the dead, who not merely appeared as cured and risen, but were constantly present, not only while the Savior was living, but even for some time after he had gone, so that some of them survived even to our own time.[2]

In his attempt to defend Christians against Roman persecution, Tertullian (AD 155–230) points out the foolishness of such persecutions:

> But who would rescue you [if Christians were to withdraw] from those secret enemies that everywhere lay waste your minds and your bodily health? I mean, from the assaults of demons, whom we drive out of you, without reward, without pay. Why, this alone would have sufficed to avenge us—to leave you open and exposed to unclean spirits with immediate possession.[3]

In a similar vein, in his letter to the Roman official Scapula, Tertullian refers to the healings of well-placed Roman citizens:

> For, the secretary of a certain gentleman, when he was suf-
> fering from falling sickness caused by a demon, was freed
> from it; so also were the relatives of some of the others and
> a certain little boy. And heaven knows how many distin-
> guished men, to say nothing of common people, have been
> cured either of devils or of their sickness.[4]

Due to immorality, spiritual dryness and incompetence, and cold
formalism, the miraculous nature of Jesus' kingdom has waned in
some periods of church history.[5] But in the last century, especially
since around 1970 or so, the church has recovered certain aspects of
biblical teaching that lay largely dormant for a long time, and as a
result, miracles done in Jesus' name and in the power of His kingdom
have multiplied like rabbits around the world. Here is an example
that comes from the highly regarded *Jesus* Film Project and Campus
Crusade for Christ. It's a bit long, but as you will see, it's well worth
reading.

The film project involves showing a movie of Jesus' life as depicted
in the Gospel of Luke, and hundreds upon hundreds of millions of
people have seen it so far. Here is an eyewitness account from a team
showing the film in villages in the bush area in deeply Muslim territory.
The team was showing the film about six times a week in dangerous
locations. They were headed toward a large village and had sent a
coworker ahead to arrange a meeting with the chief to ask permission
and announce the showing of the film. Here, in the team leader's own
words, is what happened:

> When I arrived, the worker was trying fruitlessly to per-
> suade the chief. He wanted nothing to do with *Jesus* and
> declared, "I am a Muslim...I am a Muslim leader. I lead
> the mosque and I'm the chief of the village. Since this vil-
> lage has existed we have never allowed any other religion.
> You will do NOTHING here!" With the Holy Spirit as my
> guide, I respectfully replied, "We are coming here to show

you and your people the *Jesus* film, preach the gospel, and heal the sick." He responded, "What did you say? Heal the sick?...Really?...Is that possible?" "Yes, if you allow us to show the *Jesus* film and preach the gospel." He looked at his second-in-command and fell silent. There was a pause as he thought. The chief turned back to me and said, "Really!? Heal the sick...Okay, we want to see this." With his permission, the film team went to work at a large soccer field. They unloaded the projection equipment, generator, threaded the film, set up the screen, speaker and lights. Then, they went about announcing the film. Around 5,000 people came that night and filled the soccer field. It was standing room only. Something was happening. As the projector started I went to the car and prayed, asking God to give me a word for these people when the film concluded. They were deeply moved by the *Jesus* film...Over the microphone I called out, "How many here recognize a need for a Savior?" Almost everybody raised his hand. There was a group of young people on my right. Some raised their hands and voices, "We want our sins to be forgiven!" Then others on the other side cried out, "We want our sins to be forgiven." Everyone began crying out to God for mercy. So, in that moment, I led the entire group of 5,000 in the prayer of salvation. Then I spoke to the crowd. "This Jesus is not only a Savior, but He is a Healer, and today He wants to heal anybody who is sick. Bring your sick forward." So, one by one they came—first about 12 men and women with back problems. He healed them all, instantly. They brought a young deaf boy, about 8 years old. The Lord healed him. People kept coming, and kept being healed. God was at work affirming His Word and His Son! It was simply incredible. On my right stood the chief, the leader of the village and the mosque. Now I turned to him and said, "Do you see what is happening?" He answered, "Yes. Can

I say something to my people?" I gave him the microphone and he stepped forward. To the 5,000 he spoke: "What you have just seen is real because there is no man who can do what you have seen unless God is with him and with these people who have come to us. The Lord is with them. Now, bring all the sick from the village! Go home and bring them here!" As I continued to pray for the people, a father came running. He was holding his daughter. She was 7 years old, born totally blind. He pleaded with me, "Please pray for my daughter." I said, "Do you believe Jesus will heal her?" He answered, "That's why I brought her!" I prayed and then moved my hand across her face. She started to move, and followed my hand. She was able to see. She moved her head to the left, to the stage and lights. She was just amazed by the lights and everything she was seeing. Still in her father's arms, he asked her, "Do you see? Do you see?" She turned her eyes to him, and looked on her father's face for the first time in her life. She knew his voice but had never seen his face. The look on both their faces was amazing. She answered, "I can see you."[6]

Miracles like this are breaking out all over the world today, and there are too many credible reports to dismiss it all as urban legend. My own story is not as dramatic as this, but it is my story nonetheless, and I am immensely grateful for it and for the chance to share it with you.

My Love Affair with the Son of God

If you and I were talking over coffee, I would look you in the eye and say with complete honesty and conviction that my life cannot be explained without the existence of the Christian God and the truth of Christianity. I want to share my story in the hope that it will encourage you to consider becoming—or rededicating yourself as—a disciple of

Jesus. I wish to say at the outset that I have had periods of dryness in my pilgrimage, times when God seemed absent and hidden, numerous times when God said no to my prayer requests and other times when I sensed no answer at all, just complete silence. I am selecting times when God's presence has been manifest to me, not to mislead you about my journey, but to present evidence from my own journey that convinces me, and I hope you, that the life of following Jesus is real and true.

I was born on March 9, 1948 in Kansas City, Missouri, and was raised in Grandview, Missouri, a Kansas City suburb. My father died when I was in second grade, and I was raised largely by my mother, though she did marry again during my seventh-grade year. My mother and stepfather were good to me, though neither could help much with my religious instruction. Neither were educated beyond high school. My mother worked in a paper cup factory, and my stepfather was a welder. My mother was a very anxious person, and because of this and the death of my father, I entered early adulthood with a significant predisposition toward anxiety and depression.

Through high school I attended a mildly liberal United Methodist church, and as a result, I saw Jesus as a fairly boring, middle-class white person who espoused a somewhat benign set of moral platitudes. I was an honor student and a decent athlete with a good social life, so I was simply uninterested in learning anything more about Jesus Christ. God's existence seemed likely to me, but my religious affections toward Him lay dormant.

I received a scholarship to study chemistry at the University of Missouri, so in the fall of 1966, I set out for Columbia, Missouri, not knowing that during my tenure there, I would make a decision that would forever alter the course of my life. I had two goals for college: to prepare for a Ph.D. in chemistry so I could become a university professor, and to date as many attractive girls as possible to increase my chances of obtaining a wife. So I joined a social fraternity and took all the chemistry, physics, and math courses I could. I had a disdain for the humanities, but like most undergraduates then and now, I was virtually ignorant of what they were.

Through the '60s, I lived a fairly typical pagan lifestyle. I never took drugs, but I drank and partied hard, and I was very successful in school, graduating with highest honors in chemistry. On occasion I would pray to a vague father figure whose depiction I had managed to glean from the watered-down instruction I had received in Sunday school prior to college. Church attendance at college was out of the question. I recall the unrest on campus, as well as the desperate need for ultimate meaning that social and political causes afforded to many of my friends. I remember asking one friend, Carol, why she was marching against the Vietnam War. She replied that she really didn't know the issues and didn't actually have much of an opinion on the war, but she still felt a need to count for something, and the antiwar rallies satisfied that need.

Encounters like the one with Carol regularly shook me out of my lethargy about life. As a chemistry major, I could easily hide in the lab, proud to be a scientist, without giving much thought to larger, ultimate questions. But I regularly sensed a large emptiness inside me, and I knew that if God did not exist, life in general, and my life in particular, were without ultimate significance. One tragedy of religious liberalism is its inability to provide reasonable answers to the sort of hunger I regularly suppressed inside me, so I simply did not know where to go with my doubts and desires. I redoubled my efforts in school and social life, not knowing they were like Turkish delight—the more I got of them, the more I was addicted to what could not satisfy the vacuum in my heart. Still, my busyness kept me from feeling the anxiety and depression that characterized my empty life.

In November of my junior year (1968), some Campus Crusade for Christ speakers came to my fraternity house and shared an intellectual case for the deity of Jesus Christ, along with a presentation of the gospel. I was simply shocked. Here were attractive, intelligent people talking about Jesus outside the church walls. They obviously had something I didn't know anything about, so I began to meet weekly with Bob Farnsley, a Campus Crusade worker. I asked questions and read the New Testament, and after about a month and a half, I became convinced that the New Testament was probably true and that Jesus of Nazareth was most likely the Son of God. One evening, I went up to my dorm room, closed and locked the door, and knelt by my bed. I accepted Jesus Christ as my Savior and set my heart to being His disciple for the rest of my life. I simply asked Him never to leave me and to walk with me wherever I went—a request, I would learn, He was quite eager to grant.

That very evening I had a sense of Christ's presence that was so vivid that I was afraid of opening my eyes for fear I would see a form standing in the room! Since that day, I have had numerous additional visitations by the Lord Jesus, and they have continued to strengthen my life as His follower. In the next weeks and months, my life changed dramatically. That may sound like a cliché, but it is simply the truth. A new power, calm, strength, direction, and reality came into my life. I instantly became celibate and refrained from sexual activity until I was married in 1977. I also became an underground radical for Jesus, speaking at free-speech rallies, distributing Christian literature on campus, and seeking to evangelize others. The Bible came alive to me and it, along with the fellowship I discovered with other believers, provided such sustenance to me that I can only say I have never recovered from the life-changing power of God that I experienced in those early years of my newfound knowledge of God.

When I graduated in 1970, I turned down a fellowship to do doctoral studies in nuclear chemistry, and I joined the staff of Campus Crusade, serving in Colorado from 1970 to 1972 and in Vermont from 1972 to 1975. Those were incredible days of growth and ministry. I was hungry to grow as a believer, so I read as widely as I could in apologetics (the study of the reasons for thinking Christianity is true), theology, and devotional literature. I also witnessed genuine acts of God in my ministry. I will share one of them.

In 1972, two staff women and I went to the University of Vermont to start a Campus Crusade ministry from scratch. We had no student contacts at all, so we started doing evangelism. We desired to make a substantial, initial impact for Christ on the campus so the university community would be put on notice that followers of a supernatural Jesus were there. So during the first week of classes, the three of us knelt in prayer in my apartment and asked the Lord Jesus to lead us to a fraternity or sorority house in which He had prepared hearts to respond to His gospel. We wanted very much to see conversions that would generate momentum and help make Jesus Christ the central issue on campus. The university had 30 or so fraternity and sorority houses, and after prayer, I opened the university catalog and picked the Alpha Chi house for our first meeting. That evening, we talked to the Alpha Chi president and set up a team meeting for the next week.

To make a long story short, that evening, 25 out of 45 women in the house became Christians. Three different women confessed to me that throughout the week before the meeting, they had been dreaming about God at night and had been talking about how to find God. Those 25 converts were genuine—all of them stayed strong in the faith the rest of their college days, and five of them went into missionary work from that one sorority house. More than half the Alpha Chi house had found Jesus Christ. In a little over a year, we had won more than 150 students to Christ on a campus of 8000, and our Christian group was three or four times larger than any other group of any kind on campus, including the ski club! The gospel of Jesus Christ was the most commonly discussed issue on campus, and a spiritual revolution came to pass.

In my evangelistic and discipleship ministry, I saw that if Evangelical Christianity was going to make an impact on individuals and social structures, we needed more leaders who were spiritually vibrant and intellectually trained. So I left Campus Crusade and attended Dallas Seminary from 1975 to 1979. There I made the second-greatest decision of my life, my decision to marry Hope Coleman. I had met

Hope in 1971 at a Campus Crusade training conference. She was on Crusade staff and was a dedicated disciple whose life exuded the spirit and kindness of Christ Himself. But we had never been assigned close enough to each other to spend time together. The year before I left for seminary, Hope was reassigned by Campus Crusade to live in Dallas, and shortly before I arrived, God spoke to her in clear terms that she and I were to be married. She never put it to me in those terms; she merely said that God had given her a desire to be with me. But that assurance helped her persevere through our rocky dating experience while I dealt with intimacy and commitment issues resulting from the death of my father.

I finally worked through my psychological difficulties, and we were married in May of 1977. We now have two lovely daughters who have finished college, married, and given us two wonderful grandchildren at the time of this writing. Our devotion to Jesus provided the wisdom and glue that held our family together as a flourishing unit. Hope and I are more convinced than ever that a marriage in which husband and wife individually seek Jesus Christ with all their hearts is far richer than anything that can be achieved without His lordship. In a day in which marriage is being defined in increasingly arbitrary and meaningless terms, people need to study the lives of dedicated, Spirit-filled marriages to keep before them the nature of marriage itself.

Since graduation from seminary in 1979, Hope and I have helped to plant two churches, and I have taught at various institutions, including Talbot School of Theology since 1990. From 1981 to 1985, I earned my M.A. and Ph.D. in philosophy and was privileged to have Dallas Willard as my chief mentor. I have always believed that philosophy, properly approached, is simply a way of enriching the life of discipleship to Jesus, and when I teach or write on philosophical themes, that belief is always in the background.

Psychologists claim that purpose must inform daily life. Recent studies have shown how dangerous retirement can be if it results only in a life of leisure with no goals for living besides that. In the past 15 years of my life as one of Jesus' students, five values have informed my own sense of vocation:

1. The value of love and devotion to the triune God, with special focus on Jesus Christ, along with an intentional plan to make progress in spiritual formation.

2. The value of the mind and a developed intellectual life in which truth and reason are central.

3. The importance of being a Christian activist, one who seeks to penetrate the world with a Christian worldview, with special emphasis on the Great Commission.

4. The value of friendship and community in the body of Christ, in which one learns to give honor to others and to be genuinely enthusiastic about their successes and concerned about their hardships.

5. The importance of learning how to live a supernatural Christian life, in which the miraculous power of God's kingdom breaks through in such a way that I become "naturally supernatural."

These five values are expressions of a central truth I have learned over the years of being one of Jesus' followers: Being a Christian was never meant to be an extra religious compartment added to an otherwise secular life defined independently of Christianity. Rather, being a Christian is an entire way of being present in the world, and it informs, permeates, and shapes every single aspect of one's thinking, feeling, and acting. Being enraptured with Jesus Himself is the central core to growing as His follower, and because Jesus is completely worthy of such devotion, I have without reservation continued to make Him Lord of my life as best I can and within the limits of my own frailties. I have come to know that following Jesus is the wisest, smartest, best thing one can do with one's life.

The Evidence from My Own Journey

At this point, I believe the testimony of God's Holy Spirit and, more generally, the value of religious experience enters the picture. Without trying to provide a technical development of an argument for Christianity from religious experience, let me say simply that I believe it to be fruitful to consider the following sorts of religious experiences as evidence for the truth of Christianity.

Biblical Wisdom

I constantly find that biblical teaching accurately describes me, my family, and the social, ethical, and aesthetic world in which I seek to live a good life. Time and time again, I come away from Scripture with the deep impression that it is absolutely correct in its insights into virtue and vice, individual and structural good and evil, parenting, sexual love in marriage, and a host of other things. Moreover, I find that when I internalize biblical wisdom, my life changes for the better, and I become a better person, father, husband, friend, and professor. I don't know how many times my Christian friends and I have said that we have no idea how people live without Jesus Christ and the Scriptures. When we say this, our hearts are not filled with arrogance and pride, nor are we trying to put others down or say that no one can do anything good without being a Christian. Rather, we are expressing the fact that most of us have lived on both sides—we were all unbelievers at some point— and having tasted the goodness of Jesus and His Word, we realize that life without Him is mere biological existence compared to the deep flourishing that comes from knowing and living the wisdom in the Bible.

Specific Changes in One's Life

As I noted above, William James argued that real effects require real causes adequate to explain those effects, and moreover, the changed lives of religious believers is best explained by the existence of God. In a similar way, Patrick Sherry argued that a careful study of the Christian church, as a collective whole and as a group of individuals, justifies the claim that distinctively New Testament conversion and discipleship is far superior to alternative worldviews or paths in life in the depth, degree, breadth, and profundity of its impact in producing virtuous heroes and saints who have changed the world, often at great personal cost, and who have flourished as humans in unparalleled ways.[7] This does not mean that no moral heroes exist outside the church or that everyone in the church is a moral hero. It does mean that an honest evaluation of history justifies the conclusion that authentic Christianity changes lives in an unparalleled way.

Here is a very simple story of this sort of thing. My mother smoked cigarettes for 54 years. She wanted to quit, but she could not bring herself to do so. One afternoon, a few years after her conversion to Christ in 1969, she lay in a hospital bed after a successful back surgery. As she tells it, that afternoon, the Lord Jesus spoke to her in clear terms that He wanted her to stop smoking and that He would help her do it. She stopped cold turkey and never touched a cigarette again from that day until her home-going in 2004. Instantaneously, her desire for cigarettes vanished, and she had no struggle at all, not even once, in her resolve to stay away from the habit.

This is a simple, small story, and it could be multiplied by ten thousand in my life and among those I personally know as Christian friends, not to mention the testimony of Christians in church after church and throughout history. I do not deny that, in current American Christianity, the spiritual vitality of Jesus' followers is not what it once was. However, that is not the fault of Christianity itself, but of our current grasp of spirituality. And even with our shallow contemporary discipleship, God still changes lives far beyond what should be expected, given the Americanized Christianity that far too often substitutes for the real thing.

Specific Experiences of God's Presence

In my own life, I have experienced times in which God Himself has been directly present to me in one way or another. I have also experienced times in which God has spoken to me in a way I will make clear shortly. A few years ago, I entered a period of about three months in which Jesus Christ came to me vividly on several occasions. During this time, I had nine or ten different occasions when I could sense His presence in a very real, unmistakable way. One morning I was at home studying when I became overwhelmed with the presence of God. For about the next hour, I just sat alone in my living room and wept with joy.

On another afternoon while sitting in my backyard meditating on some verses I had memorized, I had the sense that Christ was near me in an unusual way. A specific thought and feeling came to me with a texture that made clear to me that the thought and feeling came from the "outside" and not from within my own subconscious. I was led to pray specifically for my younger daughter, who felt terribly isolated socially. I prayed specifically that by the end of that week, at least two of her three closest acquaintances would call and invite her to play. She had not received a call of this sort for several weeks, and none from these three girls for months. Within three days, two of the girls had called and invited my daughter to play. The time with them really lifted her spirit.

A few days later, I was on a plane to Illinois to deliver an academic paper when Christ became so vivid to me that I started laughing with joy in my seat! Pity the poor fellow next to me! He must have thought I was crazy! At that moment, I had the strong sense that God was asking me if He could do something specific for me. The evening before, my other daughter came down with a migraine headache. In her case, these usually lasted from a full day to two days. I asked God to take her headache away that very moment, and the sense came back to me that it had been done. That evening, I arrived at my hotel and called my wife, and she informed me that my daughter's headache had left that morning, the time I was praying.

During that three-month period, I was caught up in a season of closeness to God that was even evident to others. A group of my students actually came to me after class and asked me what was happening to me. They sensed a glow on my face, a sense of peace and calm that was out of the ordinary. At the end of the three-month period, I had the distinct sense that God was going to hide His presence from me so I would seek Him during a dark period, Since that time, I have had other periods of intense awareness of God's presence along with times of dryness. I share all this because this sort of thing happens to mature believers regularly. I believe many people have times in which the Lord Jesus manifests His presence to them in a special way. The experiences are very hard to explain away, and in my view, only a defective worldview renders impotent the intellectual value of religious experience like this.

Answers to Prayer

I have already shared examples of answered prayer, and I have been strengthened considerably in my faith by their presence in my life. Disciples experience unanswered prayer as well, but in all honesty my family, close Christian friends, and I have seen enough specific answers to prayer that for me to doubt that prayer actually works is no longer reasonable.

To illustrate, early in my ministry I attended a seminar in Southern California, where I heard teaching on how to pray specifically. In a few weeks, I was to return to Colorado to start my ministry at the Colorado School of Mines in Golden with Ray Womack, a fellow Campus Crusade worker. Unknown to anyone, I wrote a prayer request in my prayer notebook and began to pray specifically that God would provide for Ray and me a white house with a white picket fence and a grassy front yard, within two or three miles of campus, for no more than $130 per month. I told the Lord that this request was reasonable because we wanted a place that provided a home atmosphere for students, accessible from campus, that we could afford. I also told Him that I was experimenting with specific prayer and wanted my faith to be strengthened.

I returned to the Golden area and looked for three days at several places to live. I found nothing in Golden, and in fact, I only found one apartment for rent for $135 a month, and it was about 12 miles from campus. I told the manager I would take it, and she informed me that a couple had looked at the place that morning. They had until that afternoon to make a decision, and if they did not want it, I could move in the next day. I called late that afternoon and was informed that the couple took the apartment, the last available one in the complex. I was literally back to ground zero.

I had not mentioned to anyone that I had been praying for a white house. That evening, Kaylon Carr (a Campus Crusade friend) called me to ask if I still needed a place to stay. When I said yes, she informed me that earlier that day, she had been to Denver Seminary. While there, she saw a bulletin board on which a pastor in Golden was advertising a place to rent, hopefully to seminary students or Christian workers. Kaylon gave me his phone number, so I called and set up an appointment to meet the pastor at his place at nine the next morning. As I drove up, I came to a white house with a white picket fence, a nice grassy front yard, about two miles from campus. He asked for $110 per month rent. Needless to say, I took it, and Ray and I had a home that year in which to minister.

A few years ago my family and I were hit with an unexpected financial crisis. Shortly thereafter during a morning walk, I told the Lord that I was at a point where I really needed to see Him intervene for me. Suddenly, a thought came to me: *Why don't you ask Me to do something for you now?* I wasn't sure it was the Lord or my own thoughts, but I responded to what I thought was His prompting and asked that He bring my family $5000 that very day. My faith was not particularly strong at this time. The mail came and went with no check. But at

5:40 that evening, completely out of the blue and totally unexpectedly, I received more than $5000 from someone who knew me but knew nothing of my situation. It was simply incredible, and besides the wonderful provision from God, this answer to prayer engendered faith in my entire family and me.

With God as my witness, I have a prayer notebook that contains dozens upon dozens of specific answers to prayer like these. Remember, I have had numerous prayers go unanswered, and I do not view God as a celestial bellhop who should give me what I want. I am simply a broken, needy person who has learned that I may bring my request to a loving and living God who answers prayer. I've seen too many prayers answered to doubt the power of God and the importance of petitioning Him honestly.

Providential "Coincidences"

On numerous occasions, God has done something for me at exactly the right time when His action was most needed. These experiences have given me the joy of knowing that I am not alone and that God is not too busy to take notice of me. Here's just one of many, many examples.

A few summers ago I suffered from a series of anxiety attacks that led to a debilitating seven-month depression. Almost immediately after sinking into an emotional and spiritual abyss, I began to be plagued with doubts and self-criticism about my academic, scholarly work. My self-talk, which I believe was energized by demonic attacks, was filled with repeated accusations that I had wasted my life studying, writing, and lecturing, and that my intellectual endeavors for the cause of Christ had achieved very little by way of impact. This repeated thought plagued me for several weeks, plunging me deeper into depression. I felt my work had been meaningless and, as a result, my life was basically meaningless. In the midst of this plunge, I went to Columbia International University in Columbia, South Carolina, to deliver a five-day lecture series. I live in Southern California, and South Carolina seems halfway across the world to me. I knew no one in Columbia and had never been there before.

One day while I was in Columbia, just before dinner, I came down with an extreme migraine headache. I can go five years without even a small headache, so this was a first for me. I took Tylenol, canceled my evening lecture, and went to bed in my dorm room. But things got worse. My head was wracked with pain. Around six p.m. I received a phone call from a conferee who lived in the area. He said he was taking me to the emergency room. I slumped into his front seat, and he drove me to a walk-in clinic about 15 or 20 miles away. I staggered in, left my driver's license at the front desk, and was whisked away to the emergency room. Immediately, two nurses hooked monitors to my chest and brain and began testing me to find out what was wrong. My blood pressure was off the charts. They gave me an injection to alleviate the headache, and it began to work quickly.

After about five minutes of this, the doctor on call that evening walked in the door. Holding my driver's license he said, "Are you J.P. Moreland? The one who teaches at Talbot Seminary?" Taken a bit off guard, I nodded. "I don't believe this! There are nurses here who would give their eyeteeth if a movie star walked through those doors. In my case, if I could pick one person in the entire country to come in here it would be you. Dr. Moreland, I can't thank you enough for what you have done in the intellectual world for the cause of Christ! I have read almost all your books, and hey, you know that book *Body and Soul* you wrote with Scott Rae? I teach ethics at a local community college, and I use that as a text. I can't believe I am getting to meet you!"

It turned out that I had most likely eaten some bad shrimp at dinner the day before this happened, and the food poisoning takes about 24 hours to hit someone. But as soon as this doctor shared with me the impact I had had on him, the Lord spoke to me: *I am well-pleased with your academic work for My name's sake. You have done well. Keep trusting Me.*" At the very moment of my need to be reassured of the meaning of my intellectual work, I met a doctor who "happened" to be on duty that evening in a city in which I've never been who valued the very work for which I needed consolation during my depression. What a "coincidence"! My repeated meditation on things like this in my own life has reassured me that God knows about my needs and that I can trust Him to act when He knows the timing is right.

Miraculous Healings

I have seen and heard eyewitness testimony to miraculous healings too numerous to mention. During the past two years, our church alone has seen at least six cases of cancer miraculously healed, some of them terminal and beyond medical intervention. One person instantly received complete eyesight after significant, partial blindness. A Vietnam veteran blinded in one eye for 25 years by a grenade explosion received full sight after only 20 minutes of prayer by a team of several people. A young deaf boy received miraculously full hearing after a friend of ours laid hands on him and prayed.

These stories are real, in most cases we know the people involved in praying, and the stories could be multiplied many times over by other examples of miraculous healing. For four years, I have been in the habit of asking congregations or other Christian groups to whom I speak to raise their hands if God has miraculously healed them in such a way that they are convinced it could have not been a coincidence or a form of self-suggestion. About 5 to 10 percent raise their hands. When I ask if they personally know someone who was so healed, around 70 percent of people raise their hands. No, this is not a scientific survey. But who cares? These people can't all be liars or duped, naive people. Who says God has stopped doing miracles!

Spiritual Reflections on My Journey

I can't explain all I have seen, heard, and experienced unless the Christian God is real. And it should be obvious by now that a life of following Jesus involves intellectual, emotional, spiritual, and supernatural components. The divisions between these aspects of one's Christian life are somewhat arbitrary. The so-called intellectual parts of the Christian life are crucial to a vibrant spirituality, and conversely, the spiritual insights, practices, and habits of a person are important for informing a distinctively Christian intellectual life. Learning to cooperate with God's Spirit and kingdom to see overtly supernatural things happen is crucial to the growth of faith and a holistic relationship with God. Conversely, a holistic intellectual, spiritually formative walk with Jesus provides crucial balance for the overtly supernatural so that it does not become out of balance or inappropriately weird. Having said that, however, it still remains fruitful to reflect on factors central to one's spiritual progress in a way that does not make explicit reference to the intellectual relevance of those factors.

A host of things have been helpful to me in my own spiritual life, and some of them are typical—worship, Bible study, and so forth. But certain ideas and certain activities are of special importance to me, and I would like to share some of them with you.

For one thing, I repeatedly return to the conviction that Jesus of Nazareth is simply peerless. He is the wisest, most virtuous, most influential person in history. I can't even imagine what the last two thousand years would have been like without His influence. No one is remotely like Him. The power of His ideas, the quality of His character, the beauty of His personality, and the uniqueness of His life, miracles, crucifixion, and resurrection are so far ahead of any other person or ideology that the greatest honor ever bestowed on me is to be counted among His followers. Early in my Christian life, I was debating about Christianity with a Marxist radical, and I recall vividly how overwhelmed I was with the superiority of Jesus over Marx. I left that dialogue with tears in my eyes at the simple thought that I had the chance of aligning myself with the matchless Christ. I cannot imagine someone truly understanding who He is and what He offers and refusing to become His disciple, though I know it does happen.

Becoming one of Christ's followers is not only an unspeakable honor but also the greatest opportunity by far anyone will ever have of gaining a life of meaning and of becoming what we all know we ought to be. Sometimes people say that following Jesus is hard. In a sense

I agree, but in a more fundamental sense I could not disagree more. Following Jesus is indeed difficult in the sense that exemplifying the traits characteristic of His teaching and kingdom takes more effort and practice than "doing what comes naturally." But if by "difficult" one means a life that is painful, sad, lonely, depressing, or anxiety-filled, then a really difficult life is one lived contrary to the way of Jesus. All one needs to do is to compare the lives of those most in conformity with the New Testament with those most contrary to it and ask, soberly and honestly, which one flourishes in a distinctively human way. It will become obvious that the way of Jesus is far easier than the path in the opposite direction. Here is one simple example: Though it may be hard to learn, it is actually much easier to love one's enemies than to hate them. The latter causes one to be upset, angry, anxious, and controlled by others. The former is a life of ease in which God is trusted to bring about justice and vindication when (and only when) it is deserved.

Second, the history of God's people is a history of the richest community the world has ever seen. The greatest music, the best literature, the most profound ethics and philosophy, the most influential moral saints and heroes, and the richest treasures on spiritual formation are found among the followers of Jesus. I am not saying the church has been perfect. However, I would argue that when the church has been ugly and hideous in its actions, it has strayed from the New Testament charter it received from the Master Himself. Nor am I saying that no good things have come from outside the church. As John Wesley noted, "To imagine none can teach you but those who are themselves saved from sin, is a very great and dangerous mistake. Give not place to it for a moment."[8] I heartily agree. Still, Christians need to remind themselves regularly that by and large, it was our people who started the universities; nurtured art, music, literature, and philosophy; and sacrificially went to the four corners of the world to establish orphanages, care for the sick, champion human rights, and raise the literacy level.

A few weeks ago, I attended a Talbot School of Theology graduation banquet. After dinner, we enjoyed a chronological video depiction of some of the great ones in the Way: Justin Martyr, Augustine, Francis of Assisi, and on and on. A deep sense of pride and gratitude rose up in all of our hearts that evening as we contemplated afresh what a wonderful community God has placed us in.

Finally, Christian marriage and Christian friendship is so rich that I cannot imagine living without it. To be sure, my marriage has problems and struggles just like everyone else's, and my close band of Christian friends has its own share of interpersonal conflict and difficulty. Still, I know that these problems would be far worse if we were not Christians. And I have tasted the tremendous benefits of knowing Christ Jesus in these two areas of life.

At the end of the day, we all need to have a worthy purpose in life sufficient to justify our fourscore and ten on this earth. And as Jesus reminded us in Matthew 16:24-27, in order to gain a life of spiritual vitality and flourishing, one needs to develop the practice of giving oneself away to others for Jesus' sake. I certainly have a ways to go in my journey, but one thing has become abundantly clear: When it comes to a life of purpose, when it comes to finding something worth living and dying for, discipleship to Jesus is the only game in town. Because of the spiritual richness, supernatural vitality, and intellectual credibility of the Christian religion, I have made Jesus Lord of my life and sought, within the tapestry woven by my own frailties, to live out that commitment with others of similar passion as best I know how. And with God's help, I plan to enlist to that Way as many as I can before this stage of my journey passes into the next one. And you are one of those people. Besides these brief, concluding reflections, the rest of this book focuses on ideas that have been of great help to me in my sojourn as a follower of Jesus. I trust that they will be useful to you too.

Part 3

HOW CAN THE SOLUTION HELP ME CHANGE?

Rethinking the Whole Thing

As I write, the Christmas season has just passed, and only a few bowl games are left. Something very interesting happened this season. As parents who raised two daughters, we tried to instill in them a number of values and attitudes we thought would help them through the teen years and into adulthood. Both girls have been married for a few years, they became pregnant at the same time, and glory to God, they have given my wife and me a grandson and a granddaughter. They and their husbands are trying to move back to Southern California, and in the meantime, they came home and lived with us a few weeks this Christmas season.

Now here's what's interesting. Time and time again my wife and I saw or overheard the two couples make statements or decisions that reflected values we had tried—and seemingly failed—to impart to the girls. They went to bed early, saved their money, and, well, acted like maturing adults. Do you know what happened? To use a biblical word, they repented. This term has a lot of negative, confusing baggage surrounding it, so let me clarify it. To repent means to rethink things, to adjust one's attitude, viewpoint, or approach in light of some new fact. Now that they are parents, our daughters and sons-in-law have suddenly rethought life and changed their approach accordingly in light of this new fact. It's amazing how the birth of a child causes the new mom and dad to adjust their lives!

Repentance was at the very heart of what Jesus was about. But we must be careful to understand what He meant by this, and shortly, we will examine the matter more carefully. For now, I assure you that Jesus' invitation to repent is really an invitation to a dramatic, deeply meaningful, hope-filled life. It moves me to be able to share this great invitation with you, and with all my heart I want you to enter into what repentance opens up to you. For the rest of our time together, I will talk with you about the deeply personal and practical aspects of following Jesus.

There's a second reason why I mention repentance, and that has to do with the place to which we have come in our conversation. I have been laboring to get before you two important facts. First, happiness, meaning to life, and human flourishing are impossible if there is no God. Your only hope for having a deeply important and rich life is if God, particularly the Christian God, exists. Second, the Christian God is a real and living God. Not only is He real, but also you can *know* He is real. I have provided a small sample of the evidence for this. If you are with me up to this point, then in light of these facts, you face a momentous, life-or-death decision about what to do with all this for the rest of your sojourn on this earth and beyond. And it is time for you to repent—to rethink your life, to start all over again, and to inventory your priorities, values, attitudes, and beliefs, in light of the reality of the triune God.

I want to help you with this if you'll let me. In the following chapters I plan to put pieces of a puzzle together that I trust will lead you to a new sort of life. And in this chapter, I will begin with first things first. Two extremely important pieces of good news lie at the very heart of Jesus' and His friends' view of life and their mission. Both of these will require that you rethink your life in light of them. I will explain these pieces of good news, try to unpack their relationship to one another, and give you help for appropriating them into your own life.

The Gospel of the Kingdom of God

Part of your very nature is to desire a life of drama, meaning, and significance. You naturally long to be a part of something bigger than you that is really important. And though our culture traffics in triviality, according to Jesus, you were made for this sort of greatness. So you must ask yourself this fundamental set of related questions: *In all honesty, what am I about? Why do I get up each day? What is a successful person and how do I think I can become one?*

Psychologists have long understood that a deep sense of purpose and meaning must inform our daily lives. And the Bible says that history is not just one darn thing after another. No, history has a purpose, a telos, a goal toward which it is moving and in light of which your own journey can take on meaning. Only—I repeat, *only*—as you subordinate and intertwine your daily life with this broader purpose for why God made the world—and why He brought you into it at this particular point in time and geography—can you experience the drama of a life of purpose. Your work, marriage, play, money, sense of self—all of your life—must be brought under this broad "divine conspiracy," as Dallas Willard calls it.

So what is God about? If you study the Bible carefully and then reflect on human history, the following, I believe, is not too wide of the mark.

God is establishing a community of people.

- Its members join voluntarily,
- its center is the triune God,
- it will progressively experience the kind of wise, loving, creative relationships (toward God, each other, and the created world) that take place among the members of that Trinity, and
- it will, together with God, defeat evil and rule over creation by creatively producing and finding truth, beauty, and goodness.

As a result, God Himself will receive honor, and our affection will be directed toward Him.

I recognize that this is a mouthful, so may I suggest that you pause and read it over a few times before proceeding? This is your life, your destiny. This is what you were created to do, and it shows how you can function most fully and most humanly. Note carefully that your Christian life is not a religious compartment in a broader life defined largely in secular terms. Your life as a disciple of the Lord Jesus is an entire way of being in the world. You are not a human being seeking a spiritual life. You are a spiritual being seeking a human life. That is, you were made for the purpose stated above, and you are to seek to live out this purpose in a distinctively human (as opposed to an angelic) way. To do so is to live fully as a human being made in the image of God Almighty. More specifically, you are to live out this purpose in a distinctively individual way. For example, I am to do this in a J.P. Moreland sort of way, in a manner appropriate to my strengths, weaknesses, gifts, personality, job, family, and so forth.

This purpose lies behind the broad gospel Jesus preached, taught, and demonstrated—the gospel of the kingdom of God. At the beginning of the launch of His movement, Jesus established the framework for His mission: "From that time Jesus began to preach and say, 'Repent, for the kingdom of heaven [God] is at hand'" (Matthew 4:17). "Jesus was going throughout all Galilee, teaching in their synagogues and proclaiming the gospel of the kingdom [of God], and healing every kind of disease and every kind of sickness among the people" (Matthew 4:23). The kingdom of God is the realm of reality over which the rule of God is exhibited—primarily the laws of nature, the individual hearts of men and women who have entered that kingdom, and the social structures they form.

Think of the kingdom as a country, say the United States. There are ways to live and flourish in the United States and ways not to. People in this country have privileges, rights, and responsibilities. They have established a hierarchy of authority and agreements about loyalty, obedience, provision, and protection. And the same is true of the kingdom of God. Or think of it this way. A kingdom is the range in which the king's will has say. You have a kingdom. It is the realm of life under your authority and control—your body, your children (allegedly!), people at work under your authority, your money, and so forth. As part of living out the purpose stated above, *the major daily orientation of your life* is to learn to get good at living according to the nature of the kingdom of God, working for its expansion, using the power it offers you within the protective arms of its King. In short, your job description is to get good at life, and this is what that means. This is your fundamental calling; this is why you are here.

Becoming Jesus' Apprentice

The basic means for advancement in this calling is to enlist as Jesus' apprentice in the school of life. Note carefully that growing as a disciple does not mean learning to add and get good at distinctively religious activities (prayer, Bible reading, church attendance, evangelizing) that are alongside the rest of your life. Jesus is profoundly uninterested in you becoming religious. No, discipleship involves learning from Jesus—primarily through His Word, fellowship in His body of followers, and interaction with Him and His Spirit daily—how to live your life well and for His honor. As Dallas Willard puts it, a disciple is someone who is learning from Jesus how to live his (the disciple's) life as Jesus would if He were the disciple. You are not supposed to live Jesus' life. He already did that and did it very well. So don't grow a beard, get sandals, and start speaking in parables! No, you have a life—a home or apartment, a job, friends, family, certain habits, and so on. Your daily reason for getting up is to learn how to take this kingdom of yours, place it under the kingdom of God, and learn from Jesus how to get good at your life so it reflects the nature of God Himself. This is what it means for you to become like Jesus.

When Jesus told us to repent because the kingdom of God was

and is near, He meant something very specific and deep. Paraphrased, Jesus meant this: "Rethink and change your approach to life in light of this new fact. My person and actions—especially My crucifixion and resurrection—open up to you through Me a completely new sort of life lived from a new place within a new realm." Jesus does not offer a new layer to your life. He invites you to a completely different life altogether. To love and be devoted to one's country is appropriate, but Jesus demands no less than our entire and ultimate allegiance to Him and His kingdom, and we are to get our fundamental sense of identity from our relationship to Him and our citizenship in His kingdom. Now.

This must become the internalized framework in light of which you approach life. It must lie at the core of your self-talk and become the way you define success. It must be your passion, your very breath, the fabric and substance of who you are in the depth of your self. This is what you have been looking for. Playing church or adding a religious layer to your life is boring and deeply wrong. But investing all your energy in growing as an apprentice of Jesus is the most wonderful, meaningful thing anyone could possibly do. And that is the sober truth.

In subsequent chapters I will flesh out some details about how to grow in and maintain this orientation. But for now, I want to emphasize how radical it is to become Jesus' disciple and adopt a kingdom orientation to all of life. We live in a predominantly secular society, and the processes of secularization pull at our minds, emotions, and will on a daily basis. Craig Gay clarifies the nature of secularization as...

> a subtle and largely inadvertent process in which religion— at least as it has traditionally been understood—forfeits its place in society. Secularization describes a process in which religious ideas, values, and institutions lose their public status and influence and eventually even their plausibility in modern societies.[1]

In a secular context, a religious life becomes one private, arbitrary expression of taste alongside being a sports fan, enjoying photography, or listening to certain kinds of music on an iPod. Religion is tolerated in our secularized society as long as devotion to it does not rise above the level of a hobby.

Discipleship to Jesus is no hobby. More of our brothers and sisters have been murdered for their commitment to Jesus in the twentieth century than in any other century, and we dishonor them and insult God Himself when we merely dabble in devotion to His Son. People who play at Christianity just don't get it. So the first thing I want you to plant firmly in your mind is that the good news Jesus proclaimed about the kingdom of God requires a totalizing response in which we do the best we can to bring all of us and place it under the authority of God and His kingdom, especially as that is spelled out in the inerrant Word of God, the Bible.

Loving God

A second defining feature of the good news about the kingdom of God goes alongside this first point and, I believe, actually helps to sustain commitment to the life of discipleship. I am speaking about the absolute centrality of learning to receive God's love for you and falling madly in love with God Himself, and cultivating the kind of intimacy appropriate to that loving relationship. I put the point in colloquial language to demystify what it means to love God and, more importantly, to divest it of a religious tone or spirit. Christians are nuts about Jesus; they can hardly stop talking about Him, and they love to think about Him, to please Him, to go everywhere with Him. Quite frankly, I can't see how anyone wouldn't be a bit crazy about Jesus Christ with even a miniscule sense of who He is and what He has done for us.

Jesus was very clear about the core of apprenticeship in His kingdom. That core amounts to nothing less that loving God "with all your heart and with all your soul and with all your mind" (Matthew 22:37). There are too many aspects to loving God for me to cover within the space limitations of this book. For example, I have devoted an entire book to the issue of loving God with your mind.[2] Here I want to focus on two things.

First, we love God because He first loved us (see Romans 5:8; 1 John 4:19). Therefore, growth in your love for God requires that you make it your life aim increasingly to understand and to experience God's love for you. This is not easy because we bring to this task a lot of internal recordings and past experiences of love—and some of its modern substitutes—that hinder us from grasping and experiencing God's love. The truth is that God actually likes you. He thinks about you constantly, He takes delight in you, and He is concerned about your well-being. Get this: He wants to be called your friend! He is eager—*eager*!—to show kindness, affection, and generosity to you. And if you have embraced His Son (which I will clarify in the second section of this chapter), no one can condemn you anymore. You must understand that all these feelings, thoughts, and attitudes flow from the sort of person God is, not from the sort of person you are. You cannot earn God's favor, nor can you lose it. The key is to live under the protective wings of Jesus.

When you need discipline, God will provide it. But He does so as a loving, wise father who is invested in your well-being and growth. And He stands ready to receive you warmly if you return to Him. Recognizing that God will never be harsh with you is supremely important. If you sense such harshness, the impression does not come from God. It is your own self-talk, your own projection of your own father figure or some such thing onto God. God's acceptance, love, and lack of a condemnatory attitude color His interaction (including His discipline) with His children—those of us in Christ.

In the Old Testament book of Isaiah, numerous passages describe how the Messiah will act and the texture of His heart toward His followers. Jesus is the exact representation of God, so these texts accurately describe how God sees you, even when you need correction. Please take a moment to read Isaiah 42:1-4,6-7; 50:4-11. They reveal God's heart toward you. We see that God will not break a bruised reed or extinguish a dimly burning wick (He will be especially gentle and careful with His broken and extremely needy children), He will hold us by the hand and watch over us, and He will exercise His skill to sustain us when we are weary.

If you are to make progress as a follower of Jesus, your first order of business is to replace your view of God with this tender, gentle, loving picture. This, in turn, should help you to seek to love God intimately and from the deepest recesses of your heart. Besides internalizing the way God feels toward you, I have two further suggestions for falling in love with Him. First, remember that Jesus and Paul both addressed God as *Abba,* a term used by little children for their fathers and best translated as "Daddy" or "Papa." This is not the only way to address God, but it is one important, legitimate way of approaching Him. I urge you to practice times when you address your loving Father as Daddy or Papa. This term not only invites a warm, intimate connection with God but also carries a feeling of putting yourself in the place of a little child who is deeply needy and dependent on your loving Father for safety and help. I say again that this approach does not exhaust your relationship with God, but it is at the core of developing an intimate walk with Him.

Second, the Bible invites us to use imagery and the imagination to foster such intimacy and dependency on God. Some people have rejected imagery on the grounds that it is too New Age or somehow inappropriate. But this rejection is naive and harmful. New Age people eat food, quiet their emotions, help the poor, and so forth. I am not practicing New Age activities when I do those things. Further, the Bible itself uses imagery all the time. Indeed, the detailed descriptions of Jesus' life in the Gospels and the vivid pictures in His parables all invite us to imagine Jesus doing this or that or to attempt to picture the content of a parable.

Returning to my main point, the Bible invites us, God's dear children, to take refuge under the shadow of His wings (Psalm 17:8; Matthew 23:37), and like a weaned child who no longer fidgets at the mother's breast, to lean against God's bosom in intimate connection and gentle hope and protection (Psalm 131). Using these images has been helpful for me. While praying, I will picture myself standing behind the Lord Jesus as He protects me, or crawling up into His lap, leaning my head against His chest, and feeling His loving and protective arms around me. Using biblical imagery like this fosters a feeling of warmth and intimate love toward God.

More than half century ago, A.W. Tozer made this note:

> The [experiential manifest] presence of God is the central fact of Christianity. At the heart of the Christian message is God Himself waiting for His redeemed children to push in to conscious awareness of His presence...The world is perishing for lack of knowledge of God and the Church is famishing for want of [an experiential awareness of] His presence. The instant cure of most of our religious ills would be to enter the Presence in spiritual experience, to become suddenly aware that we are in God and God is in us.[3]

Obeying His Commands

So the first aspect of loving God is to develop a sense of intimate, experiential connection with Him, to fall deeply in love with God. The second aspect of loving God is learning to obey and follow His commands to us. Jesus once said that if we love Him, we will keep His commandments. And if we do this, said Jesus, He will disclose Himself to us, that is, make Himself real to us and let us feel or sense His presence (John 14:21). It is crucial to understand that obedience to God's commands is actually an invitation to a life of well-being, joy, and flourishing. If I say, "Obey the multiplication tables" or "Change the oil in your car every 4000 miles," these are not arbitrary injunctions imposed on you by a cranky old man (me!) who is a killjoy. No, if you want to be good at math or have a well-functioning car, these commands will help you. In the same way, if you want to be good at life, then you should obey the commands of a good God who knows what you must do to function best the way you were designed to function. Obeying God's commands is actually acting on *an invitation to a fully human, rich, thriving life.*

While interviewing me on a radio talk show, the host asked me why I was against homosexuality. For the same reason, I responded, that I am against driving a new car on the bottom of the Pacific Ocean. Cars aren't made to thrive that way, and given that God knows best the way for us to thrive, His prohibitions against homosexuality are provisions for a thriving life and protection against a flawed, difficult life. In the same way, God's commands about sexual purity and abstinence outside of marriage do not rob us of real joy in life, and God has nothing against sex. No, God is the author of sex, and His commands are rooted in the way it—and we—function best.

The bottom line for me is this: I may be dumb, but I'm not stupid. And to live contrary to the commands of God is stupid. If you don't believe me, just compare the long-term lives of those who do and do not follow those commands and see who's life thrives best.

Obeying God's commands is a skill that takes time to develop, but it is the path toward a thriving life. It is also an expression of deep love and respect for God. When children obey their parents, especially if they do so for the right reasons, they express respect and love toward their parents. In the same way, obedience to God's commands is a way of expressing respect and love for God.

In sum, the only appropriate response to Jesus' proclamation of the gospel of the kingdom of God is to become an apprentice of Jesus in His school of life, to enter a life of deep meaning and thriving. This involves focused concentration on learning increasingly to grasp and experience God's love for you and, in response, to fall more and more in love with Him through tender, familial intimacy and obedience. This in turn will lead to human flourishing and express respect and love for God.

The Gospel of Justification by Faith

The gospel of the kingdom of God requires that we learn to trust Jesus Himself. But the New Testament contains a second gospel that requires that we trust not only Jesus but also something He did for us. This gospel has been identified with justification by faith, the announcement that through the death and resurrection of the God-man, Jesus, God's wrath has been propitiated (satisfied), we have been ransomed from the ravages of evil and the pillage of the devil, and we are declared righteous through our trust in the accomplished work that Jesus did. Before I clarify this second gospel, the question arises as to the nature of its relationship to the gospel of the kingdom of God. Here is my answer to that question:

> The direct rule of God is now available to everyone immediately. We no longer need to go through the Old Testament ceremonial system.
>
> Beginning with forgiveness and justification through faith in Jesus' death and resurrection, and by repeated repentance and trust in Jesus as our daily teacher and guide, we can choose moment by moment...
>
> - to live within the power and protection of God's kingdom,
> - to live according to its nature, rules, and structure (that is, to have God as our King, to be His servants ready to do His bidding, and to relate to other members as part of our family),
> - to seek to be its ambassadors,
> - to get our core identity from it and its triune King, and
> - to experience intimacy with the triune God and our brothers and sisters within its provision and boundaries.

Again, I recognize that this is a mouthful. And it is so pregnant with meaning that I encourage you to do two things. First, find biblical texts that undergird the different components of this statement. Second, meditate on it phrase by phrase and talk over its implications and applications with others.

In my view, the gospel of justification by faith is to the gospel of the kingdom of God as a part is to its whole or as the beginning of a journey is to the rest of the journey. The gospel of the kingdom includes justification as an essential ingredient. And it specifies the purpose of justification, namely, to be the start of a journey. The point or telos of becoming justified is that it is the way we begin a life of sanctification. The gospel is an invitation to an entirely new, rich life lived from the resources of and according to the nature of another realm. We become justified so we can enter into and learn this new life, a life that will be ours forever.

Starting a journey is different from the day-by-day carrying out of that journey, but the reason we start is to take the journey. Similarly, we accept the free grace of God in justification in order to enter a life of progressively having Jesus as our Lord in this life and the next. The gospel of the kingdom bids us to start by trusting something Jesus did for us (He died and rose for our justification) and to continue by enlisting daily as Jesus' pupil so He can teach and guide us how to live our lives as He would if He were us, that is, living out the kingdom in our own settings.

That said, let's probe more deeply this crucial notion of justification by faith. God loves you and sent His Son, Jesus, so that you might have abundant life—full, deeply meaningful, and rich (John 10:10). But we are all sinful and separated from God (Romans 3:23). As a result of our active rebellion or passive indifference toward God, we are spiritually dead, that is, separated from God (Romans 6:23). Our just desert is separation from a holy God now and for eternity. But Jesus Christ died in our place and rose from the dead to stand in our place, to take our punishment for us, and to pay the just demands for our sin against God and others (Romans 5:8; 1 Corinthians 15:3-6). Jesus Himself, then, is the only way to God, the only basis of forgiveness, as He Himself said (John 14:6). Through repentance, acceptance of God's grace in Christ, and faith in what He did for us, we are declared righteous, we are forgiven, and we receive Christ into our lives.

Jesus Christ becomes our substitute, His death and resurrection atone for our sins, and God's just and completely understandable wrath toward sin and evil is propitiated (that is, God's wrath is satisfied, and He turns away from it with respect to those who trust in and accept His Son's death and resurrection on their behalf). We are purchased out of the slave market of sin, and we are reconciled with and have complete peace with God. There is no longer any condemnation for those who are in Christ.

Wrath

I want to probe this incredible message more deeply in a moment, but let me address a few possibly confusing points. First, God's wrath and anger toward sin are easy to misunderstand. Our own anger is often immature and self-absorbed, so we can easily project a similar pettiness onto God. As a result, some Christians are embarrassed to talk about God's wrath. But this is a great mistake. In point of fact, respecting God would be difficult if He were not wrathful and angry about sin. Four points are relevant here:

1. As people mature in their moral sensibilities, they recognize and hate evil more and more. For example, I am not a vegetarian, but I have become sensitive to genuine cases of animal suffering.

2. Psychologists correctly note that the most pervasive human defense mechanism is denial. To defend ourselves, we are inclined to minimize sin's damage. Consider an act of speaking harshly to a stranger. One may be inclined simply to move on after doing such a thing and never ponder accurately the degree of harm it may have done to someone. Because God is infinitely holy, He is extremely sensitive to evil, He has a clear grasp of the depth of wrongness of sin, and

He has a profound understanding of the actual dire consequences of sinful attitudes and actions that we may deem minor. To be sure, God correctly grasps that some evils are worse than others, but the point remains that He does not minimize the things we are wrongly inclined to minimize.

3. God's wrath is not petty, picky, or trite. It is the mature, appropriate response to sin.

4. God's righteousness and wrath do not exhaust His character. He is also kind, gentle, and merciful.

One Way

Besides God's wrath, you may be having difficulty with the exclusivist claim that Jesus Christ and His death and resurrection provide the only way to God. I will address this more fully in chapter 11, but for now I will make one simple point. Suppose I stole $500 from you, you discovered what happened, and upon confronting me, I responded by saying, "I tell you what. Let's be reconciled with one another. To secure your forgiveness, I'll give you $25 back." Now, what's wrong with this picture? For one thing, it's the repayment of $25 for a $500 debt. But something deeper is here. You are the wronged party, so you are the one who should establish the terms for reconciliation, assuming you are a fair person. I am the offending party, and it is not my place to dictate to you the terms of my reconciliation. Similarly, God is the offended party when we sin against Him, and it is not our place to dictate to Him the terms of our reconciliation. He has done that in a most fair, gracious way.

Substitution

Third, you may not like the idea that one person can take the rap for another, but the idea is pretty commonsensical. Suppose a young man was sentenced by the judge to pay $273 for a traffic violation he could not pay. On pain of injustice, the judge has no alternative but to continue to hold the violator responsible for paying the fine or spending the specified time in jail. Now, suppose that the judge was the young man's father. After his gavel goes down, declaring the young man guilty, the judge takes off his robe, writes a check for $273, tells his son that he will pay his fine for him, and offers the check. The young man now has a choice. Either he gratefully receives the payment offered for his offense, or he rejects it and goes to jail. In like manner, we either receive the payment God has offered for a debt we could not pay (separation from God) or we justly remain separated from God forever.

If you have never accepted Jesus Christ as your Lord and Savior, now is the time to do so. Do not wait. And I must warn you that God will not take it lightly if you reject His Son and what He did for you now that you have heard and understood this good news. To see why, consider this.

Once upon a time, there was a man who operated the drawbridge for a train that passed over the river. His job was to lower the bridge so trains could pass. One day at the usual time, he climbed into the tower to push the lever that lowered the bridge. To his horror, as the train approached, he looked below and saw his ten-year-old son playing among the gears. He had to make a split-second decision: He could refrain from pushing the lever, save his boy, and send hundreds of passengers to their deaths in the river below, or he could push the lever, save the passengers, and allow his son to be killed. Knowing what he had to do, he watched in agony as his own son died in the gears as the train went by. The passengers went about their business. No one waved, no one thanked him, no one paid any attention to him. Imagine his justified outrage if someone subsequently found out what had happened and never expressed gratitude to the man for what he had done. I think the parallel with Christ's death is obvious.

Here is a prayer similar to the one I prayed in November 1968. The attitude of your heart is what matters, not the words. Still, why not make these words your own, receive the forgiveness God offers you, and enter His kingdom and the greatest adventure life has to offer?

Lord Jesus, I need You. I admit that I have done things displeasing to You, and I have failed to do the right thing many times in my life. I thank You that You died on the cross for my sins and rose from the dead. I gladly accept the forgiveness You offer me, and I ask You to come into my heart, forgive me, make Yourself real to me, and make me the kind of person You want me to me. Amen.

Whether you just now asked Jesus Christ to save you or you have followed Him for some time, consider some important advice about the cross, forgiveness, and gratitude.

The Cross

Jesus knew what He was doing by submitting Himself to death by crucifixion, as opposed to, say, being killed with a sword. The cross is a powerful image. In fact, it is the single most powerful, best-known image in the world and towers over other images, such as the hammer and sickle. You must stay close to the cross if you are to make progress as Jesus' disciple. You must return to it day after day.

We Christians cling to the cross, we embrace it, we boast about it, we honor it…we can't get enough of it. We all face deep issues of loneliness, shame, and guilt, and the power of the cross addresses each of these. As Christians, we must regularly imagine the crucifixion; we must regularly picture ourselves clinging to the foot of the cross. We must never stray too far from making it a regular part of our thought life and self-understanding.

By regularly embracing and clinging to the cross, I mean the regular practice of reminding ourselves that our standing before God is unalterable. We may come boldly into His presence. We need never hide from Him again. We are safe with God. He is not angry with us and never will be. He will never treat us harshly. His discipline is kind and with a view toward our good. Conversely, if you find yourself feeling guilty or ashamed before God, if you fear His discipline or project onto Him that He disapproves of you, if you believe He is tired of you confessing the same old thing again and again, then you are wrong. You need to go back to the cross and stay there in your imagination and in reflection about what it accomplished until you feel and grasp the truth again.

I absolutely love college football. You don't have to put a gun to my head to get me to watch a good game on television. I just love it, period. Now let me tell you something about God, something He absolutely loves as much as He loves beauty, spending time with you, and so forth. God absolutely *loves* to forgive. He *loves* it. He can't wait to do it. It is part of His generous, overflowing sense of goodness. He never tires of it. Forgiveness flows out of Him eagerly and with real joy and excitement. That's just how wonderful a person He is!

In this regard, I want to say something important about confession. In 1 John 1:9 we are told that if we confess our sins, God is faithful to forgive us. However, we can practice the regular confession of sin to God in two ways. For years, I practiced a self-destructive approach. On this view, if you do something wrong, you confess it as soon as you recognize what you did. This cleanses you afresh, and then you can enter into God's presence again.

This approach has two problems. For one thing, you subtly come to believe that your confession—for example, how earnest you were this time, how much you really felt sorry, how ready you were to acknowledge it, how well you have done since the last time you confessed something like this—earns you the right to walk with God again. This is deeply harmful. For another thing, you form the habit of giving a surface treatment of what is causing you to sin and what is really going on in your heart. As a result, you are more likely to engage in the sin repeatedly.

By contrast, here is a more helpful approach. When you sin against God and become aware of it, you immediately run to Him and invite Him into your situation. You immediately ask Him to search your heart and show you what is going on in the depths of your soul. This does two things. First, it is the practice of all the

New Testament teaching that you stand before God as clothed with Christ's righteousness and are no longer subject to condemnation. It is based on grace and mercy. It celebrates the unconditional love God has for you.

Second, this approach is the opposite of hiding, especially of using 1 John 1:9 as a way to avoid addressing the depths of evil in your heart. By inviting God into your predicament, you run to Him. Instead of hiding, you invite Him to search you and reveal to you more deeply what is going on, and you are then more adequately prepared to confess your sin to God—to agree with Him about it. To repeat: When you become aware of sinning, you cling to the cross, run to God, invite Him to search the depths of your heart, and then agree with Him about what you see. This is an expression of your confidence in His mercy. You do not become aware of sinning, hurry and offer a superficial confession as a quick fix, repeatedly do this as a way of assuring yourself you are worthy of walking with God, and never get beyond the surface.

Forgiveness

Our treatment of the cross has already passed over into the issue of forgiveness. In the Lord's Prayer, Jesus intimately linked the forgiveness we receive from God with the practice of forgiving others. This would include learning to forgive yourself as God has. The best book I have ever read on forgiveness is R.T. Kendall's *Total Forgiveness*.[4] Kendall explains what forgiveness is and is not. According to Kendall, when you forgive people, you do not...

approve of what they did

excuse what they did

justify what they did

pardon what they did (release them from consequences)

reconcile with them (they may be unsafe or unwilling to reconcile)

deny what they did

blind yourself to what happened

forget what happened

refuse to take the wrong seriously

pretend you are not hurt

Instead, forgiveness is the act of—and process of growing in—not holding things against people. Kendall says we prove that we have forgiven when we honestly petition God to let the people who harmed us off the hook. We are aware of what people have done, and still we forgive them. Kendall offers some ways to determine whether you are growing toward total forgiveness: You do not keep a record of what they did, you refuse to punish them, you don't tell others what happened, and you seek to be merciful, gracious, and free of bitterness. You do not intimidate them or seek to expose what they did (unless, of course, you need to in order to protect others, the church, and so forth). You let them save face and pray they will be blessed and will forgive themselves.

Two points of clarification are in order here. You would do well to have a very small group of intimate friends, perhaps your spouse, with whom you can process your life. This is where you can share what someone did to you. Usually, when we first do this, our intent is to dump on the offenders and marshal support for our side and against them. Since we are imperfect, my sense is that this is permissible under one condition: Our purpose in sharing what happened must be to process everything in a healthy way so we can eventually move on and forgive. Our intent over time should not be to harm the people and beat up on them in their absence! But we all have to start somewhere. Keep the circle of confidentiality small; otherwise, you end up justifying gossip.

Second, forgiveness is both a decisive initial act and a progression. We must eventually reach a particular moment when we choose to let go and forgive our offenders. At that point, we enter a process in which we use the yardsticks above and grow toward totally releasing and forgiving them. This process may take a long time, and we may regress and need to regroup as the case may be.

I have found these factors to be helpful in moving toward total forgiveness:

- Fear of losing control hinders progress in forgiveness and mires us in the desire to punish. Thus, the more you can focus on your safety in God's arms, the easier it will be to release offenders.

- Forgiving is actually easier than not forgiving because if you don't, people will continue to have "free rent" in your head. They will continue to control your thoughts and feelings as you battle them in your mind and waste emotional energy on them. Life is much better if you can let things go so people no longer control you.

- Try to picture offenders as little children who are being hurt by their friends, family of origin, and so forth. Try to picture them as weak, vulnerable individuals who hurt inside and are trying to cope with their own weaknesses inappropriately. This will help bring out your empathy.

- You need to forgive yourself in these ways. Try to be gentle with yourself. To be gentle toward something, like a little puppy, we need to see it as both precious and vulnerable. Try to see yourself through God's eyes as both precious and vulnerable and forgive yourself as God has forgiven you.

Gratitude

I close with a word about gratitude. In chapter 2, I mentioned that UCLA neuroscientist Jeffrey Schwartz has done experiments monitoring people's brains as they watch videos of carnage at automobile accident scenes. The anxiety center of the brain goes wild. Then he tells them to pretend they are paramedics who must make snap decisions about whom to treat first and what to do. When showed the same scenes, the anxiety center remains calm. We can alter our brain and its role in facilitating anxiety, anger, and so forth by changing how we think and adjusting our perspective. Here was Schwartz's punch line: People who see the glass half full regarding their lives are healthier, happier, and more functional than those that don't. And, he said, Christian theists who have a background belief that God is real, good, and caring will have a leg up on those without such a belief.

This harmonizes well with the findings of empirical psychology. As we saw in chapter 4, power (for example, money, education, and success), health, sexual attractiveness, and being youthful are not all that important as factors conducive to happiness and human flourishing. Instead, many psychologists list the factors that are in fact conducive to happiness and human flourishing: At the top of the list is living in a constant spirit of gratitude—a sense of thankfulness in life. Next were unselfishly caring for and helping others, learning to give and receive forgiveness, and finding a deep and real sense of meaning and purpose in life by giving ourselves to a larger framework than our own lives.

Does all this sound familiar? Gosh, you'd almost think that we were designed by God for life in His kingdom. You'd even be tempted to think that God's offer of the gospel of the kingdom and of justification by faith were expressions of His knowledge of what we need to function best according to the way He designed us. Well, guess what—if you thought these things, you'd be right. And remember, each and every day you need to practice the act of expressing gratitude to God for all the little and big things in your life. Learn to see things through grateful eyes. It is a fitting response to God. And it just may be good for you!

Two Essentials for Getting Good at Life

Americans are preoccupied with youth. We want to stay young, look young, and feel young. Based on the evening news, we pretend to care what young people think. Part of this infatuation with youth is completely understandable. All things being equal, who wouldn't want to look and feel young? But I suspect something deeper is going on here. In fact, I think two things are going on: (1) We have lost sight of the possibility of having a real purpose in life bigger than we are, one that is true and can be known as such. As a result, we have given up on living wisely in light of truth and settle for a life of immediate gratification and the satisfaction of bodily desire, and youthfulness has become the focus. (2) The loss of conviction in an afterlife has led to a culturally elevated fear of death. Staying young is a way of denying our mortality.

In the thirteenth century, Thomas à Kempis wrote *The Imitation of Christ,* one of the most influential books ever written. He warned that "it is vanity to wish to live long, and to be careless to live well."[1] Long ago, Plato (428–348 BC) wisely noted, "There is no question which a man of any sense could take more seriously than...what kind of life one should live."[2] Elsewhere Plato observed that it would be a tragedy if a person could be content with life by having good health, wealth, great looks, and a lot of ease and pleasure while, at the same time, not giving a moment's thought to the cultivation of skill at living life as a whole with virtue and character.[3]

A more profound thinker put the point quite succinctly: "For what will it profit a man if he gains the whole world and forfeits his soul? Or what will a man give in exchange for his soul?" (Matthew 16:26) Thomas à Kempis, Plato, and Jesus knew that learning to get good at a life of virtue and character—in short, getting good at the things described in chapter 7—is the very essence of a flourishing life. In his *Newsweek* review of Martin Seligman's magisterial work *Authentic Happiness,* Geoffrey Cowley summarizes Seligman's findings:

> Our circumstances in life have precious little to do with the satisfaction we experience. Married churchgoers tend to outscore single nonbelievers in happiness surveys, but health, wealth, good looks and status have astonishingly little effect on what the researchers call "subjective wellbeing."... [Authentic happiness] is about outgrowing our obsessive concern with how we feel...Is our life productive or meaningful? Does it stand for anything beyond itself?[4]

I want you to grasp and sense the importance of this. And I want to help you internalize this approach to life as your basic orientation. As doctors and biologists know, if people or animals become disoriented, they will get sick and die more easily. In the last chapter, I laid out what I believe should be our fundamental orientation to life—what we are about and why we get up each day. When I played high school football, our coach repeatedly reminded us that the game was about two fundamental things—blocking and tackling. And as the saying goes, the three things that really matter in real estate are location, location, location. In just this way, besides the topics about which we talked in the last chapter, I believe two habits lie at the heart of learning to get good at life in the kingdom. A habit is a tendency to act, feel, or think a certain way without choosing to do so. And time and focused effort are required for many habits to form, such as a good golf swing or good penmanship. Based on my understanding of the Bible and 40 years of walking daily with Jesus, I believe that these are two skills, two sets of habits that you simply must develop if you are going to thrive as a human person. Let's look at them.

Getting Good at Self-Denial

In 2001, Hollywood publicist Michael Levine wrote a cover article in *Psychology Today* in which he argued that constant exposure to beautiful women has made men less interested in dating if single or in their wives if married.[5] Levine cited studies in which men were exposed to (non-pornographic) pictures of beautiful actresses. Subsequently, single and married men were asked to rate the desirability of a typical woman in their social environment or of their wives, respectively. In both cases they were much less interested in the women available to them. Levine points out that for all of human history prior to the automobile and television, the average man was exposed to very few people in general or extremely beautiful women in particular. Limited in travel and with no television, most men learned to relate to women on a basis other than beauty. But today, says Levine, the average man sees hundreds of absolutely gorgeous women each night on television shows and commercials and gradually loses interest in less beautiful women.

These findings are not hard to believe. What is surprising, and relevant to our present discussion, is his explanation for this loss of interest. It is not that such exposure to television makes men think their partners are less physically attractive. Instead, men think, *My partner is fine, but why settle for "fine" when there are so many beautiful women out there! I can do a lot better than this!*

This is the deepest insight Levine offers, but I offer one deeper still. Why is it that men think this way? Answer: They are empty selves, drunk with seeking happiness, and as a result, they are individualistic, narcissistic, infantile people who approach others as objects that exist merely to make them happy. Many people today of both sexes are the products of an approach to life according to which they focus on their own needs and desires 24 hours a day and treat everything else as means to that end. We were not made to live that way, and when we do, we eventually break down.

Jesus had an entirely different take on the nature of a thriving life and how it is obtained:

> If anyone wishes to come after Me, he must deny himself, and take up his cross and follow Me. For whoever wishes to save his life will lose it; but whoever loses his life for My sake will find it. For what will it profit a man, if he gains the whole world and forfeits his soul? Or what will a man give in exchange for his soul? (Matthew 16:24-26).

It is of critical importance to grasp the core of what Jesus is asserting. A mistake at this point has frequently led folks to adopt a life strategy that has harmed them greatly, for example, by taking Jesus to be affirming the idea of justification by works or a gruesome, negative form of self-hatred. In context, Jesus is actually expressing a crucial insight about the nature of human beings and how they function best according to the way they were designed. Properly understood, Jesus' statement is an invitation to a life of drama, well-being, wisdom, and peace—what may be described as the classic (as opposed to the contemporary) sense of happiness—along with a description of how to enter into that life. He is not presenting His followers with a command that He knows they may choose to disobey. No, He is providing a description of reality. If you want to learn math, you have to practice multiplication. If you want to get good at Spanish, you have to memorize vocabulary. If you want to get good at life, you have to learn to give yourself away to others for Jesus' sake.

The self-absorbed, narcissistic life of seeking pleasurable satisfaction is heavily dependent on external circumstances, such as performing well in a game or even at church, enjoying a movie, and so forth. As such, it is relatively unstable and comes and goes with the flux of the circumstances of life. Living in the kingdom as Jesus' apprentice in the school of life provides a sense of well-being that springs from within as a process of maturation shapes our internal character. This deep sense of well-being becomes increasingly stable, permanent, and tied to a life of goodness, truth, beauty, and discipleship. It has less and less to do with external circumstances.

Like Turkish delight in *The Lion, the Witch and the Wardrobe*, contemporary happiness becomes addictive and enslaving if it is too central to our sense of self. Such an overemphasis makes us people who cannot live without happiness, who live an adrenalized life, whose empty self must constantly be filled with calories, romance, consumer goods, and social status. In this way, contemporary happiness becomes addictive and enslaving. Satisfaction of desire and the right to do what we want are the goals of this kind of life.

Life in Jesus' kingdom is deeply liberating as we increasingly become unified persons who live for a cause bigger than ourselves. Advancing the kingdom of God, living in intimacy with God and others, and honoring God by reflecting His good nature are the goals of this life. We seek the power to live as we ought and are not preoccupied with the right to do what we want.

People who manage to consume chunks of contemporary happiness can have pockets of happiness in their lives that are entirely split off from and unrelated to the rest of their lives. For example, a sports fan can get a bit of happiness by watching a game, but after it wears off, the impact of being happy does not necessarily make him satisfied by his marriage or work. By contrast, a life of classical happiness—virtue and deep well-being lived according to God's kingdom—colors everything because it forms the core of our lives and becomes the integrative center around which all aspects of our lives are unified.

The difference between the two senses of happiness should be clear, but is classical happiness really what Jesus is talking about in Matthew 16:24-26? Yes it is, and Jesus and other New Testament writers give it a distinctive texture. Jesus is not talking about going to heaven and not hell, nor is He teaching His followers how to avoid a premature death. Matthew writes, "What will profit a man if he gains the whole world and forfeits his soul?" Luke clarifies Jesus' meaning for "soul" by simply using the word "himself." The idea is finding one's self instead of losing one's self. More specifically, to find one's self is to find out what life is to look like and to learn to live that way. It is to become like Jesus Himself and have a character that manifests the radical nature of the kingdom of God and the fruit of the Spirit. It is to find out God's purposes for one's life and to fulfill those purposes in a Christ-honoring way.

The concept of eternal life in the New Testament is not primarily one of living forever in heaven, but of having a new *kind* of life, a new *quality* of life so different that those without this sort of life can, in a real sense, be called dead. This is a life of human flourishing, a life lived the way we were made to function, a life of virtue, character, and well-being lived like and for the Lord Jesus.

This is what people hunger for whether they know it or not. We were created for drama; we were meant to live dramatic lives as part of a worldwide movement, a divine conspiracy to trample the forces of darkness and replace them with goodness, truth, and beauty. Such a dramatic calling makes the presence or absence of a fleeting amount of pleasurable satisfaction simply beside the point and, frankly, not worth worrying about. We love movies that feature drama because that is how we are to live our own lives. We are to be dramatic even in the little things that grace the daily routines of our ordinary lives. As part of a pursuit of classical happiness, little things and ordinary activities become big and quite extraordinary pretty quickly! No wonder people who are preoccupied with pleasurable happiness become empty selves! Their vision is too small, too confining, too mundane to justify their fourscore and ten, too little to demand their best effort over the long haul! No wonder people would rather spend themselves for an important cause—specifically, the cause of Christ and leading a life well lived—than enjoy a pampered idleness. No wonder the primary problem of contemporary culture is boredom!

Self-denial in this text does not mean living without money, goods, recognition, or pleasurable satisfaction, though it certainly implies that seeking these things should not be our life's objective. Neither is self-denial the attitude of putting ourselves down. Sadly, I sometimes meet people who cannot take a compliment or who feel guilty because they receive satisfaction from an achievement or from having a new car. Nor is self-denial the idea that we should not have boundaries but, instead, should just give ourselves away to others anytime they ask. If you try that, you'll burn out in six months!

No, self-denial means something very specific. Note that Jesus uses "take up his cross" to characterize self-denial. Jesus did not literally mean this (though a willingness to die is clearly implied) because Luke adds the word "daily" (Luke 9:23) to the assertion. If Jesus meant this literally, we obviously could not take up our cross each day! Rather, taking up our cross daily means to form the daily habit of going through our day with a certain orientation and attitude, namely, that our passion is to give up our right to make ourselves the center of concern that day but, instead, to live for God's kingdom, to find our place in His unfolding plan and play our role well, and to give our life away to others for Christ's sake.

Like learning to be good at anything, such as bowling or Spanish, learning to get good at life by getting good at self-denial is a skill, a set of habits, that takes time and focused attention to cultivate and retain. So how do we make progress in this? I have four suggestions.

Become a Strong Person

First, you have to be a fairly strong person to do this. If not, your self-denial can turn out simply to be a way of hiding because you don't like others to focus on you. If that's your problem, then real self-denial for you might actually be engaging in the difficult task of letting others focus on and value you. Also, to get good at biblical self-denial, you must feel safe and secure in the world. If you don't, you will be too insecure, too afraid, too defensive to follow through. Because of these factors, the development of a life of self-denial must come after the realization and internalization of the things mentioned in chapter 7.

To get good at self-denial, you must first practice the presence of God, learn to feel and grasp His affection for you, learn to approach Him as your tender *Abba* or Papa, and learn to receive and give forgiveness. I am not suggesting that you have to become expert at these before you should launch out and practice self-denial. I am simply pointing out that biblical self-denial assumes a framework within which it makes sense and within which life is safe and secure before a constant, loving God. And that framework was presented in chapter 7. Here's a test: If you find yourself drawing back from a life of progressive self-denial, you may have stopped believing or feeling the things discussed in chapter 7. If so, you have to go back and re-appropriate them.

Counting the Cost

Second, you have to count the cost as Jesus Himself pointed out (Luke 14:25-35). This is actually a lot simpler than you might expect. Why? Because the cost is pretty low compared to the dividends. On a strictly cost-benefit analysis, a life of self-denial for Jesus is a bargain. To be honest, it's a no-brainer. I have grown in this approach to life for close to 40 years, and two things have been uppermost in my mind as I count—and recount—the cost of discipleship.

For one thing, I seek exposure to—and constantly remind myself of—what life is like outside discipleship unto Jesus. That was one reason I started this book in chapters 1 and 2 with a depiction of typical secular life (or lukewarm Christianity) in our culture. For example, the bankruptcy of atheism has been one source of inspiration for me to continue to dedicate myself to God. So be on the alert to stay connected to the emptiness of life outside of abandonment to Jesus Christ, not so you can look down on others, but so you can stay grateful for and accurately appraised of the value of life as Jesus' apprentice.

Additionally, stay in touch with the incredible rewards of discipleship. Four things can help you do this:

- Never stray far from reading the psalms. They help you feel close to God and stay in touch with your need for Him.

- Stay close to the Gospels as well. They remind you of what an incredible person Jesus is and what an honor it is to be associated with Him.

- Face and feel your brokenness, your sin, your smallness, and your childhood hurts. This will help you remain desperate for God. Denial and repression deaden the soul and undermine the passion we need to be desperate for God.

- Read Christian biographies or stories of what God is doing around the world today. This will make you proud to be a part of the body of Christ and remind you of what a privilege it is to be involved in the advancement of the kingdom.

Practicing Self-Denial

Third, you have to practice self-denial. Like any habit, you get good at this through daily practice, starting with small things and growing into larger ones. Here's something to try. Get up in the morning, and while you prepare for your day, focus on your needs or worries, and bring them before God. Once that is done, tell God you want to give yourself away to Him and others for His sake between now and lunch. Then look for every opportunity you have to practice this. During lunch, refocus on prayer for your own needs and worries. Then dedicate your afternoon to self-denial until dinner. And so forth. Find a specific regimen that works for you. And remember, the key thing is that you actually practice. Of course, as you practice, don't do it alone. Constantly invite the Holy Spirit to be your friend, guide, and power source. Yield yourself to Him and His control at various times of the day.

Fasting

Fourth, as part of the practice of self-denial, I suggest the regular practice of fasting, not only from food but also from anything that controls you. Remember, to fast from something does not mean the thing is intrinsically wrong. Rather, it means you want to train yourself to learn to go without things, to get good at saying no to yourself. Going without television, different forms of entertainment, or the use of something you own can be a great training forum for learning to engage in a broader, life-permeating self-denial.

If you want to learn to fast from food, I suggest you start by going without breakfast every Monday morning, then work up to breakfast and lunch, and eventually go without dinner Sunday night and breakfast and lunch Monday. Celebrate Monday dinner by taking your spouse or a friend out to eat (just don't pig out mercilessly!). Remember, when learning to fast, go without food during a time when you are busy and preoccupied with other things. Don't start off thinking you should fast and pray or fast and seek solitude and alone time. Why? It will drive you nuts! Learn to fast first—and practicing while you are busy is the way to do it—and later you can graduate to fasting and praying or being in solitude.

Biblical Self-Talk as a Way to Redefine Success

A critical aspect of growing in self-denial and becoming like Jesus is to practice proper self-talk. We constantly talk to ourselves, and when we do, much of it is a form of self-appraisal—self-congratulations for various successes, self-soothing by reassuring ourselves that we are safe, self-loathing for being stupid, embarrassed, guilty, or ashamed. In truth, our main agenda each day is to be safe, to appear well in others' eyes, and to hide our inadequacies and expose our successes.

This is a failed project. It produces self-absorption, it sustains a false self (a self we want others to think we are), it consumes a ton of energy to prop up that false self, and it makes us addicted to the approval of others and the appearance of success. Count me out. Life it too short to get bogged down in such a demeaning, trite, hypocritical life. But the problem is that we are all enslaved to such a life unless, with God's help, we find a way of escape. And in the remainder of this chapter, I want to describe that exit strategy.

In Colossians 3:1-17, we have what may be the best description in the entire New Testament of what life is like in the kingdom of God. It is permeated with authenticity, hope, and power. Clearly, this is one of the greatest pieces of literature in world history.

> Therefore if you have been raised up with Christ, keep seeking the things above, where Christ is, seated at the right hand of God. Set your mind on the things above, not on the things that are on earth. For you have died and your life is hidden with Christ in God. When Christ, who is our life, is revealed, then you also will be revealed with Him in glory.
>
> Therefore consider the members of your earthly body as dead to immorality, impurity, passion, evil desire, and greed, which amounts to idolatry. For it is because of these things that the wrath of God will come upon the sons of disobedience, and in them you also once walked, when you were living in them. But now you also, put them all aside: anger, wrath, malice, slander, and abusive speech from your mouth. Do not lie to one another, since you laid aside the old self with its evil practices, and have put on the new self who is being renewed to a true knowledge according to the image of the One who created him—a renewal in which there is no distinction between Greek and Jew, circumcised and uncircumcised, barbarian, Scythian, slave and freeman, but Christ is all, and in all.

So, as those who have been chosen of God, holy and beloved, put on a heart of compassion, kindness, humility, gentleness and patience; bearing with one another, and forgiving each other, whoever has a complaint against anyone; just as the Lord forgave you, so also should you. Beyond all these things put on love, which is the perfect bond of unity. Let the peace of Christ rule in your hearts, to which indeed you were called in one body; and be thankful. Let the word of Christ richly dwell within you, with all wisdom teaching and admonishing one another with psalms and hymns and spiritual songs, singing with thankfulness in your hearts to God. Whatever you do in word or deed, do all in the name of the Lord Jesus, giving thanks through Him to God the Father.

For my purposes, the key here is the first paragraph. At first glance, you might not think much of these verses. In fact, for years, their point was simply lost on me. To seek things above and keep my mind there was, well, sort of irrelevant, or so I thought. I imagined I was supposed to try to sustain a picture of God on some throne with Jesus sitting next to him and angels flying around. Somehow, if I paid attention to this picture and not my daily trials, life would turn out well. About ten years ago, I decided to do something truly novel and radical: I actually studied the passage! Was I in for the surprise of my life. The passage turned out to be so practical that when I shared my findings with my good buddy Bill Roth—a well-respected Christian therapist in the area and faculty member at Loma Linda University Hospital—he insisted that we memorize verses 1-17 together (which we did).

We all have an affective coloring, a tone, a personal presence we carry with us throughout the day. This tone is so pervasive and subtle that it usually lies in our unconscious life. But it is so real that it determines how others experience us day by day. And like soft background music at a restaurant, it colors how we see and feel the world and shades every thought we have. Would you like to know the main factor that determines this tone? It's largely the product of our mental preoccupation. It results from the habits of our mind. We have habits about what we are preoccupied with hour by hour—largely, appearing successful—and the content of that preoccupation, along with the feelings associated with it, determine our affective coloring.

That's the bad news. The good news is that we can change our feeling-tone by forming new habits of the mind, fresh mental preoccupations, and that's where Colossians 3:1-4 comes in. When the passage admonishes us to "keep seeking the things above" and to "set [continually be intent on] your mind on things above, not on the things that are on earth," we are challenged to do two things: Learn to set aside the mental preoccupations I have mentioned a few paragraphs ago, and replace that preoccupation with the steady, constant, habituated, and nearly unconscious engrossment with three specific things. These three, I believe, must become our new sense of self and success.

Our Core Identity

First, I constantly remind myself that my core, fundamental identity is my connection with Jesus Christ along with the person into which He is shaping me and to which He has called me. I am identified with Jesus' resurrection—I have a new power and authority over evil. Jesus Christ is my very life. He is the source of my new life in the kingdom; He is closer to me than my next breath; He is my purpose, my job, my dearest friend, my Master, my everything. I am His disciple at my core. Further, my life is hidden in Him. I think this means that I am protected in Him but more importantly, it also means that my true self—not my false self, the self I have fabricated to be safe, the self I project so others will like me—is hidden in two senses:

1. It is so deeply interwoven with Jesus' own life, so pervasively connected with what Jesus is doing in me, so wrapped up in Jesus' purpose for and calling upon my life, that where I end and He begins gets fuzzy. We are so tight that our lives interpenetrate each other. He

is a friend who sticks closer than a brother, and I cling so tightly to Him each day that I can't imagine going to work or doing anything else without fiercely acknowledging that He goes with me.

2. What He is doing in me, the person I am becoming, and the person I will eventually be is not clear yet. So while others (and I myself) have a right—indeed, a duty and privilege—to exhort and admonish me when I need it, no one—including me—has a right to condemn and look down on me. I have got to get out of the comparison game. How do I know where others started in their Christian journey? Maybe they were ahead of me when I started due to a better childhood and so forth. Maybe God has very different aims for each of us.

Here's the point: My goal is to get good at being who I am in Christ, and much of what that means, most of what I will eventually become, is hidden now. So I must be grateful for where I am at, not get discouraged if things move slowly sometimes, and draw comfort that I will eventually be at such a wonderful place that I would not recognize myself if I saw it now, nor would I believe it were it told to me!

By way of application, we need to constantly let go of the need to succeed and the fear of failure. It is normal to want to do well at work, to have wonderful children, to make a good income. And it is normal to want to avoid being lazy, getting fired, and so on. But we have to let go of the drivenness we have about these matters. They play too big of a role in our lives. So each day, learn to take the significance out of these. If you do well and get rewarded or recognized for it, be grateful for a time, receive it gladly, then let it go and move on. And the same goes for failures.

By contrast, you need to constantly remind yourself of the core of your identity. I am a father, husband, grandfather, university professor, author, and so forth. These are all part of my identity, and it is normal to get some strength of identity in these. But I must be careful here. For one thing, my goal is to be a *Christian* father, husband, professor, and so on, so even these aspects of my identify should eventually be caught up in my life as Jesus' follower. For another thing, I must constantly talk to myself about my ultimate core identity: I am a disciple of Jesus. It doesn't get any better than that. So when I shower in the morning, when I drive to work, just before and after student appointments, on the way home, and as I lay in bed before drifting off to sleep at night, I speak to myself about being hidden in—identified with, caught up into—the very life, kingdom, and purposes of the living God. When a problem comes to mind, I immediately invite my Friend, Lord, and co-laboring God to search my heart, help me see the truth, and work with me in resolving it. You must practice the presence of God in this manner, and your identity and relationship with Him is to be the fundamental orientation of your hour-by-hour life. This is the first thing it means to keep your mind on things above.

Our Mission

Second, as the Blues Brothers reminded us, I am a man on a mission from God! As I have already noted, part of what it means to be hidden in Christ is that I have been put here for a purpose. In verse 17, this aspect of "setting your mind on things above" is further elaborated: "Whatever you do in word or deed, do all in the name of the Lord Jesus, giving thanks through Him to God the Father." There is a reason why you are here. As a master conductor brings in the flutes at just the right time and then the French horns, so God has brought you into the world at your specific time and location to play your role—not Billy Graham's or Rick Warren's role—in His grand symphony.

By way of application, you should never treat an aspect of your life as something secular, something to be defined apart from God's kingdom purposes and your role in them. Remember, this does not mean that you are to find a way to do Bible study or evangelism or Scripture memory while you sell insurance or play golf. If this seems appropriate, well and good. But if you think primarily in these terms, then you haven't gotten it yet. You conceive of aligning yourself hour-by-hour with kingdom purposes in terms of adding a religious layer to your life that, in turn, is defined outside of the kingdom. That leads to a fragmented secular versus sacred life. It's also very tiring because it means you have to add religious activities alongside your work, family life, recreation, and so forth.

Instead, rethink everything in light of your own unique calling and role in the kingdom. What would it mean to be a Christian insurance salesman? What would you do and not do? Perhaps more importantly, how would you view your work and conduct it differently if you saw it as a ministry, an expression of discipleship to Jesus? How would you approach exercise, recreation, family life, and so on? For example, if you go to a bookstore, don't just buy and read books that help you grow personally. Also read books that help you discover and develop your gifts and talents for the body of Christ. Read books about important moral and cultural issues so you can be a better ambassador for Christ. Spend mental energy getting good at locating yourself for the good of your church, your workplace, your customers, your family, and the broader kingdom enterprise. Rethink it all. Inventory your time, emotions, energy level—all of it—and ask God to search your heart and help guide you as you do. And do this on a daily basis. Make it a *daily practice* to orient your day in light of your aim to serve, honor, and walk with Jesus Christ throughout that day, and interpret all your activities in light of your commitment to Him and His kingdom. This is the second thing it means to keep your mind on things above.

Our Character

Third, form the daily habit of being passionate about and completely absorbed in developing character, a tender inner life, and a heart for God and others. This is clarified in verses 5-16. In the next chapter I will offer some suggestions for doing this, but for now I simply note that learning to set aside sinful habits, to replace them with good ones, and to learn to focus on others and be concerned for their welfare is far more important than learning how to talk all the time so you impress others, to dress well or obtain the right consumer products so others envy you, to look sexually attractive and be an attention-getter, or to receive lots of respect for your various successes in life.

To keep seeking the things above and constantly to set your mind on them, then, means this: forming the habit of constantly being pre-occupied with your core identity with and in Jesus Christ, with finding and learning to play your role well in every aspect of your life, and with becoming a loving person with a tender heart and Christ-honoring character.

ABC's *20/20* recently did a special on happiness. For an hour, the show discussed the results of happiness research done by interviewing hundreds of thousands of people from more than 160 countries. The results? Three things stood out:

1. The happiest people in the world are those who take themselves to be following their calling in life, including treating their job as a calling. I don't think there can be a calling without a Caller. Without a knowable God of a certain sort, most especially the Christian God, "calling" language becomes an empty metaphor that expresses a vague, vacuous placebo constituted by the hope that there is some bigger something, somewhere, to which I am contributing.

2. We were made for community, and the importance of nurtur-ing meaningful relationships and having an intimate community to which we belong cannot be overstated. Christianity predicts this. At the very heart of existence stands a triune God, a community of three centers of consciousness in one being who love, adore, and respect each other. The Trinity shows that individuality and community are both fundamental and of equal importance. As those made in God's image, we are born to be connected to others, most especially God Himself. And besides the Trinity itself, the richest community in the world is the body of Christ.

3. Only 10 percent of happiness comes from one's external circum-stances. By contrast, 40 to 50 percent of our happiness is the result of free choice—specifically, the choice of what we will focus on mentally throughout the day. Happy people are those who are optimistic about

the future (and if God doesn't exist, why should we be optimistic about a future that isn't really going anywhere?). They see the glass half full and practice gratitude (you can only be grateful for life if you are also grateful to Someone). They choose to forgive and focus on counting their blessings.

I think it should be obvious that these discoveries prove we were made for God and His kingdom as revealed in the Bible. We were made to practice and get good at self-denial and the three mental preoccupations that constitute the continual seeking of things above. This is your only hope for a thriving, flourishing life. I'm not kidding. This is the way, walk in it.[6]

Avoiding the
Three Jaws of Defeat

On a few occasions over the years, I have tried to diet. Have you tried it? I hate it. If you don't succeed, you feel terrible, and if you do succeed, you feel terrible during the diet and in anticipation of a relapse in the months ahead! I like win/wins, not lose/loses! My last dieting attempt was a real bust. I faced a number of distractions in the form of special desserts, dinners, and parties during the weeks leading up to Biola University's graduation celebration. It was hard to diet during these distractions. Then there was my own weakness of will. If either chips or ice cream are in the house while I am dieting, it's all over. And then there were temptations from my "friends," who reminded me, "You don't really need to diet, and besides, just one evening of overeating isn't going to hurt anything."

Failing in one's diet is not the end of the world unless serious health considerations are lurking. But failing in combat is another matter. A friend of mine fought in the Vietnam War and had to kill someone with a knife in hand-to-hand combat. He told me that several times during his stay in 'Nam, he had to avoid outward distractions: hard living conditions, lack of sleep, and "friendly" approaching Vietnamese who may be the enemy in disguise. He also had to keep in check his own inner fears, desires to be back home, and faintness of heart. And if these were not enough, constant enemy propaganda proclaimed that the war effort by the Americans was not worth it, that we were losing, and that the Americans back home hated the soldiers (which, sadly, was not entirely propaganda).

Failing to fight well in a war is far more serious than failing at a diet. It can lead to an early and untimely death. But there is an even more important context in which failure is even more serious: the task of getting good at life in God's kingdom as Jesus' student for the honor of God Himself. To fail here is to miss life itself. And that is even worse than dying. In the last two chapters, I have spelled out a fundamental orientation for growing toward a thriving life according to God's design and purpose. In this chapter I must bring up something uncomfortable. It certainly is not the sort of thing I would lead with if I were talking about the joys of following Jesus. I am speaking of three sources of destruction, three "jaws of defeat," three areas of life from which hindrance and harm will come to you in your journey toward deeper discipleship if you let them go unchecked.

Jesus was very clear about these three sources of attack on human flourishing. During the early months of His movement, we have no evidence that Jesus taught in parables (pithy stories). He seems instead to have engaged in public lecture (like the Sermon on the Mount) or conversation. But about halfway through His public ministry, Jesus turned to parables as His main vehicle for teaching, and His very first recorded parable may be the most important. It sets the context for all His other parables, and it is found in Matthew 13:1-15, Mark 4:1-12, and Luke 8:4-10. Given its prominence, if you want to be a growing follower of the Lord Jesus, you would do well to consider its message. In it, Jesus is preoccupied with identifying and warning us against three "jaws of defeat." Here is Luke's version:

The sower went out to sow his seed; and as he sowed, some fell beside the road; and it was trampled under foot and the birds of the air ate it up. Other seed fell on rocky soil, and as soon as it grew up, it withered away, because it had no moisture. Other seed fell among the thorns; and the thorns grew up with it and choked it out. Other seed fell into the good soil, and grew up, and produced a crop a hundred times as great…He who has ears to hear, let him hear.

In His own interpretation of the parable, Jesus identifies three sources of concern (Luke 8:11-15): The world, the flesh, and the devil. The devil may snatch the seed from one's heart (verse 5), the person's own inner shallowness and fleshly habits may keep the seed from taking root in his or her life (verse 6), and the worries and distractions of the world may choke out the seed (verse 7). The Bible encourages us not to love or be conformed to the world (Romans 12:1-2; 1 John 2:15-17), to resist the devil (James 4:7; 1 Peter 5:9), and not to live according to the pattern and desires of the flesh (Galatians 5:16-21). Considerable and harmful confusion surrounds these three, so in the remainder of the chapter, I will try to clarify these three areas of harm and offer help in defeating them.

The World

I don't mean this to be mean-spirited, but I have to warn you that the Christian community is terribly confused about the world. People have been hurt deeply, deprived of much good, and judged harshly because of the ignorance among Christians about what the world is. It is said that the Amish had a saying: "Don't go out there among them English." The phrase assumed a rigid moral and theological division between the Amish and everyone else (the English), and the English were to be avoided at all costs. Why? Because supposedly, nothing good can come from the English. In 40 years, I have spoken to college groups from 200 campuses and in hundreds of churches in 43 states. I have repeatedly heard this very thing asserted with an Evangelical twist.

The idea is that there are solid believers and everyone else, particularly unbelievers, who are identified as "the world." And we are to avoid unbelievers—their culture, ideas, habits, moral values, music, literature, behavior, and so on—like the plague. This advice is an expression of ignorance, though it is usually well-intentioned.

What, exactly, is the New Testament conception of the world? The Greek word *cosmos* is translated "world" in the New Testament, and it is used 185 times, 105 in John's writings. It has three meanings, and a fourth is conspicuous by its absence. It can mean the created world, the universe (Acts 17:24), or the inhabited world, the earth in so far as it is the place human beings dwell, human beings taken as a group. (John 3:16). In these senses, the world is good. It is the third sense of *cosmos* that is inherently evil: an ordered system, headed by Satan, that stands opposed to God; organized, synergistic flesh; the realm of ideas, feelings, beliefs, actions, cultural artifacts—such as music, movies, and books—that are contrary to the nature of God and His kingdom" (John 12:31; 1 John 2:16).

Do you see what is missing? The world is *not* identical to the culture, ideas, habits, moral values, behavior, attitudes, and artifacts made and embraced by non-Christians. Jesus' followers in the West regularly make this mistake. The result? The Christian community tends to become—and comes off as—defensive, ingrown, silly, withdrawn, unattractive, and out of touch with people's lives. I do not mean to insult anyone, and I take no joy in saying this. But I cannot in good conscience fail to bring this to your attention. Here's why: This (in my view) largely accurate description of the Christian community is bad enough, but to make matters worse, this communal dysfunction (resulting from a mistaken view of the world) tends to produce a judgmental, harsh, arrogant, ready-to-attack religious (Pharisaical) spirit in Christians quite at odds with the tenor and tone of Jesus' Holy Spirit. This view of the world actually expresses a small, petty self-image on the part of Christians who try to protect themselves from the power of their culture by rejecting all of it as worldly.

The Bible does not identify the world with the sum total of non-Christian culture, but rather with that aspect of non-Christian culture (and that aspect of Christian culture!) that is contrary to the nature of God and His kingdom. That means that non-Christian culture is a mixed bag—some of it is worldly, and some of it is the expression of truth, goodness, and beauty that results from the image of God still present in non-Christians. The Bible sometimes praises the wisdom (including moral wisdom and practical wisdom for being good at life) of non-Christians and their culture, along with their (admittedly limited) ability to listen to and learn from wise people (1 Kings 4:29-31; Jeremiah 49:7). Scripture acknowledges the truthfulness and accuracy of non-Christian thinkers (Acts 17:28), and it quotes approvingly from the non-Christian book *The Assumption of Moses* (Jude 1:9). Believers and nonbelievers can learn things about God and right and wrong from creation and conscience (Matthew 5:43-45; Romans 1:18-23; 2:12-16).

Given that we are to not love or be conformed to the world, and given that the world is not identical to the whole of non-Christian culture, we followers of Jesus have to do something truly painful if we are to obey biblical teaching about the world: We have to *think hard* and *well* and *biblically* about life! If something from culture contradicts Scripture, it would be foolish to believe it. Millions of pilgrims have put the Bible to the test, and it has proven itself true and reliable time and time and time again. When properly interpreted, Scripture is our ultimate authority concerning all it teaches. Put the Bible to the test and see for yourself if you don't believe me. But be warned: If you believe or do things contrary to Scripture, it will eventually catch up with you. On the other hand, if something from culture does not contradict the Bible, should a Christian believe it or not? In this case, believe it if the evidence for it is good and it seems wise, true, good, and helpful. Otherwise, reject it. In other words, assess things on a case-by-case basis by consulting the evidence and Christian wisdom. Here are four pieces of practical advice for learning how to deal with the world (properly understood).

Love God with Your Mind

Constantly renew and feed your mind biblically and theologically, and develop biblical categories and ways of thinking. Pay close attention to your thoughts, beliefs, and emotions, and evaluate them carefully in light of biblical teaching (Romans 12:1-2; 2 Corinthians 10:3-5). You have to make it a priority to fill your mind regularly with the Bible. Some find it helpful to read it each day. That has not been my experience. Instead, I have done three things. First, I have memorized five key passages (ranging from two to sixteen verses), and I repeat them to myself and meditate on them all throughout each day of my life. These key passages have become the habits of my mind and the rails on which my life runs. I have found this more helpful than trying to memorize dozens and dozens of verses, though others would disagree with me. Second, I try to find an hour or so once a week where I sit at a specific (and comfortable) place in my home and give myself time to be quiet and read or study the Bible. Third, I purchase and study a good commentary on the book that my pastor or Bible study leader is working through in my church or small group. This forces me to study the Bible instead of just reading it, and my study supplements a portion of Scripture already in focus in my local fellowship. You may have to ask for the preaching calendar ahead of time, but it is worth it.

In Addition to the Bible...

Become a chowhound for Christian input. Constantly listen to good teaching live or on your iPod or CD player while jogging or riding in your car. Set aside time two nights a week for one hour each (and you may need to get some physical exercise to be able to say awake and have energy for this) to read good Christian books. I suggest you start with these in this endnote.[1]

Doubts

Face honestly and deal with your doubts. Some doubts are unknowingly fed by ideas absorbed from the plausibility structure of the surrounding culture—that is, the things our culture tells us we should and should not believe and the things that are silly to believe or not believe. People with these kinds of doubts are unaware of how they have been influenced by the assumptions made by the surrounding culture. Even though such assumptions are usually easy to answer, finding such answers does not, by itself, resolve the doubts. This can only be done by making these cultural assumptions explicit, exposing them for the intellectual frauds they actually are, and by being vigilant in keeping them before one's mind and spotting their presence in the ordinary reception of input each day from newspapers, magazines, office conversation, television, movies, and so on.

Said differently, it is not enough to find good answers to these doubts as it is for more specific intellectual problems. The real solution here is the conscious formation of alternative, countercultural ways of seeing, thinking, and being present in the world. If this is not done, these background assumptions will bully us Christians to live secular lives, and they will squeeze the spiritual life out of us. Enjoy magazines, novels, music, television, and movies. But don't consume them passively. Pay attention to the values and messages they convey. Process them with Christian friends. As a good introduction to learning to get better at evaluating movies and television as a Christian, I recommend R. Douglas Geivett and James S. Spiegel's book *Faith, Film and Philosophy*.[2]

In contrast to the vague doubts subconsciously absorbed through the perpetrators of secularism's plausibility structure, another sort of doubt is a horse of an entirely different color: a specific intellectual doubt.[3] The doubting person is clearly aware of it and can write it down on paper. The doubt is quite precise and explicit. Here are eight steps for removing such doubts and increasing your God-confidence.

1. Approach the issue with the hope that you will find an intellectually satisfying answer. In his study of doubt, Christian Smith reports one Christian woman who, typical of many, opined, "I do not do anything to try to resolve my doubts, I just live with them. They don't worry me. I have accepted that I am going to have some doubts. Someday,

I will find out if I am right or wrong."[4] This defeatist approach—the ostrich approach—is *not* the one to take. Remember, when believers seek hard after answers to doubts, they often find intellectually satisfying answers. This has surely been my experience. It is highly unlikely that someone in the history of the church or in contemporary times has not dealt with the problem adequately.

2. *Be sure the doubt is really intellectual.* As I mentioned near the beginning of the book and in a different context, I once had a roommate who was debilitated by fear that he had committed the unpardonable sin. For weeks I reminded him of the main interpretations of what this sin is and of why it was impossible for him to have committed it. But this was to no avail. Only when I approached the source of the doubt as an emotional problem was it removed. Due to early childhood attachment issues, he felt unloved by and disconnected from people in general and God in particular, and rather than face this head-on, he projected his emotional insecurity onto the unpardonable sin as a more manageable center of focus. Here's how to tell if your doubt is not largely intellectual: If you have received an intellectual answer to the doubt that satisfies most other believers, especially those more knowledgeable than you, and it doesn't help you, the problem probably isn't intellectual.

3. *If the doubt is sourced in the challenges presented by another person, don't assume he or she has considered fairly the available answers to the issue.* Sometimes you may have relatives, coworkers, or professors who seem smarter and more knowledgeable than you, and they may harass you with intimidating, opinionated questions you can't answer. When this happens, don't assume that they really know their stuff and that their attack is the result of a well-reasoned investigation of the issue. Instead, if this happens and you don't know the answer, do three things. First, if the objection is expressed with a lot of anger, mocking, and intimidation, chances are the issue is emotional and not intellectual. Don't allow yourself to internalize the attacker's feelings. Set an emotional boundary and don't take on the responsibility to fix that

person's problems. If it really is an intellectual problem, the challenging point is usually made with an honest, inquiring tone.

Second, tell the person that you don't have an answer now but that you will get one for him or her. Then either read up on the topic yourself or, if you feel inadequate, find someone in your church who is able to handle the question and arrange a lunch for the three of you. Third, express this to the questioner: "I am sure you have formulated your viewpoint against Christianity in a fair-minded and intellectually responsible way by studying *both* sides of the issue. So tell me, what were the four or five best books you have read that *defend* the Christian answer to your claim? And what were the three or four best arguments *against* your conclusion that you had to address in arriving at your skeptical stance? How did you answer these arguments?" In my experience, hardly anyone has fairly done this kind of homework. This is especially true for most evolutionists who mock intelligent design theory. Note that this approach removes the responsibility for you to provide an instant answer, and it calls the attacker to intellectual honesty.

4. *Write your doubt down on paper.* Work and rework it until you are satisfied that you have clearly stated your doubt in all its facets. Carry this around with you, especially when you plan to meet other Christians or when you attend church.

5. *Doggedly find an answer.* Don't give up. Take out your paper (step four) when you are around someone who might have an answer and jot down his or her response. Ask your pastors for help; ask them for the name of someone in the congregation who knows about the issue. Ask a librarian or someone at your local Christian bookstore for a book or books on the topic. If you live near a Christian high school or college, find a teacher or professor who can help, get an appointment with him or her, and take your paper with you.

6. *Doubt your doubts.* Write down on paper several reasons why your doubt isn't that good after all. Use these reasons as ongoing self-talk. When the doubt comes up in your mind, train yourself to immediately turn your attention to your doubts about the doubt.

7. *Remember that knowledge is partly communal.* We know many things, not because we can prove them, but because several genuine experts with knowledge about the subject know the answers to the question. For example, I used to have questions about the historicity of Moses and other portions of the Old Testament. But I have had neither time nor the desire to independently find specific answers to these questions. Instead, I know that hundreds of Evangelical Old Testament scholars are fully aware of the objections and have solid answers to them. Knowing everything is impossible, and so we must be willing to rely on other members of the body to help us. This is no different from non-Christians. No one can know everything available in a culture, and we all have to trust genuine experts who know, for example, that such and such medicine is safe. What a predicament we would be in if no intellectuals were solid believers. Fortunately, many scholars in virtually every academic discipline are solid Evangelicals who know full well the problems in their fields and who are able to answer them satisfactorily.

8. *Remember that atheists and skeptics have as many or more doubts than we do.* When people are vulnerable and afraid, they often believe others have more power and less fear than they actually have. We tend to maximize others and minimize ourselves when we feel weak. When you have questions about faith, you can easily believe that atheists and other skeptics have great confidence in and little doubt about their views.

But this is not true. For example, atheists are plagued with doubts, and in fact, many of them pray regularly. They really do repress or suppress the knowledge of God, as Paul tells us in Romans 1:18. As comedian Woody Allen noted, "I'm not afraid to die. I just don't want to be there when it happens." On a more serious note and in a moment of rare frankness, atheist philosopher Thomas Nagel made this admission:

> I want atheism to be true and am made uneasy by the fact
> that some of the most intelligent and well-informed people

I know are religious believers. It isn't just that I don't believe in God and, naturally, I hope that I'm right in my belief. It's that I hope there is no God! I don't want there to be a God; I don't want the universe to be like that.[5]

Influential young atheist Douglas Coupland discloses this:

Now—here is my secret: I tell it to you with an openness of heart that I doubt I shall ever achieve again, so I pray that you are in a quiet room as you hear these words. My secret is that I need God—that I am sick and can no longer make it alone. I need God to help me give, because I no longer seem capable of giving; to help me be kind, as I no longer seem capable of kindness; to help me love, as I seem beyond being able to love.[6]

So remember, our critics are not as sure of themselves as they want us to believe. Come to think about it, they too are made in the image of God, so that's what we should have expected all along.

Guard Your Heart

Work hard at balancing your growing knowledge with a tender heart for God and others. Avoid developing a religious spirit, an argumentative personality according to which you are ready to jump on people with a different viewpoint and you look down on less-informed folk. Paul says that "knowledge makes arrogant, but love edifies" (1 Corinthians 8:1). But for two reasons, this is not a rejection of the incredible value of spiritual and theological knowledge. First, we actually know the principle itself, that is, that knowledge puffs up. Second, Paul is rejecting the abuse of knowledge, not its proper use. The correct response to his teaching is humility and a tender heart, not ignorance.

The Flesh

For the most part, you are your habits, especially habits of thought, feeling, and behavior. These habits are largely products of your conscious choices and the unconscious influences on you of your culture, friends, family, routine, and so on. In dealing with the flesh, your goal as Jesus' disciple is to remove, with God's help and in dependence on His Spirit, those habits contrary to God's kingdom and to a thriving life according to the way He made you, and replace them with those that reflect the kingdom and human flourishing. In this regard, a number of New Testament texts seem a bit odd at first glance. It's hard to know how to take them if we do the right thing and interpret them literally.

> Therefore I urge you brethren, by the mercies of God, to present your *bodies* a living and holy sacrifice, acceptable to God, which is your spiritual service of worship (Romans 12:1).

This verse is unpacked earlier in Paul's letter:

> Even so consider yourselves to be dead to sin, but alive to God in Christ Jesus. Therefore do not let sin reign in your mortal body that you obey its lusts, and do not go on presenting *the members of your body* to sin as instruments of unrighteousness, but present yourselves to God as those alive from the dead, and *your members* as instruments of righteousness to God...I am speaking in human terms because of t*he weakness of your flesh.* For just as you *presented your members* as slaves to impurity and to lawlessness, resulting in further lawlessness, so now *present your members* as slaves to righteousness, resulting in sanctification (Romans 6:11-13, 19).

> Therefore, *consider the members of your body* as dead to immorality, impurity, passion, evil desire, and greed (Colossians 3:5).

> *Discipline yourself* for the purpose of godliness; for *bodily discipline* is only of little profit, but godliness is profitable for all things, since it holds promise for the present life and also for the life to come (1 Timothy 4:7-8).

As mentioned above, at first glance these texts—especially the itali-cized words—may seem a bit puzzling, but as we will now discover, they express insights about human nature and flourishing so very deep that, once again, the insights of the Bible expose the shallowness of our own culture in breathtaking fashion. To understand this biblical teaching, we must first clarify four concepts: *habit, character, flesh,* and *body.*

A *habit* is an ingrained tendency to act, think, or feel a certain way without needing to choose to do so. The way people write the letters of the alphabet is not something they need to think about. It is a habit, and they concentrate on what they are writing, not on the habitual style of handwriting used. *Character* is the sum total of one's habits, good and bad. Penmanship character is the sum total of one's good and bad writing habits; it is one's handwriting style.

Biblical terms such as *flesh* (*sarx*) or *body* (*soma*) have a wide field of meaning. Depending on the context, they can mean many differ-ent things. Sometimes *flesh* and *body* mean the same thing, but in the passages above, each has a unique and important meaning. *Body* is pretty obvious. In contrast to the soul, it refers to one's living, animated physical aspect. The body can be seen and touched, and it is composed of tissue, skin, bone, and various organs and systems. The *flesh* in these texts refers to the sinful tendencies or habits that reside in the body and that are opposed to the kingdom of God. To understand these more fully and to appreciate their importance more deeply, let's return to learning to play golf.

When people play golf, they have a "golf character," that is, the sum of good and bad habits relevant for playing golf. The "golf flesh" is the sum of a person's bad golf habits. Where do these bad habits reside? They dwell as ingrained tendencies in specific body parts, in particular members of the body. A golf game may be weakened by bad habits in the wrists, the shoulders, or somewhere else. People may have good habits in their legs but bad habits, or golf flesh, residing in their shoul-ders. Golf flesh resides in the specific members of golfers' bodies.

How does one develop a good golf character? Not simply by daily golf readings coupled with regular exposure to motivational golf music! No, golfers must present their members to a golf instructor at a driving range as instruments of "golf righteousness" instead of following their golf flesh as an instrument of "golf unrighteousness." These are not figures of speech. They are literal indeed. By so presenting their members, they gradually get rid of bad golf habits and replace them with good ones.

How do golfers present their members to a golf instructor? Two things are involved. First, they must dedicate themselves to the pursuit of golf righteousness (to getting good at golf) and choose to submit as apprentices to a teacher. Second, they do not simply engage in a one-time act of dedication to the teacher. To present their bodies to a golf instructor requires repeatedly engaging specific body parts in regular activities done over and over again, with the instructor in charge, and practicing different movements. For example, golfers may present their wrists to the instructor by practicing over and over again a specific wrist movement, a particular swing. The result of such habitual bodily movement will be the replacement of bad habits in the wrists with good habits. The golf flesh that resides in the wrists will give way to golf righteousness in those members. Later, the instructor may require the habitual presentation of other members, say the hips, to replace bad habits that reside there.

A golf discipline is a repeated golf exercise, a bodily movement involving specific body parts that golfers repeat over and over again so they can get rid of golf flesh and gain golf righteousness in their bodies. Some golf disciplines are practiced in a different way from how they are done in the game. Like playing piano scales, they are performed to prepare the player for a different movement that actually takes place in the game. Like scales, the practice activity drops out during the real game. For example, a golfer may practice an exaggerated swing to compensate for the tendency to hook the ball. Other practice activities are also done in the game, such as keeping the head down while swinging. But the important thing is this: A golf discipline is repeated not to get good at the discipline, but to get good at the game of golf.

The parallels with becoming good at life should be clear. Presenting our bodies to God as living sacrifices involves not only a one-time act of dedication but also a habitual, repeated bodily exercise (1 Corinthians 9:24-27; 1 Timothy 4:7-8) involving specific body parts (Romans 6:11-13,19). This results in putting to death our bad habits (Colossians 3:5), that is, removing the flesh that resides in those body parts and replacing it with righteousness that comes to reside in them. A Christian spiritual discipline is a *bodily practice, repeated over and over again,* in dependence on the Holy Spirit and under the direction of Jesus and other wise teachers in His way, *to enable us to get good at certain things in life that we cannot learn to do by direct effort.*

In the same way that golf flesh resides in specific body parts, such as the wrists, so sinful habits often reside in specific body parts. For example, anger can reside in the stomach area, anxiety in the chest or shoulders, gossip in the tongue and mouth region, and lust in the eyes and other areas. A spiritual discipline is a repetitive practice that targets one of these areas in order to replace bad habits with good ones in dependence on the Spirit of the living God. Some disciplines, such as playing scales on the piano have no value in themselves and are totally means to an end—gaining the technique required to play beautiful music. Other disciplines, such as practicing putting in golf, are valuable not only as a means to an end but also for their own sake during the game itself.

In the same way, some spiritual disciplines, such as journaling (that is, the habit of writing down our prayers to God), are mere means to an end (learning to express ourselves to God and remember His answers). Other disciplines, such as ongoing prayer, are both means to an end when done as disciplines and intrinsically valuable in their own right in the actual game of life.

To help you get good at dealing with your flesh, I want to recommend two books (see the endnote) and briefly mention two combinations of spiritual disciplines I have found to be most helpful.[7] But first, consider the following two categories of spiritual disciplines: some of abstinence or detachment, and others of engagement:[8]

DISCIPLINES OF ABSTINENCE	DISCIPLINES OF ENGAGEMENT
solitude	study
silence	worship
fasting	celebration
frugality	service
chastity	prayer
secrecy	fellowship
sacrifice	confession
	submission

In disciplines of abstinence, we unhook (for short intervals and to varying degrees) from the satisfaction of normal, appropriate desires—food, sleep, companionship, sex, music, comfort, financial security, recognition, and so forth. These disciplines help us address sins of *commission*. In general, when we detach from something, we should fill the resulting void with attachment to something positive. Thus, disciplines of engagement go hand in hand with those of detachment, and the former help us address *sins of omission*.

Worship and prayer are so important that I will postpone treatment of them until the next chapter. Besides these, one discipline of abstinence and one of engagement have played a deep, central role in my own journey: (1) solitude combined with silence, and (2) fellowship, including celebration.

Solitude

In solitude, we seek to form the habit of being alone and learning to be quiet. When we add silence, we do not speak to anyone and are not subjected to noise. When practiced regularly, solitude refreshes our soul, helps us set aside our false self and reconnect with (and hear from) our true self, and opens us up to communing deeply and intimately with God, who seeks our companionship. I have found four effective ways to practice solitude:

1. Find a place in your home and schedule at least two or three times each week when you can go there, be alone, and be quiet. I do this four times a week for one or two hours. I also go to bed about 45 minutes before I need to go to sleep. While lying on my bed, I invite the Lord's presence, I express my love for Him, and I recall my day and my concerns while asking Him to search my heart and to consider my petitions. I also express to Him a half-full perspective on my next day by thanking Him for the things I am grateful for, by giving thanks for the things I look forward to, and by telling Him how glad I am that He will walk with me tomorrow. This is a mouthful, but please look it over again. These are not empty words to me. They are the very substance of my life, and at this point in my journey, I can't imagine living without these habits.

2. Find time regularly to walk, jog, or ride a regular or stationary bicycle. During some of these times listen to CDs in order to grow. But during other times, seek to be quiet. Make the activity a time for solitude and silence.

3. Make your car a chapel for worship, a classroom for instruction, and a retreat center for solitude. In all honesty, I thank God for my commute to work, for time in my car, and for traffic (which forces me to spend more time in my car). Stop listening to talk radio (to the degree you deem important for your discipleship) and seek silence, solitude, and prayer. You may think this sounds silly, but I also suggest you drive in the slow lane. I'm not kidding. When I start driving fast, changing lanes regularly, and so forth, I know something is wrong with my soul. I am overly impressed with my own importance and my own control over my life, so I try to save all the time I can. (If I don't, who's gonna take care of me!) When I am at peace and in

solitude and prayer, I drive more slowly and don't want my time in the car to end.

4. Once or twice a year, go to a retreat center, a cabin, or something similar and spend two days and one night (at least!) in a solitude retreat in which you seek do two things: Spend time walking and communing with God, and spend time on your knees or in a comfortable chair in worship and prayer. Take the Bible and a hymnbook or collection of praise songs and sing them.

Celebration

Regarding celebration and fellowship, seek regular—at least weekly—times to be together with a Christian friend or small group of such friends. This is so important to me that I have met one evening a week with a dear Christian brother, Bill Roth, for 20 years. My wife, Hope, and I also have a group of five couples with whom we share a meal once a month, and we are in a weekly house church of 30 people associated with our church.

In that time, enjoy each other, seek to focus on each other, and find out what is going on in each other's hearts. Try to stimulate each other toward growth in discipleship and commitment to stepping out in faith for the cause of Christ. A study was done of people who have changed the world politically, economically, spiritually, or in other ways. The people were quite diverse, but they had one thing in common. They each had a small number of close friends who shared their passion for the same mission and to whom they could come for healing, help, and strength to reengage the struggle for their cause.

Celebration refers to the act of gathering together with other believers for good food and drink and to spend time celebrating the goodness of life from God. During these times, people should share openly the things they have seen God do for them. It is to be a time of joy and celebration, not a time for expressing needs (which is very important but should be reserved for other times of fellowship).

The Devil

The devil and demons were originally angels who served before God Himself, but because of their rebellion, they are now fallen angels who oppose God's purposes in the world. And don't think for a minute that they aren't real. Whether or not we like it, demons are very real and constitute part of the unseen supernatural world.

We Westerners readily accept psychological explanations for a wide range of phenomena—such as multiple personality disorder and schizophrenia—and we are correct in doing so. But we would be foolish in our journey as Jesus' disciples if we failed to avail ourselves of spiritual warfare principles and acknowledge the presence of demonization when circumstances warrant it. My purpose here is not to provide detailed teaching about demonization and its recognition, but I do want to make two points.[9]

First, Christians and non-Christians alike can be oppressed and harmed by demons to one degree or another. The Bible uses the notion of possession only with respect to God and those of us who have trusted His Son: We are God's own possession (Ephesians 1:13-14). Thus, Scripture does not distinguish between demon possession and oppression or even use these notions. Instead, the Bible uses "to be demonized" as its primary descriptor. Demons can influence and attach themselves to anyone, but the degree of influence is greater in general for unbelievers than for believers.

Second, when (but not only when) at least one of three criteria is satisfied, we are justified in believing a demon is present:

- The alleged demonized person cannot do things that Scripture says cannot be done by a demon (such as confess Jesus as Lord).

- During a deliverance session, the person expresses private (usually embarrassing) details of the life of someone in the prayer team, details that the demonized person simply could not have known. (This happened to two friends of mine—on different occasions—who were embarrassed in front of others as a demon accurately accused each of a specific sin and supplied details!)

- Overt physical phenomena occur, such as moving objects.

As we said above, demons are real indeed. A few years ago, a Biola University undergraduate began to experience sudden and unexpected episodes of a racing heart. The episodes were so severe that she would pass out on the spot, sometimes in the middle of class. She saw several doctors and underwent various tests, but no cause was found, so she wore a heart monitor to enable the doctors to gather more data on her condition. Desperate for help, the student and a friend visited the office of Biola professor Clint Arnold. Dr. Arnold is a world-renowned New Testament scholar, and he is an authority on demons. Dr. Arnold told me that when the girls entered his office, he clearly sensed an evil presence. He offered a deliverance prayer, all three sensed the malevolent spirit's departure, and the girl was instantly and irrevocably healed of the condition on the spot. The incident was so incredible that it was reported in the Biola student newspaper.

Another friend of mine whom I'll call Dr. Smith (not his real name) took his Ph.D. from one of the top ten universities in America, has published a technical monograph with what may be the top academic publisher in the world, and teaches at a well-respected university. Dr. Smith lives alone, and he told me recently that for a period of two months (which ended about two months ago as of this writing) he had seen overt demonic phenomena in his condominium. It began with a specific piece of furniture moving in his living room, an event he witnessed with his own eyes. Next, his phone began to ring repeatedly with no one on the line. Shortly thereafter, when he went downstairs for breakfast, he found a large wreath which had been hanging on his wall lying in the middle of the floor about 12 feet from the wall as though someone had tossed it there. Note carefully that no one had entered his home during the night, nor does Dr. Smith walk in his sleep.

Finally, he has discovered pictures in his bedroom turned around 180 degrees from their ordinary position, and no human could have done this. Dr. Smith has lived in his home for eight years, and nothing has ever happened like this until a friend came to stay with him. The phenomena began a few weeks before the friend's arrival, lasted for the two weeks of his stay, and continued for a few weeks after his departure. Frustrated and frightened, Dr. Smith enlisted the help of a prayer team from his church, who came and prayed over each room in his home. As of this writing, the manifestations have ceased.

These two incidents involve highly educated, credible people who are not hysterical, gullible, or liars. In fact, the most recent addition of our university's alumni publication, *Biola Connections;* features a story on demons.[10] The story contains interviews with six professors, all of whom have Ph.D.s in their respective fields. All have witnessed demonic phenomena, including flying objects at a home plagued by demons, supernatural knowledge, induced nausea, and an oppressive sense of evil.

The danger we Westerners face is to go to opposite extremes regarding demons and the devil: to see everything as involving their direct presence and influence (this leaves out the role of the world and the flesh as sources of evil) and to see nothing in this manner (perhaps because we are secular or we believe falsely that demons are active only in less developed countries). In my opinion, Charles Kraft's excellent work *Defeating Dark Angels* is the most balanced and helpful treatment of the demonic in print. In the remainder of this chapter, I want to highlight and apply some of Kraft's insights.

Keep in mind that demons are persons—angelic, not human persons. That is, they are substantial centers of consciousness, including will, thought, desire, emotion, beliefs, and so forth. As with persons generally, demons are social creatures. A satanic kingdom structures demons into a social hierarchy of principalities and powers with greater or lesser authority and power. Not all evil and disruption on earth is due to demons; nevertheless, they are involved in all kinds of disruption. They can delay answers to prayer (Daniel 10:13) as well as fester and agitate vice, sinful behavior, and evil and harmful thought and emotional patterns.

A helpful way to think about demons is as rats—they need garbage to feed on. Thus, when garbage is in our lives, we give them an entry point and permission to make things worse. Conversely, once a demon is properly rebuked and dismissed, we must then deal with the garbage (through therapy, spiritual discipline, confession of sin, and the like) or else the problem itself won't go away, and an opening to future demonization is retained. The worst thing you can do is to think of demonic influence the way it is depicted on television and in movies. To be sure, in extreme cases, violent behavior, different and horrible voices, and vomiting are present, but these are extreme cases. Typically, when one or more demons are influencing you, your ordinary destructive, sinful self-talk, emotional dysfunction (anxiety, depression, anger, fear), thought patterns, behavior, and interpersonal problems are agitated beyond what is reasonably explained by your own spiritual and psychological baggage. Something else—and more—is going on. And based on years of experience, Kraft says that the strength of demonic influence can be depicted on a scale from one to ten (one being weakest). And believers are seldom if ever in the seven to ten range. Still, they can and often do experience mild to fairly strong intimidation and influence.

Here are six points regarding relief from demonic influence:

1. Deliverance is not always a one-shot deal. Inner healing, therapy, and spiritual formation to rid ourselves of sinful patterns is often required over a period of time. As we grow stronger, resistance to demonic influence grows stronger. These activities, combined with repeated prayers for deliverance over time, are sometimes required.

2. Believers are not to be afraid of the devil or demons (Isaiah 41:10; 2 Timothy 1:7). We have authority over them because of Jesus' shed blood for us and because we stand in the kingdom of God and may act as its ambassadors on its behalf by bringing the authority of Jesus to

any situation. George Otis Jr. has traveled around the world numerous times, he has been in extremely remote areas all over the globe, and he has taken written and video documentation of the supernatural acts of God's kingdom and the kingdom of darkness all over the world. He may be the leading researcher alive on these matters. I had the honor of speaking to him a few years ago in my office at the university. He told me that in areas where people have never heard of the Bible or the name Jesus, the authority of Jesus triumphs over the demonic, but the names of other, even local deities fail. This reinforced what he already knew: that demons are real and not merely psychological. Otherwise, why do people respond to a name about which they know nothing, yet fail to respond to names that are familiar in their culture? Answer: It's the demons, not the humans, who are responding! Otis' experience also shows that Jesus' name has greater authority than any other. "Greater is He who is in you than he who is in the world"(1 John 4:4).

Interestingly, a few years ago a woman came to Christ from occult involvement and told her new Christian friends that they had no idea how much power they had. As a follower of Satan, she had known that Christians had greater power than she, but (from her old point of view, fortunately) they did not recognize the power they had.

3. Demons can attach to people through conscious invitation, unconscious invitation (such as constant wallowing in negative attitudes, lust, greed, and so forth), through the invitation of someone in authority over them, and for other reasons. In these cases we are admonished, "Do not give the devil an opportunity" (Ephesians 4:27). Deal with sin when it surfaces, and don't foster and hold on to it. Instead, retain intimacy with and obedience to Jesus as best you can.

4. Demons make bad things worse, they are one source of temptation (and when they are involved, they make it worse than usual), they seek to keep people ignorant of their activities and strategies, they try to make people fear them, and they deceive, accuse, hinder the good, foster compulsions, and harass us. In all these cases, we must resist them, and the devil and demons will run from us (James 4:7).

5. We can resist the forces of darkness by doing the things that promote spiritual growth: disciplining ourselves to remain focused on God, filling our minds with truth, learning to give our burdens to Jesus day by day, and turning away from evil. We can also actively resist demonic forces by telling them to leave us alone in the name of Jesus and on the basis of His shed blood for us.

6. We can engage in self-deliverance as stated above, but sometimes we should invite a group of friends over to lay hands on us, and pray for deliverance, healing, and restoration. This may take from 30 minutes to a few hours.

Conclusion

Whether you like it or not, you are in a battle for your own heart and soul, and others who live around you fight similar battles. And when you sign up to be a follower of Jesus, you must fight to make progress in becoming like Jesus and having an impact for His purposes in the world. The world, the flesh, and the devil are the three sources of attack you will have to negotiate. From personal experience and on the basis of biblical authority, I have tried my best to warn you about this and to provide you some brief and helpful advice about winning the battle. Now I'd like to share one more word of wisdom. With God's help, you will win this battle as you focus on (1) progressive detachment from the lure of the world, the lust of the flesh, and the lies of the devil; and (2) progressive attachment to a God, who wants to have an intimate relationship with you, and to giving your life away for Jesus' sake. This fundamental orientation toward daily life is the foundation for success.

How to Unclog Your Spiritual Arteries and Develop the Heart to Work with God

By now you know that I enlisted as one of Jesus' followers in 1968. You also have a sense for why I believe that Christianity is both true and can be known as such. And you've given me a chance to share with you my take on what it means to follow Jesus and how to go about it.

But my treatment has been sadly lacking because I am inadequate to do justice to these topics, and even if I were satisfactory, these issues are too pervasive and profound to discuss in one volume. Many, many things have been left out—community, the local church, the ministries of the Holy Spirit, Bible study, and so forth.[1]

But there are two topics I can't afford to set aside. And here's what is so curious about them. In the first two or three years after my conversion, they were important to me, but then I entered into an odd time. For the next handful of years, I still affirmed that I cared about them, and in a way I did. In fact, I practiced them pretty routinely. But I would never have written on them because, to be honest, I didn't have much I could share with passion and integrity from the depths of my heart. And I'll tell you the truth—the things I am covering in this book are matters I take myself to know and about which I am deeply passionate. In short, they are the substance of my very life. I want them to be so for you.

But for 20 years or so regarding one of the topics and for about six years for the other one, my life has been revolutionized. And I don't say that lightly to people. This is, quite simply, the truth. I am speaking about worship and prayer. I say again that volumes could be written on each, and I won't try to offer a comprehensive treatment of worship and prayer. Instead, I will mention some facets of each that I believe will help you as much as they have me. So let's dive in and see what we can learn.

Worship and the Manifest Presence of God

The God We Worship

Christian philosophers call God a "Maximally Perfect Being." This sound pretty heady, but in reality, it is a crucial concept. To see why, think of people who are phenomenally gifted. Now, these folks deserve respect for their attributes, abilities, or whatever. How much respect? They deserve a degree of respect proportionate to their excellence in their area of giftedness, such as intelligence. But these people do not deserve our complete or full respect. Why? Well, if someone more intelligent came on the scene, the new person would deserve *more* respect. So even if a more intelligent person is not around, we know such a person undoubtedly exists, so we hold back our respect a bit.

A Maximally Perfect Being is one who could not possibly be surpassed in wisdom, mercy, love, power, and so on. God is not the greatest being who happens to exist. He is the greatest being who could possibly exist. The implication should be clear: God is worthy of our complete, full, deepest, total commitment. Worship is the act of giving admiration, respect, affection, honor, reverence, and adoration to God. And given the nature of God, worship should be unreserved and total.

Practicing a Specific Type of Worship

Wise teachers among Jesus' followers have pointed out that, strictly speaking, all of life is worship. For the believer, no sphere of life is secular. One can worship by means of cutting the grass, selling insurance, exercising, and so on. I believe this insight is true, and I invite you to meditate on it's application to your life. But for my purposes, I wish to focus more narrowly.[2] I am interested in worship as *individual or corporate acts of singing to God, expressing affection and honor to Him through praise and prayer, and seeking an adoring, intimate, loving connection with Him.* The regular practice of such worship is appropriate and fitting because of who God is, and it is also an air hose for the Christian life. Among other things, by regularly focusing on receiving love from and giving love to God, I stay focused and stable. Why? Because it keeps me from inappropriately filling these needs elsewhere.

I urge you to form a habit: Listen to worship music regularly, especially while driving in your car, and engage in worship regularly with a church fellowship. I can bear witness to three things that you must practice for this to be transforming and deeply meaningful—perhaps by writing them on a three-by-five card you will look at often—if such worship is to be the wonder and joy it was intended to be. Having practiced these for five years now, I can only marvel at how I now hunger to be alone in my car—and I can hardly wait to get to church!—in contrast to times before, when worship was pretty boring.

A Loving Father

Habituate a certain orientation to worship with four key elements. First, remember that we love Him because He first loved us (1 John 4:10,19). Second, remember that He loved us even when we were hostile toward Him and His Son, so He clearly loves us in spite of how inconsistently we walk with Him (Romans 5:8). He may discipline us from time to time, but He does it as a loving, caring *Abba*-Daddy who still has warm affection toward us. Third, remember that God Himself seeks very few things, but He does seek our worship and intimate fellowship (John 4:23-24). These are things He loves and enjoys. Fourth, remember that He rewards us if we diligently seek Him with all our hearts and don't give up (Jeremiah 29:13; Hebrews 11:6). I encourage you to write these verses down and read them regularly. Here's the bottom line: You are safe before a loving Papa who cares deeply about you, who will never remove His affection from you, and who seeks your worship and fellowship and promises to reward you for reciprocating with all your heart as best you can.

Intimacy

God seeks—and worship includes—warm, deeply emotional, tender intimacy and affection between two people (you and God) who are in love with each other. This claim has two bases. First, it is expressly taught in specific biblical texts. For example, Hosea 11:8 says this:

> How can I give you up, O Ephraim?
> How can I surrender you, O Israel?
> How can I make you like Admah?
> How can I treat you like Zeboiim?
> My heart is turned over within Me,
> All my compassions are kindled.

This is not some minor text tucked away in an obscure book in the Old Testament. Hosea is the first book among the minor (shorter) prophets, he was a contemporary of Amos, Micah, and Isaiah, and the book is quoted directly or indirectly at least 30 times in the New Testament. Here's the context of this passage: God's people (Ephraim was a tribe of Israel) had abandoned a loving, covenantal relationship with God for dead orthodoxy and vain ritual. But God cannot reciprocate and give them up. He will not destroy them as He did the cities of Admah and Zeboiim (two cities associated with and destroyed alongside Sodom and Gomorrah [Deuteronomy 29:22-23]). Instead, His heart is filled with sorrow to the point of fainting (see Jeremiah 8:18 for a text that uses the same word as in "My heart is *turned over* within Me"). Why? God has fire in His heart for His people; He is filled with passion for them. Think of this the next time you see pictures of galaxies from a space probe or look at the power of a thunderstorm or ocean swells. The very big God who made all that is passionate about you and me!

Second, the reason we know that God seeks intimacy with us is that an important analogy for our relationship with God is sexual intercourse between a husband and wife. In the Old Testament, God's people are wed to God, and idolatry is called adultery. The use of the metaphor of adultery is clearly intended to express the idea that the deepest sort of human intimacy as seen in marital union is the sort of closeness we are to have with God. Setting this aside for another god, is just like adultery. The New Testament calls the church the bride of Christ. Here again is the bottom line: An important aspect of worship is *intimate, tender, and emotional interaction with God.* Learn to be crazy about Him and to lavish praise, respect, and adoration on Him, to desire, hunger, and long for Him. Learn to be in touch with your emotions.

The Presence of God

When worshipping, invite the Lord's manifest presence and seek to affectionately experience God and His presence. David says that the most important thing in his life, the biggest thing that he seeks, is to "behold the beauty of the LORD" (Psalm 27:4) in worship amid the gathered covenant community. Commentators have provided deep insights about this text.[3] Two are of special importance. First, David intends two meanings for "beauty": (1) desirableness and loveliness, and (2) graciousness and favor. The psalmist wants to experience God's own loveliness and His favor directed toward him as God's child and worshipper. Second, "behold" means to experience directly, to look through the eyes of the soul with pleasure upon, to commune with or enter into mystical union with. This is the bottom line here: God wants us to seek to *experience His manifest presence* as we worship Him, along with His favor toward us, and we should invite that presence and prepare our hearts to be receptive toward it.

Final Suggestions

I have two further suggestions. For one thing, purchase some really good contemporary praise music and listen to it regularly. Such music has been inappropriately maligned. To be sure, some bad praise music has circulated, but in general, since the 1960s, the worship music generated by the American church has represented a substantial advance in the history of Christianity in excellence of worship within the limited framework of this discussion. When at its best, such music contains simple, profound expressions of biblical truth that are relevant to the adoration of God and an experiential, mutual exchange of intimate love.

Additionally, I urge worship leaders not simply to be song leaders or to focus only on becoming good musicians, though that is clearly important. The aims of good worship leaders are to be constant, day-in and day-out worshippers to invite God's manifest presence to come to their congregations during worship, and to invite the people to come along with them as they express intimate worship to God themselves.

Asking and Receiving Answers to Prayer

Why Petitionary Prayer?

There are many purposes for prayer, including worship, confession of sin, and giving thanks to God. But the major emphasis of prayer in the New Testament is on offering requests to God and receiving His answers to prayer (see Ephesians 6:18). Prayer changes things. Some things that happen in the world would not have happened had someone not prayed. And some things fail to happen in the world that would have happened had someone prayed. Prayer—and, more importantly, the God to whom it is addressed—is powerful. Thoughtful, devoted followers of the Lord Jesus have come to various conclusions about the precise nature of God's sovereignty and providential control over the world, especially regarding how they relate to the love of God on the one hand and human freedom and the origin of evil on the other hand. But one thing is almost universally acknowledged: If our view of these matters causes us to stop praying, to stop believing that prayer can be efficacious, to stop trying to bring about good and thwart evil through prayer, then our view is false.

But why does such an arrangement even exist? After all, God is all-knowing, all-powerful, and infinite in wisdom and love. So why has He set up an arrangement that includes prayer in the first place! Here are three reasons:

1. Prayer teaches us to depend on God. By establishing a vehicle—prayer—through which certain things do or do not come to us, we are thereby taught to depend on the Source of petition-granting. Why did God make us to be dependent? What else does an omnipotent, self-existent Being do? God alone is self-existent, and everything else by its very nature as a created thing is dependent. Being dependent is hardly an arbitrary feature of created things! And prayer is a form of dependency that is appropriate to the way we were created to function best, to our precise nature as created human persons. This leads to my second point.

2. By their very nature, people cooperate and work together through talking and communicating. That's just how persons are. Through prayer, we co-labor with God in precisely the way we do with persons, particularly unequally strong, wise, and authoritatively positioned persons. Doctors and patients provide an analogy here. Doctors are wiser, have more authoritative knowledge, and so forth with respect to health. So patients petition doctors for help. In turn, doctors may

have various alternatives they can utilize, so they may ask patients to be specific about what the patients want. And doctors respect patient autonomy—the right to accept or refuse treatment. Thus, even if doctors know that certain treatments are best, they will not administer them (except in rare cases) if patients do not want them. In such cases, doctors will apply the next-best alternatives. Take a moment to probe this analogy's parallels with prayer.

3. We were put here to count, and prayer is a way we can make a difference. God has more on His mind than simply bringing about good or defeating evil with regard to the issues about which we pray. He is also concerned to help us grow as disciples and thriving people, and He knows that learning to be effective in prayer is part of what that means. Thus, sometimes He will not do the good or stop the evil unless we ask precisely because if He always did that, we would not learn to express our nature as praying, dependent, created persons. Many times I did not give good things to my children if they did not ask me. I didn't want to force things on them, and I wanted them to learn to depend on me (and thereby on God). The same goes for intervening in the natural consequences of their bad actions. There were limits to this, of course, and so there are with God, though we often don't have the needed perspective to see what God has in mind in doing or refusing to do something.

In 2 Corinthians 1:8-11 we are reminded that sometimes God refrains from answering a legitimate prayer until several people join in. Why? Because an answer that comes with many people praying not only brings about the good thing itself but also grows, edifies, and nurtures many people who took part. This nicely illustrates the fact that God is interested in more than just bringing about even a good thing. Many times, of course, God will go ahead and bring about the good or thwart the bad even if we do not pray. But not always, and that's the point.

Two Models for Petitionary Prayer

There are two ways of thinking about petitionary prayer. Both are legitimate and, when properly practiced, mutually reinforcing, though the second model is often overlooked. The first is straightforward: Petitionary prayer is simply talking to God and asking Him to do something. This is what Paul had in mind when he wrote, "Let your requests be made known to God" (Philippians 4:6). This is a wonderful thing, and I say without apology that you cannot live a thriving life without this sort of prayer. But without the second model, there is a danger here. Put simply, it can lead one to think, *Since I have asked God to do such and such, since I have made thus and so known to Him, I'm not going to bring it up again. To do so may indicate my lack of faith.*

The second model helps to address this erroneous thinking. Petitionary prayer is a form of co-laboring with God in which I invite God's attention and direct His power on a problem and work on it with God in the very act of prayer itself. You may think of this as a form of bathing prayer: You bathe the issue in prayer; you soak it with the power and presence of God while you pray. In this sense, prayer becomes a form of spiritual labor with God, and the longer you can stay with something, the more you work on it by way of interactive conversation with God Himself. This means that continuous, repeated prayer is at the very heart of working something over and constantly or repeatedly directing God's power toward the problem. Here the issue is not to tell God what you want as much as it is speaking together about the issue and, as one who stands in the place of God's kingdom, directing the power of God onto something.

As with the first model, there is an erroneous way of thinking about the second one: *I have to work hard at this problem, so the longer I can get myself to stay focused on prayer, the more I force God to do something about it. I have to work on this problem, and my staying power is the only limiting factor to getting an answer.* One response to this faulty reasoning is to be reminded by the first model that prayer is indeed a form of co-laboring, but it is a joint exercise between non-equals to say the least! True, in bathing prayer, we co-laboringly work on something. But we must never forget that in the process, we are really asking God to act. The efficacy is in divine action, not in our ability to stay focused or to pray for a long time.

The central figures in the Old and New Testament, respectively—Moses and Jesus—provide dramatic illustrations of this form of prayer. In Exodus 17:8-13, we have an account of Moses leading the armies of Israel into battle against the armies of Amalek. Standing on a hill, Moses lifted his hands heavenward, and Israel prevailed. But when Moses' arms dropped, Israel succumbed. The position of Moses' arms and hands were so important that Moses had rocks put under his arms to keep his hands in the air!

Is this just a silly, superstitious story in the Old Testament? Hardly. It expresses a central truth about how God's kingdom and prayer work. In the Old Testament, the lifting up of hands was an expression of prayer. Even if we take the raising of Moses' hands to be symbolic, we must ask what the act symbolized. In point of fact, Moses' raised hands symbolized and expressed a form of dependent prayer that was necessary for the power of God to be unleashed on the problem. Moses' act was a form of bathing prayer. It tapped into, unleashed, and directed the power of God. It was a form of co-laboring with God such that in and during the act of prayer itself (as expressed by elevated hands), work was being done on the problem.

The same happens in the New Testament book of Mark. In chapter 5 we are told of a woman who, having suffered for 12 years with a hemorrhaging flow of blood, expressed her faith by touching Jesus' garment for healing. Clearly, Mark means this to be a form of petition—a woman coming to Jesus to solve a problem and grant a request. Jesus felt power flow out of Him and, turning, saw the woman who was now healed. As the woman contacted Jesus by the touch of her hand, the power of the kingdom in Jesus was directed to her problem.

This second model has some limits. For example, in one case Paul prayed three times for something, God did not act, and Paul learned a lesson about how to deal with weakness instead (2 Corinthians 12:7-10). But this, I think, is an exception that proves the rule. Clearly, Paul was in the habit of ongoing, continual, repeated prayer, and unless the Lord directs us to stop or we judge that wisdom in general requires taking a different direction, bathing prayer should be continued, all things being equal.

In sum, these two aspects of prayer—as a request and as a form of co-laboring with God—together provide the framework for developing a powerful, effective life of prayer as Jesus' apprentice in kingdom life.

Illustrating the Power of Petitionary Prayer

Consider this stunning answer to prayer that comes from a well-known and highly respected Christian doctor whom I know well:

> Our daughter, Ashley, who was probably about 10 years old at the time, had two parakeets. One of them had just died. She told her mother that she wanted to get another one so that she would have a couple again. Mother, however, had had enough pets for the time being and told Ashley that we weren't going to get another parakeet at this time. Ashley, however, had a mind of her own. She said that she was going to pray to God for another parakeet, which she did. The next day, Ashley was playing outside with her friends when one of the kids saw that there was a bird in the tree. They all knew that Ashley had just lost her pet. It was a parakeet, the same color as the one she had just lost! (To this point, no one could remember ever having found a parakeet in the neighborhood before—and this occurred just the next day.) You can imagine her sense of triumph as she brought the bird home and announced that God had answered her prayer.

The doctor went on to share the sense of shock he and his wife experienced as Ashley brought a duplicate of her lost parakeet into the house the next day on her finger![4] This may seem trivial to you, but I assure you it was not for little Ashley and her family. It taught her a big lesson in the power of prayer. Still, you may wonder if God ever answers bigger prayers. *Yes He does!* Consider the following.

A few weeks ago, a woman I know shared this account of a dramatic answer to prayer. Her missionary parents retired after many years of service and moved to the San Diego area. Her mother became a public school teacher, and her father helped plant churches and do itinerant preaching primarily among non-English-speaking Hispanics for no pay. One day, they called members of the extended family to ask that they pray. They had been renting and had spotted a modest, vacant house for sale. It had stolen their hearts, and they were to meet a Realtor there the next day.

The house was small and empty, so the walk-through was brief indeed. At its end, the couple made an offer to the Realtor, only to be told that it was not even in the ballpark. Needless to say, they were deeply disappointed. At that moment, a knock sounded from the front door, and upon opening it, the Realtor was greeted by a man who asked for the owner. Not knowing what to do, she pointed back to the couple, who were already approaching the stranger. What he said was truly shocking. He stated that he worked with AT&T, and if they bought the home, he was prepared to offer them $10,000 down and $10,000 per year (which later became $11,000 per year) for 30 years if they would let AT&T build a palm-tree looking signal tower in their backyard. What a "coincidence"! They agreed and have been living in a largely paid-for house ever since!

Here's my last example of answered prayer. Ten months ago as of the time of this writing, my wife, Hope, and I traveled to Sumter, South Carolina, to vacation with my brother and his wife. I also spoke at their Sunday church service, which began with the pastor announcing something truly horrible that had surfaced the previous week. A young couple in their late twenties with a little baby had just learned that the husband—Jason—had a baseball-sized tumor the doctors feared was malignant and attached to the brain such that its removal would harm brain functioning. The couple had come that morning with Jason's parents to ask the church for prayer, something the pastor did in the announcement.

After I preached, I asked Jason and his wife to come to the front of the church. With about 400 people holding their hands toward Jason, and surrounded by several elders who joined me in laying hands on him, I prayed for about ten minutes. I asked God to shrink the cancer so it disappeared or was so small as to be negligible, to come against the cancer, and to break any connection between the tumor and Jason's brain. Early the next morning, Jason had surgery to remove the tumor. To the doctor's amazement, it had shrunk to the size of a walnut, it was benign, and it was detached from the brain! Jason was back at work in two weeks and continues to be healed!

I close this chapter by acknowledging that there is much about these topics I have not treated. For example, many times God does not answer prayer according to our requests, and many of those times are downright hard to understand. But I have seen far too many answers, (and my circle of friends have witnessed even more) for me to deny the power of God in answer to prayer. As the saying goes, I may be dumb, but I'm not stupid! Prayer is powerful, and it works. And when it is fervent, worship is one of the greatest privileges of human life. As we become students in Jesus' school of life, the journey into worship and prayer is opened up to us as never before.

Part 4

IS THIS LIFE
ALL THERE IS?

11

From Here to Eternity

French philosopher Blaise Pascal once remarked that the immortality of the soul is something of such vital importance to us that one must have lost all feeling not to care about knowing the facts of the matter. Indeed. The Bible says that God placed eternity in our hearts. And nothing is more evident than that. The afterlife is associated with the earliest archaeological traces of the sons and daughters of Adam and Eve. It is depicted in cave drawings, rituals for burial, and so on. The pyramids stand as a testimony to our hunger for immortality. Something in us (unless it is repressed) reminds us regularly that this life is fleeting and that there must be more to it than our fourscore and ten.

If you think the afterlife is not real, forget about it. It is not my purpose to provide evidence for an afterlife in this chapter. I have done that elsewhere.[1] I only note that if Jesus was raised from the dead, He has been to the afterlife and is qualified to tell us about it. And He assures us that there is a heaven and a hell. Further, if the biblical God exists, God values us who bear His image too much to let us pass out of existence. And He has a project or purpose He is working out for and through us. That project will never be finished, so He won't let us go. The project—and we—mean too much to Him. No competent artist destroys his work of art he likes while he is still in the process of completing it, and God is no different with respect to His unending work in our regard.

Finally, while the Bible is our ultimate source of authoritative information about heaven and hell, there is a growing, quite substantial body of evidence for heaven and hell from near death experiences (NDEs) in which people become clinically dead; actually experience angels, demons, God, heaven, or hell; and return to life. One must always be careful not to derive doctrine from such experiences, but that they are real is, in my view, beyond question.

The Bible says that we die once, and after that is the judgment (Hebrews 9:27). But this truth does not rule out the reality of NDEs for two reasons. First, "death" in Hebrews 9:27 could mean irreversible death, and if so, it is not the same as clinical death. The latter allows for NDEs but not the former. Second, even if the passage just means death without the notion of irreversibility, it still doesn't rule out NDEs. Why? Because throughout the Bible and in periods of church history, people such as Lazarus (John 11) died, continued to be conscious, and came back to life. God can do whatever He pleases, and if He desires to make an exception to Hebrews 9:27 now and then, He can. Being relatively rare, these exceptions actually underscore the general rule.

Here are two of many, many credible NDE accounts.[2] The first involves a nurse who worked in a hospital in the Northwest. While she was attempting to resuscitate a clinically dead young patient, the patient suddenly became conscious, grabbed the nurse's arm, and reported that she had left her body, floated out and above the hospital roof, and had seen a large, old, blue shoe with a little bow worn to the threads and with the lace tucked under the heel on an upper ledge of the hospital roof. The ledge was neither accessible to anyone but hospital personnel nor visible from buildings nearby, and the patient had never been to the hospital before. With curiosity aroused about this bizarre story, the nurse was shocked to find the shoe just as the patient had described in just the correct location![3] The patient was interviewed by other witnesses that day who corroborate the incident.

A second, well-known account is about a woman who was checked into a hospital for routine gallbladder surgery. Six days after the surgery, her condition had worsened to the point that she was operated on again and died on the operating table. When the doctor said she was dead, the woman was confused. She had been in excruciating pain, but she suddenly felt a ring in her ear and then popped out of her body! She found herself floating near the ceiling and gazed around the operating room, noting a number of things, including her own lifeless body! Though the room had been sealed off for surgery, she heard voices in the outside hallway and passed through the wall, where she saw her anxious family. Immediately, she noticed her daughter, who was wearing an outfit the patient did not like (the daughter had rushed to the hospital and put on the mismatched outfit hurriedly and without thinking). She then noticed her brother-in-law talking to a family neighbor: "Well, it looks like my sister-in-law is going to kick the bucket. I was planning on going out of town, but I'll stick around now to be a pallbearer." The patient was infuriated by the insensitive comment.

She also sensed *presences* around her that she took to be angels. And get this: She could travel anywhere her thoughts directed her, so she found herself instantaneously in another city, where she saw her sister getting ready to go to the grocery store. The patient noted carefully the clothes her sister was wearing, the search for misplaced keys, a lost grocery list, and finally, the car she drove. Moments later, she was whisked through a tunnel. Space forbids me to describe all she saw, but I must mention one thing. She met a baby who told her he was her brother. She was confused because she did not have a brother. The baby then showed himself to her dressed in quite specific clothing and told her that when she went back to tell her father about all this, she should describe the clothing.

When the patient came back into her body, each and every detail I have shared was verified by the people involved, often with additional eyewitnesses. Her dad confirmed that only he, her mother, and the doctor knew about the brother who had died as an infant but about whom the father and mother had decided to remain silent (which they had done).

Make no mistake about it. The afterlife is real. In this closing chapter, I want to do two things. First, I will briefly say something about heaven and how important it is. Second, I will spend the bulk of the chapter describing the nature of hell and explaining why its existence is not only reasonable but also essential to God's purposes in the world.

Heaven Is a Wonderful Place

A human being is a unity of two distinct entities—body and soul. The human soul, while not by nature immortal, is nevertheless capable of entering an intermediate disembodied state upon death, however incomplete and unnatural this state may be, and eventually being reunited with a resurrected body. Heaven will be a place where there is no longer any suffering and where life will be filled with joy, fulfillment, and a host of interesting, meaningful things to do.

I am not an expert at describing the nature of heaven, so I won't try. Happily, others have done a fine job of this.[4] Instead, I want to encourage you about how important heaven is. The cartoon character Charlie Brown once said, "I've developed a new philosophy of life. I only dread one day at a time."[5] Archibald Hart explains how many of us adopt this stance: "All of life is loss…Life is all about loss. Necessary loss."[6]

In point of fact, in this life we experience three kinds of losses. First, we often suffer the natural consequences of our own bad choices. We lose a job, a marriage, friends, health, and much more. And these losses stay with us. They are hard to shake.

Second, we suffer losses due to the fact that we live in a fallen, imperfect world. We lose our youth, our eyesight, our physical attractiveness (such as it may be!), our athletic ability, our loved ones due to death, our children to marriage, our sexual potency, and so forth. We discover that our marriage, career, and overall life satisfaction aren't what we hoped they would be. And as we age, we realize that many of our dreams will never come to pass.

Finally, we all suffer several forms of injustice that are never made right. Friends gossip about us, bosses bully us, and more severe crimes are committed against us. The injustices of this life are not balanced, and the harm done to us is not completely healed.

This is where heaven becomes so very important. As Hart points out, a major problem with losses of various kinds is that we are overly attached to this life and the things it offers: reputation, safety, our possessions, and people who meet our deepest needs. Psychologists tell us that we need to have daily hope and optimism in life, and that optimism must be rationally based so it isn't just a form of denial or a fantasy world out of touch with reality. In my view, to do this, we need to be able to place our losses—indeed, our entire, brief lives with all their ups and downs—into the context of a broader, true, objectively meaningful picture. If we can do this, we can ease back our attachment to this life. The rational hope of heaven as the Bible presents it is just the sort of background belief we need to navigate day-to-day life appropriately and with a proper proportionality in assessing what it brings our way. And heaven gives us the rational hope that the injustices and other losses will, in fact, be made right.

This is no small deal. It's actually an essential perspective for living life well each day in God's kingdom. It's kind of ironic, really. People claim that the belief in heaven robs people of the value of life on this earth. But it's really just the opposite. In light of eternity, this life takes on incredible meaning and gives us the perspective we need to live life well with the right priorities and the appropriate degree of attachments.

Hell: A Tragic yet Avoidable Outcome

Hell is one of those back-room topics. We may think about it from time to time, and in our weaker or more fearful moments, we may talk about it with someone we trust. Some people have even pulled out the topic to scare unbelievers into making a decision of faith. Others have brought it up and thrown it into people's faces, declaring damnation on them for their harmful, disdainful acts.

But more often than not, the subject creeps up on us silently, almost seditiously. It enters our conscience and plagues us with thoughts of personal torment and judgment or the agony loved ones will face if their lives don't turn around. The topic can bring so much concern and pain into our lives that we put it into the back room of our minds and padlock the door. We do not want to talk about hell, much less dwell on it. We would rather the topic never came up.

But locking it away will not dispel its reality. In fact, throughout history the concept of hell—some kind of judgment and punishment for wrongdoing—has played a critical role in religious life individually and communally. Certainly this has been true in the history of Judaism and Christianity—two of the most dominant religious forces in Western history.

In the Hebrew Scriptures, the prophet Daniel warned, "Many of those who sleep in the dust of the ground will awake, some to everlasting life but the others to disgrace and everlasting contempt" (Daniel 12:2). Turning to the New Testament, we find Jesus Himself advising His disciples not to "fear those who kill the body but are unable to kill the soul; but rather fear Him who is able to destroy both soul and body in hell" (Matthew 10:28). Then we see Paul, the great Christian missionary, proclaiming that "these will pay the penalty of eternal destruction, away from the presence of the Lord and from the glory of His power" (2 Thessalonians 1:9).

These leaders and teachers did not attempt to prove hell's reality. They knew it existed and warned their audiences appropriately. In church history, the reality of hell was once so gripping, so pervasive, that the threat of excommunication was a powerful and feared danger.

Things have certainly changed. Today, hell is not a topic for polite conversations, and it rarely surfaces anywhere else, including sermons. We are afraid of it, embarrassed by it. Some even reject it as infantile and obnoxious. Atheist BC Johnson frankly states that "the idea of hell is morally absurd."[7] Morton Kelsey even notes that believers are ambivalent about the doctrine: "The idea of hell is certainly not popular among most modern Christians."[8]

The Scriptures on Hell

Two New Testament passages provide the clearest definition of hell we have. One is 2 Thessalonians 1:9, which we have just seen. The other passage is Matthew 25:41,46: "Then He will also say to those on His left, 'Depart from Me, accursed ones, into the eternal fire which has been prepared for the devil and his angels'...these will go away into eternal punishment, but the righteous into eternal life." These and other verses show that the essence of hell is the end of a road away from God, love, and anything of real value. It is banishment from the very presence of God and from the type of life we were made to live.

Hell is also a place of shame, sorrow, regret, and anguish. This intense pain is not actively produced by God; He is not a cosmic torturer. Undoubtedly, anguish and torment will exist in hell. And because we will have both body and soul in the resurrected state, the anguish experienced can be both mental and physical. But the pain suffered will be due to the shame and sorrow resulting from the punishment of final, ultimate, unending banishment from God, His kingdom, and the good life for which we were created in the first place.

Moreover, the flames in hell are most likely metaphorical. If metaphors for hell are taken literally, contradictions result, at least from the limited perspective of our finite minds. Hell is called a place of fire and darkness, but how could both exist together? Hell is a bottomless pit and a dump. How can it be both? In addition, Scripture calls God Himself a consuming fire (Hebrews 12:29) and states that Christ and His angels will return surrounded in flaming fire (2 Thessalonians 1:7).

But God is not a physical object as is fire, and the flames surrounding the returning Christ might be no more literal than is the sword coming out of His mouth (Revalation 1:16). Flames are often used as symbols for divine judgment.

Some Reasons to Believe in Hell

Some people think the severity and finality of the Bible's view of hell is too horrendous, too absolute, too tragic to accept. It is no surprise, then, that the biblical picture has had many detractors. So now I want to examine the justification of hell by focusing on some of the issues, objections, and alternatives that have been proposed.

A Good Fit

Oxford University philosopher Richard Swinburne has offered an important defense of the orthodox view of hell.[9] He asks why we must have right beliefs and a good will (a properly directed will, one that desires God, salvation, and heaven) to go to heaven. Why are people with wrong beliefs and a bad will left out?

His basic answer is twofold: First, heaven is the type of place where people with wrong beliefs and a bad will would not fit. Second, heaven must be freely and noncoercively chosen.

According to Swinburne, heaven is a place where people eternally enjoy a supremely worthwhile happiness. This happiness has three important aspects. First, it is not the mere possession of pleasant sensations. You could have pleasant sensations, say, by taking drugs all day or by having people constantly lie to you about how wonderful and intelligent you are. But for that you should be pitied. You would not have a supremely worthwhile happiness.

Second, you can have such a happiness only if you do what you truly want to without any conflicting desires. You could be happy doing something even if you experienced conflicting desires about that activity, but it would be better to do something you wanted to do and be free from conflict.

Third, a supremely worthwhile happiness must come from true beliefs and things that are truly and supremely valuable. We all know that happiness can be obtained from false beliefs. You can be happy in the belief that someone loves you even if that belief is false. So happiness can come from either true or false beliefs, but happiness is more worthwhile if it comes from true beliefs. If given a choice between a lot of happiness from false beliefs or a little happiness from true beliefs, we would choose the latter. Furthermore, happiness can come from engaging in silly or even immoral actions. Some people gain happiness from killing or stealing. But a supremely worthwhile happiness comes from true beliefs and activities that are really valuable.

To sum up then, a supremely worthwhile happiness is a deep happiness, not a shallow one. It does not involve the mere possession of pleasant sensations, but is obtained by freely choosing to do activities when that choice is based on true beliefs and those activities are truly worthwhile. Deepest happiness is found in successfully pursuing a task of supreme value and being in a situation of supreme value, in having true beliefs about these and wanting to be doing these tasks in this situation without any conflict of desires.

What are these supreme tasks and situations? Swinburne claims they include developing a friendship with God, learning to care for others who have that same friendship, caring for and beautifying God's creation, and the like. Heaven is not a reward for good action; it is a home for good people. Heaven intensifies and fulfills a certain type of life that can be chosen, in undeveloped form, in this life. Only people of a certain sort are suited for life in heaven: those who have a true belief about what it is like and really want to be there for the right reasons.

People with different beliefs about the good life or heaven will value and practice different activities, so even if they are seeking the good in some sense, their character will develop in a different way from the character of the Christian. For example, a Buddhist who spends his whole life trying to remove his desires would not find heaven a place that fulfills the things he really wants. People may have a bad will or a good will, but if they have false beliefs about what God, heaven, and the good really are, they will not be suited for life in heaven.

Can God force the bad to become good? No, says Swinburne, not if He respects our freedom. God can't make people's character for them, and people who do evil or cultivate false beliefs start a slide away from God that ultimately ends in hell. God respects human freedom. We could add here that it would be unloving, a sort of divine rape, to force people to accept heaven and God if they did not really want them. When God allows people to say no to Him, He actually respects and dignifies them. We may rush in to force our children to do something in their best interests, but our paternalism drops out when they grow up because we wish to respect them as adults. Similarly, God dignifies people and treats their choices as significant by allowing them to choose against Him, not just for Him.

So Swinburne's argument is that heaven is suitable for people of a certain sort (those who really want to be there and who base their choice on true beliefs), and their decision to go there must be made freely. Hell is a place for people of a different character who freely choose to be there.

Respect

As it is, Swinburne's case seems to be a good one, but we can add to it too. For example, more can be said about how hell is the result of God's respect for persons. We can reasonably argue that it is wrong to destroy the type of intrinsic value humans have. If God is the source and preserver of values, and if persons have the high degree of intrinsic value Christianity claims they have, then God is the preserver of persons. He would be wrong to destroy something of such value just because it has chosen a life it was not intended to live. Thus, one way God can respect persons is to sustain them in existence and not annihilate them. Annihilation destroys creatures of very high intrinsic value.

Another way to respect persons is to honor their free, autonomous choices, even if those choices are wrong. God respects persons in this second way by honoring their choices. Philosopher Eugene Fontinell makes this note:

> The question that must be raised here is whether the doctrine of universal salvation, highly motivated though it may be, does not diminish the "seriousness" of human experience... At stake here, of course, is the nature and scope of human freedom...There is a profound difference between a human freedom whose exercise *must* lead to union with God and one that allows for the possibility of eternal separation from God...A world in which there can only be winners is a less serious world than one in which the possibility of the deepest loss is real.[10]

God will not force His love on people and coerce them to choose Him, and He cannot annihilate creatures with such high intrinsic value, so the only option available is quarantine. And that is what hell is.

Justice and Holiness

There are two other considerations to ponder concerning hell. First, some of God's attributes—particularly His justice and holiness—seem to demand the existence of hell. Justice demands retribution, or the distribution of rewards and punishments in a fair way. It would be unjust to allow evil to go unpunished and to reward evil with good, even if the good was not sought in a genuine, informed way. Thus hell is in keeping with God's justice. As Paul put it, "For after all it is only just for God to repay with affliction those who afflict you...dealing out retribution to those who do not know God and to those who do not obey the gospel of our Lord Jesus" (2 Thessalonians 1:6,8).

Similarly, God's holiness requires Him to separate Himself entirely from evil, and hell is essentially a place away from God. Thus, hell is in keeping with God's holiness. It may very well be that our current hostilities toward the notion of hell result not from an enlightened conscience, but quite the reverse. Our culture embraces a contentless set of moral slogans, where individual liberties prevail, come what may. But as a society we have little concern or appreciation for holiness, and this dulling of our moral sensibilities may have inevitably led to our failure to appreciate the morality of hell as seen in the light of the demands of holiness and justice.

Moral Experts

This matter leads to a second point. In ethics, there is a theory known as *virtue ethics*. The details of this theory are beyond my present concern, but one thing about virtue ethics is very important to our discussion. This theory maintains that people who have a well-developed, virtuous character are in a better position to have moral sensibilities and genuine insight into what is right and wrong than those who do not have such a character. In other words, true moral experts are possible, and they are those people who have cared deeply about virtue and goodness and who have labored to develop ingrained virtues and moral sensibilities.

Jesus Christ and His apostles were moral experts. They were remarkable people who exhibited lives of staggering dedication to goodness, virtue, and the moral way of life. Now, if they, being as virtuous as they were and having well-developed moral sensibilities, did not balk at the notion of hell but even embraced it as just, loving, and fair, then our current distaste for the doctrine says more about us than about the doctrine itself. To deny this conclusion is tantamount to claiming that our modern moral sensibilities are more developed than those of Jesus and His apostles, not to say those of the overwhelming number of godly people who have followed Jesus since. But this claim is clearly arrogant and unreasonable.

This, then, constitutes some of the reasons the biblical doctrine of hell is morally and intellectually justifiable. But we must consider some other objections.

Some Objections Answered

Universalism

According to universalists, God will eventually reconcile all things to Himself, including all individuals, even if this means that God will continue to draw them to Himself in the afterlife. Morton Kelsey has said, "To say that men and women after death will be able to resist the love of God forever seems to suggest that the human soul is stronger than God."[11] John Hick claims that because of God's goodness, mercy, grace, and love, "God will eventually succeed in His purpose of winning all men to Himself in faith and love."[12]

Universalists appeal to various arguments in support of their views, but three are central. One argument is that the doctrine of eternal banishment is immoral and unjust and therefore unacceptable. Second, they argue that the doctrine of eternal banishment is incompatible with some of God's attributes, such as omnipotence, love, and mercy. God's mercy must surely triumph over human resistance. Finally, certain Bible texts (Acts 3:21; Romans 5:18; 11:32; 1 Corinthians 15:22-28; Ephesians 1:10; 1 Timothy 2:4) are cited in favor of universalism. However, these arguments do not succeed. Let's look at each one more closely to see why.

We have already considered some reasons for rejecting the first argument—the injustice of eternal banishment. The state of hell is fair and, in fact, an indication of human dignity. Heaven is unsuited for certain types of people and lifestyles. People can freely resist God. God's love respects human freedom, making human choices and human history truly significant. And God will not extinguish people of intrinsic value. Eternal punishment is sad, even to God, but we must not confuse sadness with injustice. Real, eternal gains are possible in this life, and this brings with it the possibility of real, eternal loss. And this latter possibility elevates the seriousness or significance of our world.

Regarding God's attributes, we can make a similar case.

Omnipotence has nothing to do with the issue of hell. Consider the task of creating a square circle. This is a logical contradiction. The task of creating such an entity is a pseudotask. It is not something you could do by, say, working out with weights. Power is irrelevant to such pseudotasks. The same can be said with regard to free choices. All the power in the world cannot *guarantee* that a free choice will be a good one. Determining a good result of a free choice is a logical contradiction.

Furthermore, while hell is in some sense a defeat to God (His *desire* is that all men be saved), in another sense it is not a defeat. It is a quarantine that respects the freedom and dignity of His image bearers while separating hell from His special presence and the community of those who love Him.

Finally, regarding divine love, we all know that resistance to love does not always break down. Love, even divine love, cannot coercively guarantee a proper response to it.

What about the Bible, then? Does it teach universalism? No. In fact, it contains very clear passages that contradict universalism (Matthew 8:12; 25:31-46; John 5:29; Romans 2:8-10; Revalation 20:10,15). And the passages that appear to support universalism should be understood as doing one of two things. Either they are teaching what God's desire is without affirming what will happen, or they are describing not the ultimate reconciliation of all of fallen humanity, but a restoration of divine order and rule over creation taken as a whole.

So universalism is not an adequate stumbling block to belief in hell. C.S. Lewis made this wise observation:

> If a game is played, it must be possible to lose it. If the happiness of a creature lies in self-surrender, no one can make that surrender but himself (though many can help him to make it) and he may refuse. I would pay any price to be able to say truthfully, "All will be saved." But my reason retorts, "Without their will, or with it?" If I say, "Without

their will," I at once perceive a contradiction: How can the supreme voluntary act of self-surrender be involuntary? If I say, "With their will," my reason replies, "How if they *will not* give in?"[13]

A Second Chance After Death

The Bible is clear that people do not get a second chance to go to heaven after death. Hebrews 9:27 says, "It is appointed for men to die once, and after this comes judgment." Is this teaching fair and just? Yes. At least three factors tell us why.

For one thing, certain passages indicate that God gives people all the time they need to make a choice about eternity. Second Peter 3:9 teaches that God is postponing the return of Christ because He is "not wishing for any to perish but for all to come to repentance." From this, we can infer that if all that people needed were more time to make a decision, God would see to it that they got the extra time instead of dying prematurely. No one will go to hell who would have gone to heaven if given one more chance. Those who would have responded to a second chance after death will have their deaths postponed and given that chance this side of the grave. God "desires all men to be saved and to come to the knowledge of the truth" (1 Timothy 2:4).

Second, people most likely do not have the ability to choose heaven after death. Character is shaped moment by moment in the thousands of little choices we make. Each day our character is increasingly formed, and in each choice we make we either move toward or away from God. As our character grows, some choices become possible and others impossible. The longer one lives in opposition to God, the harder it is to choose to turn that around. If God permits a person to die and go to hell, it seems reasonable to think that God no longer believes that this person would ever choose to be saved. Only God could make that type of judgment, but that judgment could clearly be true.

And if God gives people a second chance after death, why did He create this world in the first place? Why not just go straight to a world in which everyone starts in the afterlife? Particularly, if some people would reject Christ in this life but accept Him in the afterlife, why not skip this life altogether? The second-chance idea makes this world superfluous, especially for those just described.

Annihilationism

Recently, some people have argued for conditional immortality for the unsaved on scriptural and moral grounds. Scripturally, they claim that biblical flames in hell are literal and that flames destroy whatever they burn. Morally, they assert that infinitely long punishing is disproportionate to a finite life of sin. Thus, everlasting punish*ment* in extinction is morally preferable to everlasting punish*ing*.

The scriptural argument is weak. Clear texts whose explicit intent is to teach the extent of the afterlife overtly compare the everlasting conscious life of the saved and the unsaved (Daniel 12:2; Matthew 25:41,46). Moreover, as noted above, the flames in hell are most likely figures of speech for judgment (see 2 Thessalonians 1:7; Hebrews 12:29).

The moral argument fails as well. For one thing, the severity of a crime is not a function of the time it takes to commit it. Thus, rejection of the mercy of an infinite God could quite appropriately warrant an unending, conscious separation from God. Further, everlasting hell is morally superior to annihilation. To see why, consider the example of euthanasia.

Sanctity-of-life advocates eschew active euthanasia, but quality-of-life advocates embrace it. The former reject it because on the sanctity-of-life view, people are valuable not because of their quality of life, but simply because they exist in God's image. The latter accept it because they believe the value of human life accrues from the quality of life. Thus, the sanctity-of-life position has a higher moral regard for the dignity of human life.

Now, the traditional and annihilationist views about hell are expressions, respectively, of sanctity- and quality-of-life ethical stand-points. After all, the only grounds God would have for annihilating someone would be the low quality of life in hell. If a person will not be saved and if God will not extinguish one made in His image, then God's only alternative is quarantine, and that is what hell is. Thus, the traditional view, being a sanctity- and not a quality-of-life position, is morally superior to annihilationism.

The Fairness of Hell

What about people who, through no fault of their own, never have a chance to hear the gospel of Christ? Do they receive or deserve unend-ing punishing? Furthermore, why did God create people whom He knew would go to hell in the first place?

We must first affirm with Scripture that Jesus Christ is the only way to God. Christ is unique in His claims to be God (John 8:58; 10:30), His authority to forgive sins (Mark 2:10), and His miracles and resur-rection from the dead. Buddha, Confucius, Mohammad, and other religious leaders are still in their graves; Jesus is not. Furthermore, Jesus Himself claimed to be the only way to God (John 3:18; 8:24; 11:25–26; 14:6), and this claim is reasserted by Peter in Acts 4:12.

The main issue in religion is truth, not belief. Believing something doesn't make it true. If four people have different beliefs about the color of my mother's hair, they can't all be right, and believing that her hair is red does not make it so. All religions have certain truths in common; nevertheless, they significantly differ over what God is like, what God believes, what the afterlife is to be, and how we have a relationship with God. The real issue is truth, not belief. If Jesus was who He claimed to be, then He is unique and the only way to God.

We also need to observe that according to the Bible, God desires all men to be saved (Ezekiel 18:23,32; 1 Timothy 2:4; 2 Peter 3:9), and He judges fairly (Genesis 18:25; Job 34:12) and impartially (Romans 2:11). The biblical God is not a cold, arbitrary being, but a God who deeply loves His creatures and desires their fellowship and worship.

Also, all humans have some light from creation and conscience that God exists, that He is personal and moral, and that they are guilty before Him (Romans 1:18-20; 2:11-16).

Moreover, the Bible is very clear about the state of those who hear the gospel and reject it (John 3:18; 5:21-24). They will be banished from heaven and sent to judgment in hell. Remember, the most kind, virtuous person who ever lived said these words.

With all this in mind, we can begin to address the first question raised: What about those who don't have a chance to hear the gospel? The Bible doesn't address this question explicitly and for obvious reasons. The Word of God doesn't usually offer a plan B if the church chooses to reject God's plan A. Scripture commands us to go to the world and be sure no one fails to hear the gospel. It doesn't explicitly say, "Here is what will happen if you decide not to act on God's command." So whatever view we reach here must be formulated theologically from God's attributes and general considerations in Scripture.

Here is another point: We must distinguish between the *means* of salvation and the *basis* of salvation. Christ's death and resurrection have always been the basis for our justification before God. However, the *means* of appropriating that basis has not always been a conscious knowledge of the content of the gospel. Saved individuals before Christ (and surely justice includes people who lived and died within a few years after Christ's execution when the gospel couldn't reach them) were saved on the basis of Christ's work, but they did not know the content of the gospel. They were saved by responding in faith and mercy to the revelation they had received at that point (Genesis 15:6).

Furthermore, most theologians believe that those who cannot believe (infants and those without rational faculties capable of grasping the gospel) have the benefits of Christ applied to them. Many argue this on the basis of 2 Samuel 12:23, where David expresses his conviction that he will be reunited with his deceased infant in heaven. They also appeal to the fact that there is no mention of perdition for children in all the Bible, and they cite God's clear desire to save all humanity, His justice, and His love.[14]

So we believe it is certainly possible that those who are responding to the light from nature that they have received will either have the message of the gospel sent to them (as in Acts 10), or God may judge them based on His knowledge of what they would have done had they had a chance to hear the gospel. The simple fact is that God rewards those who seek Him (Hebrews 11:6). It does not seem just for others to be judged because of my disobedience in taking the gospel to them, and the gospel certainly has not been taken to others in the way God commanded. I am not sure this line of reasoning is true, but some deem it plausible in light of the information we have. However, at the end of the chapter I will offer another view of the fate of the unevangelized that is at least as plausible if not more so than the one we are now considering.

If this case is correct, then why reach out to others with the gospel? For three reasons: As I admitted, this answer is somewhat speculative (remember, the Bible does not address the question explicitly). I think it could be right, but we should evangelize just in case it is wrong. Also, God commands us to tell others about His Son, and we should obey Him out of our love for Him. We are also told to spread God's teachings and broaden His family not only for what happens in the future state but also to spread His rule now. Why delay and give evil more victory now? Why not bring people mercy and forgiveness and release from sin as soon as possible? Good news should not be delayed.

New Testament scholar Leon Morris puts this whole discussion in perspective:

> Peter told [Cornelius] that God is no respecter of persons, "But in every nation he who fears him and works righteousness is acceptable to him" (Acts 10:35). This surely means that people are judged by the light they have, not by the

light they do not have. We remember, too, that Paul says, "It is accepted of a man according to what he has and not according to what he does not (2 Cor. 8:12). Long ago Abraham asked, "Shall not the Judge of all the earth do right?" (Gen. 18:25), and we must leave it there. We do not know what the fate of those who have not heard the gospel will be. But we do know God, and we know that he will do what is right.[15]

But a final question remains: Why did God create people whom He knew would not choose Him? In my view, Christian philosopher William Lane Craig has provided a very helpful answer to this question.[16]

According to Craig, among the things God knows is His knowledge of what every possible free creature would do under any possible set of circumstances. This is sometimes called "middle knowledge." This is knowledge of those creatable worlds God can actually create. For example, I do not have a sister, but God knows a possible person who would have been my sister if my parents had married earlier and given birth to a daughter. Again, I was raised in Missouri and never challenged to become a lawyer, but God knows what would have happened if I had moved to Illinois as a teenager and what I would have freely done had I been challenged as a boy to become a lawyer. This is knowledge of what a free creature would do in certain circumstances, even if those circumstances do not happen. God knows all the possible creatures He could have created but didn't, and He knows all the free choices all His creatures—those He actually created and those He did not create—would make in all the circumstances they could be placed in (some actually happening, some not happening).

What does this have to do with the doctrine of hell? God knows every possible creature and every possible response they would make to the gospel in every possible circumstance. Given this knowledge, why did God create a world in which people are not saved (people who He knew would not trust Christ)? Furthermore, because God knows what circumstances need to happen for each person to trust Christ, why didn't God bring those circumstances about instead of other circumstances in which persons freely reject Christ?

Craig breaks down this problem into four statements:

1. God has middle knowledge.

2. God is omnipotent (all-powerful).

3. God is all-loving.

4. Some persons freely reject Christ and are lost.

According to Craig, the problem is this: If we accept the first three statements, an objector would claim that we cannot also accept statement 4. For if we accept statements 1–3, the objector holds that we also ought to accept these statements:

1a. God knows under what circumstances any possible person would freely receive Christ.

2a. God is able to create a world in which all persons freely receive Christ.

3a. God holds that a world in which nobody rejects Christ is preferable to a world in which somebody does and consequently is lost.

The objector claims, then, that since God has middle knowledge, He would know for every possible creature just what circumstances need to happen to bring him to Christ, and because God prefers a world in which nobody rejects Christ over a world in which some reject Christ, God would have the knowledge and power to create a world in which everyone is saved.

Craig's solution to this problem is to reject 1a–3a and replace them with these statements that are more likely to be true:

1b. Some persons would not freely receive Christ under any circumstances.

2b. There is no possible world in which all persons would freely receive Christ.

3b. God holds that a world in which some persons freely reject Christ but the number of those who freely receive Him is maximized is preferable to a world in which a few people receive Christ and none are lost.

Let us look at these in more detail. We have already discussed 1b in conjunction with universalism. There we saw that God cannot guarantee that a free creature would accept Christ. That is just what it means to be free. Therefore, of all the possible persons God could have created or did create, some would freely reject Christ regardless of the circumstances. How could God *guarantee* a set of circumstances for each person in which that person *freely* receives Christ? Statement 1b seems clearly true then.

For all we know, of all the possible persons God could have created, the vast majority of those who would have rejected Christ were never created in the first place. The relatively smaller number of people who reject Christ may demonstrate God's mercy. But still, Craig reminds us, the objector may respond by asking why God created *anyone* who He knew would not trust Christ.

Craig's answer is 2b. Perhaps no world could possibly exist in which all persons freely receive Christ. Now, on the surface of it, 2b does not seem plausible. Why couldn't God just create a world composed only of all the people who receive Christ? What is the problem here?

Craig's solution is this: Creating just those persons and just the right circumstances for all to be saved may not be possible. Why? Well, if God changes the circumstances so Smith will freely trust Christ, this alteration may lead Jones to freely reject Christ even though Jones would have accepted Christ in a world without the circumstances needed to bring Smith to saving faith.

An example may help to illustrate this point. Suppose God can bring about two circumstances, one in which my father is offered a job in Illinois while I am a young boy and one in which no offer is forthcoming. In the former case, suppose my father freely accepts the offer, and we move to Illinois. In the latter case, we stay in Missouri. Let us call these events *C* and *D*, respectively. Suppose further that in circumstance *D*, three years after the offer could have been given (but wasn't), I will meet just the right person in just the right circumstances and come to Christ. It is entirely possible that I would have had no such opportunity in circumstance *C*. So my salvation is dependent upon *D* obtaining as opposed to *C*. In addition, suppose that if *D* obtained, I would lead five others to Christ in Missouri in my lifetime, but if *C* had obtained, then a neighbor of mine in Illinois would have come to Christ by watching my non-Christian life fall apart, but without my bad example he would freely reject Christ. Now suppose this neighbor would have led ten people to Christ. In circumstance *D*, six people come to Christ (I and five others), and in *C*, eleven come to Christ. *C* and *D* cannot both obtain, and thus, free human choices responding to different influences make it impossible for God to bring about the conversion of all seventeen people.

This example shows that adjusting the circumstances in a possible world has a ripple effect. Not even God can change things piecemeal and respect freedom. If one thing is changed, this has an impact on other things. Additionally, the more people God creates, the greater the chance that some of the people He makes will not trust Christ. So 2b seems reasonable and quite plausible after all.

Another point can strengthen 2b. The ancient church held two major views about the origin of the soul: creationism and traducianism. According to creationism, our bodies are passed on to us through normal reproduction by our parents, but God creates each individual soul out of nothing, most likely at fertilization. According to traducianism, both the body and soul are passed on to us by our parents. Now, the soul is the thing that makes us the unique individuals we are. I could have had a different body, but I could not have had a different soul. I am who I am because of my soul.

For the creationist, I could have had different parents from the ones I had. Why? Because God could have created my soul out of nothing and placed it into a different body formed by different parents. In this case, I would have been united to a different body and born to different parents. For the traducian, I could not have had different parents from the ones I had. Why? Because the very soul is essential to my identity, and my soul is what it is because it came from just these two people. The soul is passed on from the parents—different parents, different soul.

If we accept traducianism, then God could not have created me without creating my specific parents, and He could not have created my specific parents without creating their specific parents, and so on. In other words, God could only get to me, as it were, by reaching me through my entire ancestral chain. If my great-grandparents had married different people, I could not have existed. So when God is comparing alternative possible worlds, He is not just comparing alternative individuals, but alternative ancestral chains in their entirety. God may allow some chains to come about that include some individuals who reject Christ (say, my great-great-grandfather) but which allow for others to be born who do trust Christ. In this case, God would be balancing alternative chains and not just alternative people. Of course, if one accepts creationism regarding the soul (not to be confused with creationism as opposed to evolution), then this solution would be unavailable.

These considerations show that creating a world with a large number of people may have the result that a number of them may be permitted to be lost for some justifiable reason in order to respect human freedom and accomplish some task known by God. What might that task be? Statement 3b gives us an answer: God prefers a world in which some persons freely reject Christ but the number of saved is maximized over a world in which a few trust Christ and none are lost.

Consider two worlds, W1 and W2. In W1, suppose 50 million are saved and 5 million are lost, while in W2, 5 million are saved and none lost. It is not clear that W2 is morally preferable to WI. If W2 *is* morally preferable, then hell has veto power over heaven. God's purpose becomes the negative one of keeping people from hell, not the positive one of getting people to heaven. In contrast, having more people go to heaven may be worth allowing more to go to hell. At least this is not clearly immoral. If something like this is correct, then with Craig, we can affirm the following and add it to his opening four statements:

> 5. The actual world contains an optimal balance between saved and unsaved, and those who are unsaved would never have received Christ under any circumstances.

This would seem to explain why God would create individuals whom He knew would not trust Christ in any circumstances.

The Fate of the Unevangelized

We have considered middle knowledge in order to solve the problem of why God created people whom He knew would not choose Him. Before we close the chapter, we want to relate middle knowledge to a closely related question we discussed earlier: How can God judge those who never have a chance to hear the gospel message? In our earlier discussion we suggested a possible answer to this question: Either God will get the gospel message to such people or He will judge them based on His knowledge of what they would do if they had been given a chance to hear the gospel. We now offer a third alternative solution to the question that is at least as likely to be true as the other options.

According to the third solution, no one who does not hear the gospel message and accept it will be saved. This solution can be clarified by taking it to imply the following two theses:

> 6. In unevangelized areas, some people will be saved if

someone takes the gospel to them, and they will not be saved if no one takes the gospel to them.

7. In unevangelized areas, no one will go to hell who would have accepted the gospel if someone had taken it to them.

Proposition 6 assures us that if we take the gospel to unevangelized areas, people there will be saved who would otherwise not be saved, and 7 expresses the idea that no one who does not get a chance to hear the gospel and is lost would have trusted Christ if they have been given the chance. But how can both 6 and 7 be true? How can it be the case that if we go to an unreached people, there will be people saved who otherwise would not be saved while at the same time accepting the idea that if no one takes the gospel to that unreached people group, no one will be lost who would have been saved had someone gone to them?

The answer involves God's middle knowledge. Suppose that God is contemplating some people group through its history, and He is deciding whom He will and will not create among all the possible persons He knows He could create there. Surely, the number of people in the history of the people group under consideration could have been larger or smaller than the actual number that obtains in the real world. God could have created some persons and placed them in this people group, but for some reason or another, they are not brought into the world. Now suppose that among the possible persons God knows He could create in our people group, a specific set of possible persons would respond to the gospel if they were given the chance. God would know the number of those possible persons, and He would know who they were. Let us use the name "set A" to refer to the set of possible persons in this people group who would trust Christ if given the chance.

Now God is deciding whom to create in the people group under consideration. Should He create the people in set A or not? It depends on whether or not someone is willing to take the gospel to the people group in question. If God knows someone will bring the gospel, He will create the people in set A, and some people will be saved (those in set A) who would not be saved if no one were willing to go to the people group because, in that case, God would refrain from creating the people in set A. This is what proposition 6 means. Moreover, if no one is willing to bring the gospel to this people group, then the only people God will allow to be created are unsaveable people, those who would not trust Christ even if they had a chance to hear about Him. This is what proposition 7 means. God's choice to create the people in set A depends on whether or not someone will freely go and preach the gospel to the relevant people group. This, then, is a third solution to the question within our purview.

In this closing chapter, I have tried to share with you some important facts about the reality and nature of heaven and hell. I can't think of a better summary of these things than the one offered by the apostle Paul (which I paraphrase):

> For the wages of sin is death—eternal separation from God—but the free gift of God is an eternal kind of life that begins now and lasts forever in Christ Jesus our Lord (Romans 6:23).

Epilogue

I offer you my final invitation. You are on a journey—that is not a choice, but the path you take is. I place before you what I believe are the two most plausible choices available. Some have tried to soften the atheistic, naturalist option by adding absolute values and other bells and whistles to it, but they are implausible, ad hoc revisions of atheism that do not sit well with it. And some would opt for a different form of theism, such as Islam. But based on all the available evidence, they are nowhere near as reasonable to believe as Christianity. Here, then, are your two pathways. Ponder them wisely and choose well.

Bertrand Russell (1872–1970) gives a nice description of atheism:

> That man is the product of causes which had no prevision of the end they were achieving; that his origin, his growth, his hopes and fears, his loves and his beliefs are but the out-come of accidental collocations of atoms; that no fire, no heroism, no intensity of thought and feeling, can preserve an individual life beyond the grave; that all the labors of the ages, all the devotion, all the inspiration, all the noonday brightness of human genius, are destined to extinction in

the vast death of the solar system; and that the whole temple of man's achievement must inevitably be buried beneath the debris of a universe in ruins—all these things, if not quite beyond dispute, are yet so nearly certain that no philosophy which rejects them can hope to stand. Only within the scaffolding of these truths, only on the firm foundation of unyielding despair, can the soul's habitation henceforth be safely built.[1]

Here is the other choice, stated nicely by St. Patrick (AD 387–493):

I arise today in a mighty strength, calling upon the Trinity, believing in the Three Persons, saying they are One, thanking my Creator.

I arise today strengthened by Christ's own baptism, made strong by His crucifixion and His burial, made strong by His resurrection and ascension, made strong by His descent to meet me on the day of doom…

I arise today with God's strength to pilot me, God's might to uphold me, God's wisdom to guide me, God's eye to look ahead for me, God's ear to hear me, God's word to speak for me, God's hand to defend me, God's way to lie before me, God's shield to protect me, God's host to safeguard me: against devil's traps, against attraction of sin, against pull of nature, against all who wish me ill near and far, alone and in a crowd…

Christ ever with me, Christ before me, Christ behind me, Christ within me, Christ beneath me, Christ above me, Christ to my right side, Christ to my left, Christ in His breadth, Christ in His length, Christ in depth, Christ in the heart of every man who thinks of me, Christ in the mouth of every man who speaks of me, Christ in every eye that sees me, Christ in every ear that hears me.

I arise today in mighty strength, making in my mouth the Trinity, believing in mind Three Persons, confessing in heart they are One, thanking my Creator. Salvation is from the Lord. Salvation is from the Lord. Salvation is from Christ. May your salvation, three Lords, be always with us.

Notes

Chapter 1—Why Can't I Be Happy?

1. "Happiness and how to measure it," *The Economist,* December 23, 2006, p. 13.
2. Tony Campos, "We're Healthy and Wealthy, but Not Happy," *The Orange County Register,* July 10, 2005.
3. Edmund Bourne and Lorna Garano, *Coping with Anxiety* (Oakland, CA: New Harbinger Publications, 2003), pp. xvii-xx.
4. Robert Banks, *The Tyranny of Time* (Downers Grove, IL: InterVarsity Press, 1983), p. 80.
5. Bourne and Garano, p. xviii.
6. Cited in M. Scott Peck, *The Road Less Traveled* (New York: Simon & Schuster, 1978), p. 17.
7. Thomas Nagel, *The Last Word* (New York: Oxford University Press, 2001), p. 130.
8. Douglas Coupland, *Life After God* (New York: Pocket Books, 1994), p. 359.
9. See P.C. Vitz, *Faith of the Fatherless: The Psychology of Atheism* (Dallas: Spence Publishing, 1999). See also Benjamin Beit-Hallahmi, "Atheists: A Psychological Profile," in *The Cambridge Companion to Atheism,* ed. by Michael Martin (Cambridge: Cambridge University Press, 2007), pp. 300-17.
10. Dinesh D'Souza, *What's So Great About Christianity* (Washington, DC: Regnery, 2007), pp. 261-72.

11. Aldous Huxley, "Confessions of a Professed Atheist," *Report,* June 1996. See also Ben Shapiro, *Porn Generation* (Washington, DC: Regnery, 2005).

12. Robert B. Reich, "Bush's God," *The American Prospect,* June 17, 2004, www. prospect.org.

13. Christian Smith, *American Evangelicalism: Embattled and Thriving* (Chicago: University of Chicago Press, 1998), p. 76.

14. See George Barna, *The Revolutionaries* (Carol Stream, IL: Tyndale, 2005).

15. Dallas Willard, *The Divine Conspiracy* (San Francisco: HarperCollins, 1998), p. 11.

Chapter 2—Hope for a Culture of Bored and Empty Selves

1. These studies are reported in Jeffrey Schwartz and Sharon Begley, *The Mind and the Brain* (New York: HarperCollins, 2002). See also, Mario Beauregard, Mario and Denyse O'Leary, *The Spiritual Brain: A Neuroscientist's Case for the Existence of the Soul* (New York: HarperCollins, 2007).

2. Christopher Lasch, *The Culture of Narcissism* (New York: Warner Books, 1979), p. 88. See also pp. 88-103.

3. For more on this, see J.P. Moreland and Klaus Issler, *The Lost Virtue of Happiness* (Colorado Springs: NavPress, 2006), chapters 1 and 2.

4. Philip Cushman, "Why the Self Is Empty," *American Psychologist* 45 (May 1990): 600.

5. Lasch, *The Culture of Narcissism,* p. 103.

6. Roger Cohen, "Secular Europe's Merits," *New York Times,* December 13, 2007.

7. Dallas Willard, *The Divine Conspiracy* (San Francisco: Harper, 1998), p. 92. See also pp. 75,79,134,184-85.

8. For a helpful introduction to postmodernism, see Joseph Natoli, *A Primer to Postmodernity* (Oxford: Blackwell, 1997).

9. Bertrand Russell, "A Free Man's Worship," in *Why I Am Not a Christian,* ed. by Paul Edwards (New York: Simon & Schuster, 1957), p. 107.

10. Cited in Phillip Johnson, *Darwin on Trial* (Downers Grove, IL: InterVarsity Press, 1991), p. 127.

11. Michael Ruse, "Evolutionary Theory and Christian Ethics," in *The Darwinian Paradigm* (London: Routledge, 1989), pp. 262-69.

12. Gould's statement is cited in David Friend, "The Meaning of Life," *Life Magazine,* p. 33.

13. Cushman, "Why the Self Is Empty," 599.

14. For more on the self and the soul, see J.P. Moreland and Scott Rae, *Body and Soul* (Downers Grove, IL: InterVarsity Press, 2000); J.P. Moreland, "Restoring the Substance to the Soul of Psychology," *Journal of Psychology and Theology* 26 (March, 1998): 29-43.

15. Terry Eagleton, *The Illusions of Postmodernism* (Oxford: Blackwell, 1996), pp. 27-28.

Chapter 3—The Question of God, Part 1

1. Marilyn vos Savant, "Ask Marilyn," *Parade Magazine,* October 7, 2001, p. 25.

2. Christopher Lasch, *The Culture of Narcissism* (New York: Warner Books, 1979), p. 96.

3. For more detailed overviews of this argument, see J.P. Moreland, *Scaling the Secular City* (Grand Rapids: Baker Book House, 1987), chapter 1; J.P. Moreland and Kai Nielsen, *Does God Exist? The Debate Between Atheists and Theists* (Buffalo: Prometheus Books, 1993).

4. See the objections by Anthony Flew and Keith Parsons in Moreland and Nielsen, *Does God Exist?* pp. 163-64,185-88. See also J.L. Mackie, *The Miracle of Theism (*Oxford: Clarendon Press, 1982), p. 93.

5. Michael D. Lemonick, "How the Universe Will End," *Time,* June 25, 2001, pp. 48-56.

6. Robert Jastrow, *God and the Astronomers* (New York: Norton, 1978), p. 116. Additional sources for this chapter, ranging from more basic to more difficult include: Paul Copan, *Loving Wisdom* (St. Louis: Chalice Press, 2007); Chad Meister, *Building Belief* (Grand Rapids: Baker, 2006); Lee Strobel, *The Case for a Creator* (Grand Rapids: Zondervan, 2003); Norman L. Geisler and Chad V. Meister, eds., *Reasons for Faith* (Wheaton, IL: Crossway, 2007); William Lane Craig, *Reasonable Faith* (Wheaton, IL: Crossway, 2008); Paul Copan and Paul Moser, eds., *The Rationality of Theism,* (London: Routledge, 2003); William Lane Craig, ed., *Philosophy of Religion: A Contemporary Reader,* (New York: Rutgers University Press, 2002); William Lane Craig and J.P. Moreland, eds., *A Companion to Natural Theology* (Boston, MA: Blackwell, 2009).

Chapter 4—The Question of God, Part 2

1. See Anthony Flew, *There Is a God* (New York: HarperCollins, 2007).

2. Michael J. Behe, "Evidence for Design at the Foundation of Life," in *Science and Evidence for Design in the Universe,* ed. by Michael J. Behe, William Dembski, and Stephen Meyer (San Francisco: Ignatius, 2000), p. 119.

3. See Michael J. Behe, *Darwin's Black Box* (New York: The Free Press, 1996), pp. 69-73.

4. William Dembski, *Intelligent Design* (Downers Grove, IL: InterVarsity Press, 1999).

5. Flew, *There Is a God*, chapter 6.

6. Robin Collins, "The Evidence of Physics: The Cosmos on a Razor's Edge," in Lee Strobel, *The Case for a Creator: A Journalist Investigates Scientific Evidence That Points to God* (Grand Rapids: Zondervan, 2004), p. 130.

7. Paul Davies, *God and the New Physics* (New York: Simon & Schuster, 1983), p. 189.

8. John Warwick Montgomery, *Law Above the Law* (Minneapolis: Dimension, 1975), p. 24.

9. J.L. Mackie, *The Miracle of Theism* (Oxford: Clarendon Press, 1982), p. 115. See also J.P. Moreland and Kai Nielsen, *Does God Exist?* (Buffalo: Prometheus, 1993), chapters 8–10.

10. Michael Ruse, "Evolutionary Theory and Christian Ethics," in *The Darwinian Paradigm* (London: Routledge, 1989), pp. 262-69.

11. Helga Kuhse and Peter Singer, *Should the Baby Live?* (Oxford: Oxford University Press, 1985), pp. 118-39.

12. Ernst Mayr, *Populations, Species, and Evolution* (Cambridge, MA.: Harvard University Press, 1970), p. 4.

13. David Hull, *The Metaphysics of Evolution* (Albany, NY: State University of New York, 1989), pp. 74-75.

14. See J.P. Moreland, "Humanness, Personhood, and the Right to Die," *Faith and Philosophy* 12 (January 1995): 95-112; J.P. Moreland and Stan Wallace, "Aquinas vs. Descartes and Locke on the Human Person and End-of-Life Ethics," *International Philosophical Quarterly* 35 (September 1995): 319-30.

15. For a response to the main naturalist attempt to avoid (2), see J.P. Moreland and John Mitchell, "Is the Human Person a Substance or Property-Thing?" *Ethics & Medicine* 11 (1995).

16. Laura L. Smith and Charles H. Elliot, *Depression for Dummies* (Hoboken, NJ: Wiley, 2003), pp. 305-20.

Chapter 5—The Luminous Nazarene

1. Mike Erre, *The Jesus of Suburbia* (Nashville: Thomas Nelson, 2006), pp. xii-xiii.

2. Donald Miller, *Blue Like Jazz* (Nashville: Thomas Nelson, 2003), p. 115.

3. Jaroslav Pelikan, *Jesus Through the Centuries* (New Haven, CT: Yale University Press, 1985), p. 1.

4. Philip Jenkins, *The Next Christendom* (New York: Oxford University Press, 2002), p. 1.

5. See James Rutz, *MegaShift* (Colorado Springs: Empowerment Press, 2005), pp. 1-55. Up-to-date statistics on this subject are available at worldchristiandatabase.org.

6. For moving documentary evidence of this, see the transformation videos done by researcher George Otis Jr. and the Sentinel Group at www.TranformNations.com.

7. See Edwin Yamauchi, "Jesus Outside the New Testament: What Is the Evidence?" in *Jesus Under Fire,* ed. by Michael Wilkins and J.P. Moreland (Grand Rapids: Zondervan, 1995), pp. 208-29.

8. A.N. Sherwin-White, *Roman Society and Roman Law in the New Testament* (Oxford: Clarendon, 1963), pp. 188-91.

9. See Collin Hemer, *The Book of Acts in the Setting of Hellenistic History* (Winona Lake, IN: Eisenbrauns, 1990).

10. In my view, one of the most sophisticated treatments of the dating question is John Wenham's *Redating Matthew, Mark, and Luke* (Downer's Grove, IL: InterVarsity, 1992). Wenham argues that the synoptics should be dated between the early 40s to the late 50s.

11. Martin Hengel, *Between Jesus and Paul* (Minneapolis: Fortress Press, 1983), p. 93.

12. Larry Hurtado, *How on Earth Did Jesus Become a God?* (Grand Rapids: Eerdmans, 2005), pp. 25-29,202-4.

13. See Paul Barnett, *The Birth of Christianity: The First Twenty Years* (Grand Rapids: Eerdmans, 2005).

14. G.N. Stanton, *Jesus of Nazareth in New Testament Preaching* (Cambridge: Cambridge University Press, 1974).

15. Royce Gruenler, *New Approaches to Jesus and the Gospels,* (Grand Rapids: Baker, 1982).

16. J. Ed Komoszewski, James S. Sawyer, and Dan Wallace, *Reinventing Jesus* (Grand Rapids: Kregel, 2006), pp. 33-34.

17. James D.G. Dunn, *A New Perspective on Jesus* (Grand Rapids: Baker, 2005), p. 44.

18. Dunn, *A New Perspective on Jesus,* pp. 49-50.

19. Paul Barnett, *The Birth of Christianity,* p. 113.

20. In what follows, I am deeply indebted to Paul Rhodes Eddy and Gregory A. Boyd, *The Jesus Legend* (Grand Rapids: Baker, 2007), pp. 407-454.

21. Richard Bauckham, *Jesus and the Eyewitnesses* (Grand Rapids: Eerdmans, 2006), pp. 67-84.

22. See the painstaking treatment of these historical accuracies in Colin J. Hemer and Conrad Gempg, *The Book of Acts in the Setting of Hellenistic History* (Winona Lake, IN: Eisenbrauns, 1990).

23. N.T. Wright, *The Resurrection of the Son of God* (Minneapolis: Fortress Press, 2003).

24. For more in evidence for the resurrection of Jesus, see Gary Habermas, *The Risen Jesus and Future Hope* (Lanham, MD: Rowman & Littlefield, 2003); Paul Copan, ed., *Will the Real Jesus Please Stand Up?* (Grand Rapids: Baker, 1999).

25. I'd like to recommend two books. First, for a helpful discussion of stories and illustrations for sharing your faith with others, see J.P. Moreland and Timothy Muehlhoff, *The God Conversation* (Downers Grove, IL: InterVarsity Press, 2007). For an incredibly interesting, fast-paced novel that covers some of the issues of the last three chapters in an easy-to-read story form, see Craig J. Hazen, *Five Sacred Crossings* (Eugene, OR: Harvest House, 2008).

Chapter 6—My Own Journey as Jesus' Apprentice

1. William James, *The Varieties of Religious Experience* (New York: Modern Library, 1902), pp. 506-7.

2. Eusebius, *Ecclesiastical History* 4:3, LCL 1.309.

3. Tertullian, *Apology* 37, LCL 173.

4. Tertullian, *To Scapula* 4, FC 10.173.

5. For an excellent study of this topic, see Francis MacNutt, *The Nearly Perfect Crime: How the Church Almost Killed the Ministry of Healing* (Grand Rapids: Baker, 2005).

6. *The Jesus Film Project* newsletter, September, 2006, pp. 1-2.

7. Patrick Sherry, *Spirit, Saints, and Immortality* (Albany, NY: State University of New York Press, 1984).

8. John Wesley, *A Plain Account of Christian Perfection* (London: Epworth Press, 1952), p. 87.

Chapter 7—Rethinking the Whole Thing

1. Craig M. Gay, *The Way of the (Modern) World* (Grand Rapids: Eerdmans, 1998), p. 19.

2. See J.P. Moreland, *Love Your God with All Your Mind* (Colorado Springs: NavPress, 1997).

3. A.W. Tozer, *The Pursuit of God* (Camp Hill, PA: WingSpread, 2006), pp. 35-36.

4. R.T. Kendall, *Total Forgiveness* (Lake Mary, FL: Charisma House, 2002).

Chapter 8—Two Essentials for Getting Good at Life

1. Thomas à Kempis, *The Imitation of Christ* (Chicago: Moody Press, 1958), p. 12.

2. Plato, *Gorgias* 500 c.

3. Plato, *Laws* 661 a-c.

4. Geoffrey Cowley, "The Science of Happiness," *Newsweek,* September 16, 2003, pp. 46-47.

5. Michael Levine, "Why I Hate Beauty," *Psychology Today* 34:4 (July/August 2001): 38-44.

6. For more about happiness, see J.P. Moreland and Klaus Issler, *The Lost Virtue of Happiness* (Colorado Springs: NavPress, 2006).

Chapter 9—Avoiding the Three Jaws of Defeat

1. J.P. Moreland, *Love Your God with All Your Mind* (Colorado Springs: NavPress, 1997); *Kingdom Triangle* (Grand Rapids: Zondervan, 2007); J.P. Moreland and Klaus Issler, *The Lost Virtue of Happiness* (Colorado Springs: NavPress, 2005); *In Search of a Confident Faith* (Downers Grove, IL: InterVarsity Press, 2008); Dallas Willard, *The Divine Conspiracy* (San Francisco: Harper, 1998); Nancy Pearcey, *Total Truth* (Wheaton, IL: Crossway, 2004); James Sire, *The Universe Next Door: A Basic Worldview Catalog* (Downers Grove, IL: InterVarsity Press, 2004).

2. R. Douglas Geiveti and James S. Spiegel, *Faith, Film and Philosophy* (Downer's Grove, IL: IVP Academic, 2007).

3. The remainder of this third point is taken from J.P. Moreland and Klaus Issler, *In Search of a Confident Faith* (Downers Grove, IL: InterVarsity Press, 2008), chapter 2.

4. Christian Smith, *American Evangelicalism: Embattled and Thriving,* (Chicago: University of Chicago Press, 1998), p. 156.

5. Thomas Nagel, *The Last Word* (New York: Oxford University Press, 1997), p. 130.

6. Douglas Coupland, *Life After God* (New York: Pocket Books, 1994), p. 359.

7. The two books are Richard Foster, *Celebration of Discipline* (New York: Harper and Row, 1978), and Dallas Willard, *The Spirit of the Disciplines* (San Francisco: Harper & Row, 1988).

8. Willard, *The Spirit of the Disciplines,* pp. 154-92.

9. For help in this regard, see Charles Kraft, *Defeating Dark Angels* (Ann Arbor, MI: Servant Publications, 1992); Clinton Arnold, *Three Crucial Questions About Spiritual Warfare* (Grand Rapids: Baker, 1997).

10. Holly Pivec, "Exorcizing Our Demons," *Biola Connections,* Winter 2006, 10-17.

Chapter 10—How to Unclog Your Spiritual Arteries and Develop the Heart to Work with God

1. For a treatment of some of these additional matters, see J.P. Moreland, *Kingdom Triangle: Recover the Christian Mind, Renovate the Soul, Restore the Spirit's Power* (Grand Rapids: Zondervan, 2007); J.P. Moreland and Klaus Issler, *The Lost Virtue of Happiness: Recovering the Disciplines of the Good Life* (Colorado Springs: NavPress, 2006).

2. I have addressed the topic of loving and worshipping God with the mind elsewhere. See my *Love Your God with All Your Mind: The Role of Reason in the Life of the Soul* (Colorado Springs: NavPress, 1997).

3. H.C Leupold, *Exposition of the Psalms* (Grand Rapids: Baker, 1969), pp. 236-37; Joseph Alexander, *The Psalms: Translated and Explained* (Grand Rapids: Baker, 1977), p. 121; J.J. Steward Perowne, *The Book of Psalms* (Grand Rapids: Zondervan, 1966), p. 268.

4. I first shared this story in *Kingdom Triangle*, pp. 191-92.

Chapter 11—From Here to Eternity

1. Gary Habermas and J.P. Moreland, *Beyond Death* (Wheaton, IL: Crossway Books, 1998).

2. Both are from Peter Shockey, *Reflections of Heaven* (New York: Doubleday, 1999), pp. 147-48 and 163-72, respectively. For an interesting story of an atheistic university professor who died, went to hell, came back, left teaching, and is now in the ministry, see Howard Storm, *My Descent into Hell* (New York: Doubleday, 2005). There are a number of details reported by Storm with which I disagree theologically, but the general account itself seems to me to be credible.

3. See also Habermas and Moreland, *Beyond Death*, 212-14 for more on the patient's case.

4. Randy Alcorn, *Heaven* (Carol Stream, IL: Tyndale House, 2004).
5. As quoted in Archibald D. Hart, *Unmasking Male Depresson* (Nashville: Thomas Nelson, 2001), p. 125.
6. Ibid.
7. B.C. Johnson, *The Atheist Debater's Handbook* (Buffalo, NY: Prometheus, 1981), p. 116.
8. Morton Kelsey, *Afterlife: The Other Side of Dying* (New York: Paulist, 1979), p. 237.
9. Richard Swinburne, *Faith and Reason* (Oxford: Clarendon, 1981), pp. 143–72; *Responsibility and Atonement* (Oxford: Clarendon, 1989), pp. 179–200; "A Theodicy of Heaven and Hell," in *The Existence & Nature of God*, ed. by Alfred J. Freddoso (Notre Dame, IN: University of Notre Dame, 1983), pp. 37-54.
10. Eugene Fontinell, *Self, God, and Immortality* (Philadelphia: Temple University, 1986), p. 217. See the review of this work by J.P. Moreland, *International Philosophical Quarterly* 29 (Dec. 1989): 480-83.
11. Kelsey, *Afterlife*, p. 251.
12. John Hick, *Evil and the God of Love* (New York: Harper & Row, 1978), p. 342; see also *Death and Eternal Life* (San Francisco: Harper & Row, 1980), pp. 242-61.
13. C.S. Lewis, *The Problem of Pain* (New York: Macmillan, 1962), pp. 106-7.
14. See Robert Lightner, *Heaven for Those Who Can't Believe* (Schaumburg, IL: Regular Baptist, 1977).
15. Leon Morris, "The Dreadful Harvest," *Christianity Today,* May 27, 1991), pp. 34-38.
16. See William Lane Craig, "'No Other Name': A Middle Knowledge Perspective on the Exclusivity of Salvation Through Christ," *Faith and Philosophy* 6 (Apr. 1989): 172-88, *The Only Wise God* (Grand Ripids: Baker, 1989) pp.127-52; *No Easy Answers* (Chicago: Moody, 1990), pp. 105-16.

Epilogue

1. Bertrand Russell, "A Free Man's Worship," in *Why I Am Not a Christian*, ed. by Paul Edwards (New York: Simon & Schuster, 1957), p. 107.

It's a Harsh,

Crazy,

Beautiful,

Messed Up,

Breathtaking

World...

And People Are Talking About It...

conversant **life** .com

engage your faith